Film Follies

The Cinema Out of Order

Stuart Klawans

CASSELL
London and New York

For Bali

First published 1999 by

Cassell
Wellington House, 125 Strand, London WC2R 0BB, England
370 Lexington Avenue, New York, NY 10017–6550, USA

© Stuart Klawans 1999

British Library Cataloguing in Publication Data

A catalogue record for this book is available from the British Library

Library of Congress Cataloging-in-Publication Data

Klawans, Stuart.
      Film follies : the cinema out of order / Stuart Klawans.
          p.   cm.
      Includes bibliographical references and index.
      ISBN 0–304–70053–3 (hardcover). — ISBN 0–304–70054–1 (pbk.)
          1. Epic films—History and criticism.   2. Motion pictures—
      Economic aspects.   3. Independent filmmakers.   I. Title.
      PN1995.9.E79K63   1999
      791.43'75–dc21   98–47487
                                                                                      CIP

ISBN   0 304 70053 3 (hardback)
            0 304 70054 1 (paperback)

Designed and typeset by Ben Cracknell Studios
Printed and bound in Great Britain by
Creative Print and Design Wales, Ebbw Vale

Contents

But first of all, with the help of the Muses, I'll try to explain my ancestry to you, which not very many people know. I didn't have Chaos, Orcus, Saturn, Japetus, or any other of those out-of-date mouldy old gods for a father, but 'Plutus', god of riches himself . . . And he didn't make me spring from his brain, as Jupiter did that sour and stern Athene, but gave me Freshness for a mother, the loveliest of all the nymphs and the gayest too.

ERASMUS OF ROTTERDAM
PRAISE OF FOLLY

Introduction

I am not well suited to write about big movies – although, I confess, *Ben-Hur* once gave me a thrill. As the lights came up on the William Wyler version, to which my father had treated me as a tenth-birthday present, I rubbed the sleep from my eyes and declared it to be the best picture of the year – just as the Oscar voters had decreed, and the members of the New York Film Critics Circle. Today, through misadventure, I belong to the New York Film Critics Circle. I still can muster an interest in *Ben-Hur*, especially Fred Niblo's 1925 version; but the intimate and mundane have long since displaced the monumental in my heart. For thrills, I look not to the cinema of the chariot race but to late Ozu. Give me a static camera and a middle-aged couple, who putter around fixing a midnight snack.

Yet a small group of very large movies continues to fascinate me. To suggest why, and to set the boundaries of this book, I will explain why I call them *follies*.

First, *folly* signifies an extravagant form of madness: an obsession that does not narrow one's frame of attention but broadens it to the scale of all outdoors. The movies that concern me here surpass mere grandiosity to become delusions of grandeur. It's as if a daemon had seized the reins from Ben-Hur, driving the chariot of the movie off its track and into the skies. In some cases, such as *Intolerance*, the film careens blithely, as if its maker never imagined his ambitions might be fatally outsize. In other cases, such as *Apocalypse Now*, megalomania becomes explicit as subject matter, as if the film had been made to demonstrate its own hubris. Either way, the aesthetic interest of the folly arises principally from the excitement of seeing filmmaking pushed beyond all rational limits. These are movies for people who want to die from too much cinema.

Folly also means wasteful excess, a sense of the word that takes us beyond aesthetics into considerations of film as an industry. The pictures discussed in this book were not only too ambitious but also too expensive to make. They resulted in bankruptcies and the demise of careers; even when they turned out to be profitable (as was *Apocalypse Now*) they were *said* to have been ruinous, and the reputation of financial irresponsibility added to their allure. An industry run according to sound economic principles would not have produced these movies; but they were made all the same, whether to that industry's glory (as with *Metropolis*) or to its derision (*Duel in the Sun*).

A *folly* is also a type of building: picturesque, whimsical, and useless. This sense of the word takes us beyond a single industry of the twentieth century and into the wider field of cultural history. I propose that cinematic follies, with their reliance on exotic and historicizing production design, with their crazily eclectic style, are in some ways successors to the architectural follies that flourished in the eighteenth century. These pictures testify to the ancestry of the movies, which I believe may be traced in no small measure to festivals, fairs, and amusement parks.

Finally, I call these pictures *follies* in honor of the Ziegfeld Follies, mounted for many years in the New Amsterdam Theatre, across the street from the playhouse where *Intolerance* had its New York premiere. The pictures under discussion have the character of musical revues. Given their ambition, eclecticism, and spendthrift ways, it's only to be expected that they would string together one spectacular sequence after another, rarely troubling the audience with the demands of logic or inner development.

All of which means that these films are 'Out of Order': not working properly; in violation of normal procedure; disruptive; chronologically scrambled (and scrambled in this book's scheme of presentation).

Some people enjoy the jumble, the sense of discontinuity and breakdown. Writing in *Cahiers du Cinéma* in 1955, in an article titled 'Abel Gance, désordre et génie,' François Truffaut tantalizingly declared that 'failure is talent. To succeed is to fail.' He supported this proposition, characteristically, with a list of filmmakers, each of whom was matched with his alleged shortcomings to show that strong talent, if free to follow its own path, must express itself unevenly. 'I assert,' Truffaut wrote, 'that perfection and success are mean, indecent, immoral, and obscene.' Follies interest me as the ultimate products of this aesthetic of incoherence – not just an aesthetic, as Truffaut made plain, but an ethic as well, which has appealed not just to Truffaut himself but to a growing number of people over the past two centuries. To some critics, a taste for the misshapen and the mismatched distinguishes our present era, defined loosely (of course) as postmodern. I hope my review of follies may at least broaden the terms of this discussion.

Beyond that, I hope these follies may add to our understanding of a symbolic function of the movies. When people want to talk about the desires of the individual versus the demands of a society based on mass production, they often speak in terms of filmmakers and the movie industry. The discussion of cinema turns into an allegory of the struggle for personal expression. This allegory is dominated by two figures that arose in the 1950s: the auteur, and the independent or avant-garde filmmaker.

In this scheme, one may be either a Vincente Minnelli, who works more or less comfortably within the Hollywood factory, or a John Cassavetes, who withdraws from the assembly line and everything it represents, including the annual picnic. More than forty years have gone by since these images took hold. The studios, as Minnelli knew them, no longer exist, having become financiers and brokers of films, more than manufacturers; while 'independence,' at least in America, has turned into an industry of its own, complete with a feverishly publicized festival and distributors that are subsidiaries of vast corporations. Yet the allegory persists: the filmmaker who achieves self-expression must be either a rebel drop-out or a genius employee.

To me, the use of these categories merely promotes twin attitudes that are already too prevalent: cheap cynicism and consumerist good cheer. I propose that follies might be useful to think about because they take us out of this scheme. The people who directed these pictures behaved as if they were making a glorified home movie (like Cassavetes) yet had in their hands the full apparatus of studio production.

In short, each of the movies discussed in this book is an exception to the rule – including the rule by which I have brought them together. I therefore admit that other films, which pass unremarked here, might have contributed to the discussion; and I apologize for limiting my list to pictures that are too well known. A world of cinema still lies undiscovered, and here I am, going on about the same old Greatest Hits (or, in this case, misses). In my defense, I can say only that these films have never yet failed to lead the novice to enlightenment and the savant to mirth. At some point in the tour, they will surely take over from me, as they have taken over from everyone else who has struggled with them. As for the rest: let the reader see.

The Work of Art of the Future

During the early months of World War I, while on his way home from a hanging, D.W. Griffith looked down from a hill and saw the future of cinema spread before his feet. Most likely he stood at the corner of Divisadero Street and Broadway in San Francisco.

From the top of the Fillmore Street hill, Griffith could enjoy a panoramic view of the West Coast's biggest attraction of 1915, the fairgrounds of the Panama-Pacific International Exposition. Stretching across an area of 76 city blocks, the fair was a trade show and a civic advertisement, a museum and a carnival, bringing together all epochs of history and all nations of the world in a multicolored, Orientalist wonderland of towers and domes. The Exposition was not yet open when Griffith paused to view it; the ribbon-cutting would be held on February 20. But enough of the buildings were complete that Griffith could instruct his cameraman, Billy Bitzer, to take a matte shot of one of the towers, masking the lens so the spire could later be superimposed on some other image.

Not that Griffith had an image in mind. According to Bitzer's helper Karl Brown, who left us an eyewitness account, Griffith would have been glad just to have such a shot in his pocket. He had used one in the film he had just completed, *The Clansman*; he might well want to use another in the picture now in production, *The Mother and the Law*.

A research expedition for that film had occasioned this side trip to the fair. *The Mother and the Law* called for Bobby Harron, in the role of The Boy, to be brought to the gallows for a crime he did not commit. Griffith therefore left Los Angeles with Bitzer and Brown to investigate prison conditions and learn the procedures of execution. Traveling by overnight train, the filmmakers first went to the slimily appalling city jail in San Francisco, a place that turned out to be too dark to photograph. Then they proceeded to the comparatively cheerful and airy penitentiary at San Quentin, where the warden himself conducted the tour but would not allow photography. Nor did the filmmakers get to witness a real hanging. They did see the trapdoor of the gallows sprung into action, which made a powerful impression on the 17-year-old Brown.

After that came the detour to the fair. Perhaps it was no more than an afterthought, contrived to give Bitzer some justification for having hauled along his camera. Or maybe – a more likely possibility – Griffith already felt an interest in the fair. But whatever he was planning at that moment would soon have to change, because Griffith was about to win the greatest acclaim yet accorded any filmmaker – an acclaim that recently had been unthinkable and would for a while be unique to him.

The trip to San Francisco probably happened in December 1914 or January 1915 – soon after Griffith finished *The Clansman*, but (in keeping with Brown's account) before the opening of the fair. Within weeks of that hilltop visit, the clamor began.

On February 8, 1915, at Clune's Auditorium in Los Angeles, Griffith attended the premiere of *The Clansman*, which soon would be renamed *The Birth of a Nation*. The screening ended in 'wave after wave of cheers and applause,' which washed over Griffith 'like great waves breaking over a rock,' in the recollection of Karl Brown. Ten days later came a showing at the White House for President Woodrow Wilson and his cabinet. The ovation, if any, was inaudible from the street; but the Reverend Thomas Dixon, Jr., author of the novel and play that were Griffith's source material, emerged with a memorable endorsement: 'It is like writing history with Lightning' (Schickel, p. 270). Through a spokesman, Wilson soon backed away from this blurb, which even today cannot be ascribed to him definitively. No matter. The public knew *The Birth of a Nation* had been deemed worthy of the first Presidential screening.

The crescendo reached its climax on March 3 with the premiere of *The Birth of a Nation* in America's cultural capital. Only a year before, when New York's Strand Theatre had opened as a showplace for feature films, a critic for *The New York Times* had reacted with strained humor: 'If anyone had told me . . . the finest looking people in town would be going to the biggest and newest theater on Broadway for the purpose of seeing motion pictures, I would have sent them down to my friend, Dr. Minas Gregory, at Bellevue Hospital. The doctor runs the city's bughouse, you know' (Koszarski, *An Evening's Entertainment*, p. 20). Now Griffith stood on the stage of the Liberty Theatre on 42nd Street and declared that he wanted 'to place pictures on a par with the spoken word as a medium for artistic expression appealing to thinking people.' The New Yorkers – thinking people all – cheered themselves hoarse. Reporting the next day in the *Evening Mail*, Burns Mantle confirmed Griffith's success: *The Birth of a Nation* had 'swept a sophisticated audience like a prairie fire' (Schickel, p. 277).

To other observers, the film was about as helpful as prairie fire. Responding to Griffith's coon-show melodramatics and glorification of the Ku Klux Klan, Francis Hackett of *The New Republic* described *The Birth of a Nation* as 'spiritual assassination. It degrades the censors that passed it and the white race that endures it' (Schickel, p. 284). An editorial in the *New York Globe* was even stronger: 'To make a few dirty dollars men are willing to pander to depraved tastes and to foment a race antipathy that is the most sinister and dangerous feature of American life' (ibid., p. 288). The National Association for the Advancement of Colored People mounted a city-by-city campaign against the film; and a group of reform leaders, including W.E.B. Du Bois, Lillian Wald, Rabbi Stephen Wise, and Oswald Garrison Villard gathered in the chambers of New York's City Council to denounce it. None of this could halt Griffith's triumph. As his biographer Richard Schickel observes, *The Birth of a Nation* overwhelmed its viewers, including many who might have known better. Its impact was unprecedented: 'literally, there was nothing to compare it with.'

In a word, Griffith had established the sociological phenomenon known as the movies. 'Invented' would be a gross overstatement – and yet it's clear that contemporary observers believed he had done something new. Within the wider field of film, which had already existed for twenty years, people in increasing numbers had put forward products that were more dignified than the usual items (as with the French *Films d'Art* and their offshoots) or more ambitious in scale (as with the Italian historical spectacles). Narrative films that ran for an hour and a half or more were starting to be common. But until *The Birth of a Nation*, no feature film had caught the public's imagination in quite this way. Griffith thrillingly combined the grandeur of an operatic spectacle with the narrative sweep of a popular novel; the kinetic power of images orchestrated on a large scale, with the special persuasiveness of film actors, who seemed both more imposing and more accessible than stage performers, thanks to the camera's ability to bring them close. After March 3, 1915, filmmaking would continue

7

in all its variety; but from then on, the great economic and social force within film would be the movies.*

Neither the expression 'the movies' nor a foreknowledge of its development was available to Griffith in the spring of 1915; but he surely knew that *The Birth of a Nation* had changed the terms of his business. It therefore posed an enormous problem.

His new drama about contemporary social problems, *The Mother and the Law*, was virtually complete. But however compelling the story, it now seemed woefully slight. *The Birth of a Nation* filled twelve reels; when shown at slowest speed – in those days, projection rates were variable – the film would have run about three hours. *The Mother and the Law* would have represented a major step back to something like the scale of Griffith's previous release, the six-reel *The Avenging Conscience* (1914).

By this time, Griffith also had seen the only serious competitor to *The Birth of a Nation*: the latest, grandest, and most popular of the Italian spectacles, Giovanni Pastrone's twelve-reel *Cabiria* (1914). Set during the Second Punic War, with a scenario credited to Gabriele D'Annunzio – the great man had put his name on the project in exchange for 50,000 lire – *Cabiria* offered the audience a lot for the price of a ticket: slave girls, elephants, human sacrifices to flaming idols, shipwrecks, battle scenes, and a hunk of beefcake named Bartolomeo Pagano. There were enormous sets constructed of false marble blocks, and there was genuine location footage shot in Sicily, Tunisia, and the Alps. The mere reputation of *Cabiria* (and of Enrico Guazzoni's 1912 *Quo Vadis?*) had helped spur Griffith to undertake *The Birth of a Nation*. The experience of seeing *Cabiria* helped confirm that *The Mother and the Law* would no longer do.

So, after opening *The Birth of a Nation*, Griffith continued to tinker with *The Mother and the Law*, all the while brooding upon the demands of his new stature, the need to outdo Pastrone, and the complaints of his critics. The latter could be answered in writing. In a letter to the *New York Globe*, published on April 10, 1915, Griffith asserted that *The Birth of a Nation*, a film 'based upon truth in every vital detail,' had been 'brought forth' not for financial gain but 'to reveal the beautiful possibilities of the art of motion pictures.' Still, a film was the best vehicle for his response. He was at the height of his power when making a film – all the more so because he could make whatever film he pleased. *The Birth of a Nation* had cost $100,000 to produce (of which perhaps only $10,000 had come from Griffith himself).† In 1915, Griffith's personal income exceeded $250,000. Had the need arisen, he could have

8 * Of course, it all depends on how you use the term. In 1915, Charles Chaplin became a star; even more than a star, a national (soon international) obsession. But at that moment he was a star of the nickelodeon. He became a star of the movies – and transformed his image from vulgar comedian to reputable artist – in 1916, after *The Birth of a Nation*.

financed the next picture out of his own pocket. He just didn't know what the next picture should be.

A different filmmaker might have suspended his activities until he'd formed a plan. But Griffith seems to have worked the other way around: he developed ideas out of whatever he was doing. An autodidact from rural Kentucky who had learned his profession in fly-by-night theater companies, he was long accustomed to projects that seemed to have no beginning, only a middle into which he was dumped headlong, to make whatever he could of the situation. The habit of mind he acquired from these experiences, a kind of barnstormer's Aristotelianism, had served him well when he talked his way into the film business early in 1908. In his first year alone at Biograph, he cranked out 60 one-reelers. In the spring and summer of 1915, he therefore planned his new project in the only way he knew, by reworking and expanding *The Mother and the Law*.

It was at this point (so far as we can know) that Griffith's hilltop vision of the previous winter began to change into the vision for a film.

By the time he again took up *The Mother and the Law*, the Panama-Pacific Exposition was in full operation, having welcomed 200,000 visitors on the first day alone. Like other World's Fairs, it dominated people's talk, giving citizens something to boast about and entrepreneurs a standard of comparison. One such businessman was Carl Laemmle of the Universal Film Manufacturing Company. Twelve days after the New York premiere of *The Birth of a Nation*, Laemmle had celebrated the opening of his vast new studio complex in Los Angeles, Universal City, only to find himself swamped by 20,000 curiosity-seekers. Showman that he was, he ordered the construction of bleachers for future visitors and proceeded to promote Universal City as a tourist attraction, comparable, of course, to the Panama-Pacific Exposition.

By the time Griffith returned to work on *The Mother and the Law*, someone already had thought to compare a movie studio to a World's Fair. Griffith, characteristically, went further. He would create a work of art so grand, people would have to compare the World's Fair to his movie.

Let me rein in my hobbyhorse, however briefly. I do not claim Griffith said, 'Let us create a motion picture in the World's Fair's image.' But I do believe he wanted something new; and like anyone in that situation, he could imagine the unknowable only in relation to the things at hand. One of them, of course, was *Cabiria*. But how shabby, how small, to strive against another man's picture, when the whole world was waiting

† Although 'average cost' was a very loose concept, as film historian Richard Koszarski points out, contemporary trade publications estimated that a feature might cost a manufacturer between $18,000 and $41,000.

to be filmed. If Griffith did not consciously take the World's Fair as his model, then at least he recapitulated in film the processes that gave rise to fairs.

The Panama-Pacific International Exposition was the latest in the modern series of fairs that had flourished in Europe since London's Crystal Palace Exposition of 1851 and in the United States since Philadelphia's Centennial Exposition of 1876. At first, these fairs had served as showcases of progress. They exhibited the most inspiring novelties of science, industry, commerce, and the arts, within an architectural envelope that was itself a testament to the advance of engineering. Whatever the visitor encountered of the old and quaint would come from the exotic reaches of the world; and so those items, too, paid tribute to a kind of onward march, that of European colonization.

With the World's Columbian Exposition of 1893, held in Chicago, the fairs began to look backward as much as forward. America, oscillating as ever between the desire for a self-generated culture and the longing for sophisticated traditions, had again built its aspirations upon Europe, or at least an imagined European past. The 1893 fairground was a gleaming neoclassical White City, created as if to realize, at full scale and in three dimensions, the grandiose fantasy of Thomas Cole's painting *The Consummation of Empire* (1835–36).

But a World's Fair, even in America's historicist mode, was still the vehicle of progress. The Columbian Exposition could boast of many novelties, such as the first Ferris wheel, constructed on the fair's amusement strip, the Midway. Visitors also discovered elements of eclecticism on the fairgrounds proper: Louis Sullivan's Palace of Transportation, its portal built within an enormous fanlike facade, or the wooded island that sheltered a Japanese house, which proved to be of great interest to the young Frank Lloyd Wright. Futurism and antiquarianism, patriotic swagger and a fascination with the exotic, continued to mingle in subsequent American fairs. In 1901, the Pan-American Exposition in Buffalo offered an attraction titled 'A Trip to the Moon,' one year before Méliès got around to filming the subject. In 1904, the Louisiana Purchase Exposition in St. Louis included on its grounds a miniature replica of Jerusalem.

The fair Griffith saw in 1914–15 was another of these immense but ephemeral artworks – a site for cultivated tourism, which might be fully appreciated only with the aid of guidebooks. To get the most of their visit to the San Francisco fair, or to imagine its splendors from afar, people relied on accounts such as John D. Barry's *The City of Domes:*

A Walk with an Architect about the Courts and Palaces of the Panama-Pacific International Exposition. Readers might learn that the San Francisco chapter of the American Institute of Architects had collaborated on designing the buildings, with painter Jules Guerin put in charge of the color scheme and the sculptural program delegated to Karl Bitter and A. Stirling Calder. Noting that 'ships to and from the Orient were continually plying' San Francisco's harbor, the designers resolved that 'there should rise an Oriental city,' with 'styles of architecture almost sensationally different.'

We know from Karl Brown's account that Griffith was particularly interested in the fair's most famous landmark, the Tower of Jewels, designed by architect Thomas Hastings and built at a cost of $500,000. This structure, so named because it was inset with Austrian cut glass, was reached along pink paths that led to an arched entranceway. From its base of yellow Corinthian columns, the tower ascended in stepped-back layers, which were decorated with sculpted figures appropriate to the history of California: a robed philosopher of the sixteenth century, a Spanish friar, a Conquistador on horseback. Orange banners and streamers flew from the tower, which was topped by a globe supported by a sculptural triad.

Four other towers said to be of Renaissance design (but somehow also comparable to the Giralda Tower in Seville) were arrayed around the Tower of Jewels. But this was only the beginning of the mishmash. Visitors to the fair might admire a Baroque Court of the Universe, modeled on Bernini's arcade for St. Peter's in Rome; a French-style Palace of Horticulture, with a dome based on the Mosque of Ahmed I in Constantinople; a Court of the Ages, done in Spanish Gothic, French, Romanesque, and Moorish style, with a 'quasi-Gothic' tower; a Palace of Fine Arts inspired (according to its architect) by Piranesi's fantasies of Roman ruins; and a re-creation of a Spanish mission, covering five acres. The colors chosen for the buildings' domes – color, according to Barry, being the unifying element in the architecture – were orange, blue, gold, brown, yellow, and green.

It is impossible to reconstruct with any certainty the development of Griffith's films, especially since, as we have seen, he worked with only the sketchiest of scenarios, preferring to think on his feet. But we do know what became of *The Mother and the Law* when he took it up again. Expanding the plan of the film as if it were a fairground, Griffith added to his modern-day story three more episodes, each representing a different time and place. He decided to dramatize the conquest of Babylon by Cyrus the Great in 539 B.C.; to portray scenes from the life of Jesus; and to tell of a love cruelly destroyed by the St. Bartholomew Day's Massacre in 1572. This combination was worthy of a great World's Fair; and like a fair-maker, Griffith proposed a noble excuse for his eclecticism. The American fairs used a date in history as their reason for assembling everything under the sun. Chicago had the four hundredth anniversary of Columbus's first voyage; San Francisco, the four hundredth anniversary of Balboa's first sighting of the Pacific. In a gesture that would soon baffle many in his audience, Griffith too unified his work through a theme – not a story, but a theme – which he announced in the film's title: *Intolerance*.

Earlier films, including his own, made their mark on the individual pieces of *Intolerance*; but we would search in vain for a cinematic predecessor to the scheme as a whole. *Intolerance* must have been inspired by the San Francisco fair, if only because it resembled nothing else. Besides, we know the Exposition contributed materially to the production. Griffith learned that the artisans who had built the fairground, sculpting its architectural figures out of gypsum plaster, lived on the West Coast. For all previous American expositions, the sculpture had been fabricated in New York and then shipped to the site. A. Stirling Calder had broken with this practice, recruiting Italian immigrants in San Francisco to fabricate the sculpture on the spot. Soon those same artisans were in Los Angeles, working in a plaster shop on Sunset Boulevard.

Having established the movies, Griffith chose as his next gesture to make this new cultural force aspire to the condition of a World's Fair – an ambition somewhat at variance with the celebrated formulation put forward some thirty years later by André Bazin. The great critic claimed that filmmaking and embalming are two expressions of a single psychological need, which urges us to capture and preserve reality as fully as possible. To Bazin, film was therefore an inherently realistic medium, which derives its power from our knowledge that the objects we see were truly, physically present before the camera. This theory holds up well when applied to film in general; but for the special case of the movies, it needs a corollary. Griffith, it seems to me, was not aiming to capture reality when he began *Intolerance*. He was hoping to *represent* reality, as the pavilions of a fair represent the participating nations. His new movie would be an assemblage of parts, which though world-encompassing would not be a direct transcription of the world, since it was to be didactic, commercial, and entertaining all at once.

What might it mean, to claim that Griffith had imported the institution of the World's Fair into the movies? I ask partly to move the discussion away from questions of Griffith's character. His personal make-up is fascinating, of course. No one has traced its course through the films more eloquently than did Jay Leyda in his essay 'The Art and Death of D.W. Griffith':

None of Griffith's frustrating conflicts with the banks and the exhibitors were as bloody as the conflict with his own inadequacies. An instinct for beauty clashed with a desperate wish for 'culture,' rarely finding an embodiment more substantial than big words – 'intolerance' was the biggest and emptiest of these.... In the same breath you bless and curse the idea of weaving together these stories that bear so little significant relation to each other. Here ... one sees a huge jerry-built frame of ideals enclosing a picture that strives with all its author's hampered might to fill that frame. The origin of *Intolerance* in Griffith's wish to answer the unanswerable attacks on *The Birth of a Nation* added plenty of inflated passion to the new film without a balancing amount of substance. (cited in Geduld, p. 166)

Agreed. Yet how many people, however pig-headed, have built an *Intolerance* out of their need for self-justification? As Leyda himself implied, there is more to this film than one man's wounded pride and runaway ambition; just as there are worlds concealed beneath Leyda's ironically punctuated 'culture.' I want to dig out the word from those quotation marks, to see what it meant to the desperately striving autodidact from Kentucky – to him, and to millions like him.

Such an excavation would need to bring to light a society in which World's Fairs could instruct as well as amuse, and appeal to both a middle-class public and the most advanced of artists. The 1867 World's Fair in Paris did not, strictly speaking, introduce Japanese prints to Western Europe, but it greatly encouraged an interest in Asian art that only recently had taken hold. A handful of artists were affected, directly or indirectly: Manet, Monet, Degas, Gauguin, van Gogh, Whistler, Tissot. Or, jumping to a different medium, I might mention (for the thousandth time) the effect on Claude Debussy of the 1889 Universal Exposition, where a gamelan concert confirmed him in the musical path he'd taken.

To a remarkable degree, the World's Fairs brought together the different levels of urban society. They also encompassed many of the forms of nineteenth-century spectatorship. They offered exhibitions of painting and sculpture; panoramas; waxworks displays and dioramas; showcases of consumer goods as opulent as those in the newly established department stores; rides on mechanical conveyances as exciting as a train trip, and as varied in the views they offered.

Historians have cited all of these art forms and entertainments as precursors of spectatorship at the movies. All were available at the fairs.

Griffith probably did not come into direct contact with a World's Fair until 1915. In 1893, he was an 18-year-old bookstore clerk in Louisville, who could only have dreamed of a trip to Chicago. The 1904 St. Louis fair was also unreachable; Griffith was busy then in San Francisco, making his living acting in melodramas. But he would have known of those fairs, probably in some detail, and as a man of his time would have understood them to be more than amusements, more than commercial ventures, more than didactic accumulations of this and that from every nation and period. The World's Fairs were summations of culture itself – no quotation marks – precisely because they were all of these things.

Intolerance, too, was to be all of these things. In imagining Griffith's ambitions for the film, we therefore need to crane our necks very far back just to glimpse the foothills. It's an uncomfortable position to maintain and may result in irritable judgments. But before we snap the magic word hubris, which clears away all problems of interpretation, we should recall that Griffith was not the first artist to believe he could create a work of art that would, like a fair, encompass everything and appeal to everyone, yet remain aloof from the world it summarized.

To understand his project, and to see how follies figured into it, we must continue the excavation.

The great expositions of the nineteenth and twentieth centuries might seem to have developed in a straight line from the medieval fairs. In fact, they were latter-day re-creations, resembling the old fairs much as a Gothic Revival train station resembled a twelfth-century cathedral.

The function of the old fairs, as summarized by Fernand Braudel, was to interrupt and expand the ordinary circle of exchange by superseding for a moment the local market and its day-in, day-out affairs. In ancient Greece, fairs were held under truce, allowing merchants from mutually hostile regions to do business on neutral ground, often at a border. Or, in keeping with the fair's character as a break from the mundane, the merchants would convene at a shrine during a sacred feast. Such fairs were held at Olympia, Delphi, Nemea, and Delos.

In Western Europe, this ancient institution came to life again in the eleventh century. Its first purpose, as before, was to ease long-range trade; for a set period, usually coinciding with a religious feast, wholesale merchants were entitled to do business without paying duties on their goods. But the promise of duty-free trade was not always kept, or was less compelling to the masses of fair-goers than a more general sense of liberation from the daily grind. The great fairs, writes Braudel, were 'temporary towns' of noise, music, roistering, 'the world turned upside down.'

The fair might begin with a hubbub of trumpet-blowing, drumming, bonfires, fireworks, and bell-ringing.

It would then be invaded by all the jokers, sellers of miracle-cures and drugs, 'purgative spirits' or orvietan (also known as 'Venice treacle' and once held to be an antidote against poison), fortune-tellers, jugglers, tumblers, tightrope-walkers, tooth-pullers, and traveling musicians and singers. . . . And without exception, fairs were a rendezvous for traveling players. From the time when it was held in the Halles of Paris, the Saint-Germain fair had been the occasion for theatrical performances. The 'Prince of Fools' and 'Mother Foolish,' which were on the program in 1511, represent the medieval tradition of farces and satires, of which Saint-Beuve said 'this is already vaudeville.' (Braudel, p. 85)

Bartholomew Fair, first held in a priory churchyard near London, was established in 1120 by a grant from Henry I to a monk who had once been his jester. Scheduled for the two weeks around St. Bartholomew's Day (August 24 old style, September 3 on the new calendar), it became the chief event in the textile trade in England. But that was hardly its only business. Miracles were reported to have taken place in 1144 and 1174, and at the start of the fifteenth century the fair provided an opportunity for yet another expression of religious fervor. The Archbishop of Canterbury wanted to suppress the Lollards, and Henry IV chose to help him by authorizing the useful instrument of public burnings. Bartholomew Fair was held over the ashes of heretics.

There is evidence of plays and puppet shows being performed at Bartholomew Fair as early as 1500. A wild beast show was instituted in the late 1660s, and in 1708 the fair got its first recorded menagerie. By the 1820s, the number of menageries had grown to at least four. Keeping them company were five theaters, a troupe of Chinese jugglers, a fire-eater, a Pig-Faced Lady, a diorama of the Battle of Navarino, and a display of the head of William Corder, murderer of Maria Marten. The Saint-Germain fair in Paris, though equally bustling, seems to have done a vast business in textiles. Bartholomew Fair got to the point where it retained no such purpose.

But then, when it was held for the last time in 1855, Bartholomew Fair had long outlived the world of jesters, miracles, burnings, and face-to-face trade. As economic instruments, fairs had begun to wither in the seventeenth century, their function taken over by two rising institutions: the mercantile exchange (including the stock exchange) and the warehouse. By the eighteenth century, Braudel writes, fairs persisted only in economic backwaters.

Yet the new and sophisticated instruments of trade supplanted only one function of the fairs. The other aspects – diversion, spectacle, the communication of ideas, the mingling of classes – found accommodation through another new European institution, the amusement park. These parks, the direct forerunners of the World's Fairs, developed not out of the medieval and Renaissance fairs but out of an innovation in private life: the folly.

When did great landowners begin to dot their estates with useless 'eyecatchers' shaped like obelisks, pyramids, and pagodas, decayed Greek temples, ruined medieval abbeys, derelict Crusader battlements?

In her historical survey of British follies, Barbara Jones traces their origin to the rediscovery of Nero's palace, the Golden House, in Rome. Excavations began around the palace in 1488 and in the early 1500s unearthed underground chambers, their stuccoed walls painted delicately in a style that was utterly different from 'classical' sobriety. Out of this discovery grew two fashions, which spread rapidly through Italy and then into France. First, in the gardens of their estates, wealthy people began to construct grottoes of their own: private spaces that were picturesque, antiquarian, and useless. Second, artists adopted a new decorative style, the grotesque. Obsessively symmetrical in its patterning but otherwise senseless, it was a style of eclecticism and excess, characterized by swarms of twining tendrils from which sprouted an ill-assorted lot of nymphs, satyrs, reclining youths, and carousing godlets, some larger, some smaller, all flanked by equally out-of-proportion images of wreaths, urns, columns, and scrolls.

In England, one of Francis Bacon's gentlemen built a grotto sometime after 1626 on an estate in Oxfordshire. It fitted in with a certain aristocratic taste for solitary contemplation and pastoral melancholy, which also was expressed in the paintings of Nicolas Poussin and Claude Lorrain, with their prettily ruined temples. Soon the private estates, as if in imitation of the paintings, began to produce architecture that was not only picturesque and antiquarian but also stood above ground.

Sham castles were constructed outside Dublin, at Ballymount, in the seventeenth century; but the fashion really began to catch on in 1708, when Sir John Vanbrugh built a castellated house at Claremont in Surrey. The Earl of Clare (later Duke of Newcastle) bought the estate and commissioned Vanbrugh to improve it with the Belvedere, the first 'gothick' folly, constructed in 1717. About two years later, Vanbrugh built large sham structures at Castle Howard, where he added other styles to the mix. A gate in a castellated wall was topped by a pyramid; the view down the road led to an obelisk.

By 1767, follies had become popular enough for William Wrighte to publish a kind of architectural pattern book, *Grotesque Architecture or Rural Amusement.* The book included designs for a Hut ('intended to represent the primitive state of the Dorick Order'), a Hermitic Retreat, an Augustine Hermitage in classical style, a Gothic Grotto, an Oriental Hermitage (built around a tree and fitted with a Chinese roof), a Turkish mosque, and a Moresque Pavilion.

The enthusiasm for follies spread quickly to France, where the elite of the eighteenth century already were renting 'pastoral' houses in the Parisian suburbs of Montparnasse and Saint-Germain. Within the grounds of these estates, they began to build ruined churches, Dutch windmills, Egyptian obelisks, and pyramids. But the French follies were distinct from the English. According to historian Béatrice de Andia (in the Introduction to Langlois), the country retreats with their exotic buildings were in effect 'microcosms . . . penetrated by the philosophy of the Encyclopedists,' or 'a prolongation of the collectors' cabinets.' It is notable that more than 60 of these gardens were open to visitors in the years before the Revolution. Guidebooks were available, and some places had admission tickets – which in the case of Bagatelle (built in the Bois de Boulogne by the Comte d'Artois) were designed by Fragonard. The only people who kept their properties closed to the public, writes de Andia, were the stage performers, who owned perhaps half of the follies around Paris.

In England, estates typically remained off-limits. But even so, follies gradually assumed a more public aspect, as was only appropriate. Roughly speaking, these were the years of the Enclosure Acts, when yeomen farmers were driven off the land, to emigrate to the colonies or else crowd into the cities. Where these farmers once had lived, the gentry built private parks with follies. And in the midst of the new urban masses, a folly also arose: the pleasure garden.

New Spring Gardens, better known as Vauxhall Gardens, was laid out on the east bank of the Thames in about 1661 but did not become popular until Jonathan Tyers bought it in 1732 and began to develop it as a brightly lit, colorfully painted entertainment park. (Tyers was also a great builder of follies at his country estate in Surrey. In an eight-acre wood, which he called Il Penseroso, he built a small temple, which he had inscribed with solemn inscriptions and outfitted with a concealed clock that struck once a minute. At the end of the grounds, an iron gate, its piers fashioned in the form of caskets, opened into the 'Valley of the Shadow of Death.') In 1742, a competing entertainment park opened across the river in Chelsea, on the former estate of the Earl of Ranelagh. This, too, was a place for balls, masquerades, fireworks shows, and concerts, all in a setting of calculated other-worldliness. Tobias Smollett described Ranelagh as the enchanted palace of a genie.

This institution, too, spread to France. In the north of Paris, near the boulevard theaters with their acrobats and mimes, Jean-Baptiste Torré built his 'vauxhall' in 1764: a garden with a rotunda of painted canvas, in which people would gather after watching fireworks shows. Pierre-Sauveur-Balthasar Ruggieri followed in 1766 with a garden of his own, where he mounted bigger and bigger spectacles: *The Burning of Troy* and *The Siege of Delhi by Kouli-Kan*. The cost of admission was low enough that shopkeepers, clerks, and civil servants could frequent these parks, to dance, dine, drink, listen to music, and marvel at the jugglers and horseback riders. But inexpensive did not mean free; the lower classes who amused themselves at the Saint-Germain and Saint-Laurent fairs could not easily visit the gardens of Torré and Ruggieri, nor would they have been expected to enjoy the more orderly sorts of entertainment being offered.

These first Parisian pleasure gardens were built by entrepreneurs from Italy. The next were the work of the upper classes and had a more didactic (or perhaps Encyclopedic) tone. The financier Simon-Charles Boutin, administrator of the royal treasury, built Tivoli on the rue de Clichy in 1771. Encompassing 20 acres, Tivoli offered the public three different styles of garden: Italian, English (with sham ruins), and French (with a sham classical temple). To add charm to the spot, Boutin had artificial hills constructed. But perhaps the greatest of the Parisian follies, and the one that is still visible in part, was the Parc de Monceau, built in 1773–79 and paid for by the duc de Chartres. There, visitors could stroll past artificial streams and stride over artificial hills while enjoying the sight of a ruined Temple of Mars, pyramids, a windmill. Those who felt energetic could play on the *jeu de bagues* (a kind of carousel), while the more meditative could contemplate the rustic shepherd who'd been hired to frequent the grounds.

These new parks did not replace the old fairs at once. Rather, the two coexisted and for a while evolved together. Just as the gardens combined pleasure with instruction, so did the amusements at the fairs become steadily more edifying. In the first half of the eighteenth century, theaters were the primary attractions at the fairs of Saint-Laurent and Saint-Germain. By mid-century, people were flocking instead to scientific displays, panoramas, and exhibits drawn from the world's exotic corners. In 1747–48, a Magic Palace made its appearance at the fairs, featuring automata and showers of electric sparks displayed against a backdrop painted with a forest scene. Magic lantern shows were produced in 1775 – forerunners of the instructive, quasi-scientific projections of the Lumière brothers.

With the Revolution came an intensified didacticism: under force, the fairs gave way to Robespierre's secular patriotic festivals. And even after the brief season when the citizenry mounted their pageants to Reason and the Supreme Being, the festivals retained a civic air. From 1798 to 1849, Paris hosted eleven national expositions. Outwardly, these resembled the old fairs; but they had neither a sacred occasion nor a compelling economic purpose.

It remained for Prince Albert to bring the folly definitively into modern times with his sponsorship of the first of the International Expositions, that at the Crystal Palace in 1851. Not fairs in the original sense, the International Expositions were, in the words of Eric Hobsbawm, 'giant new rituals of self-congratulation' for capitalism, 'allegorical representations of economic triumph and industrial progress' (pp. 32–3). Their function was not so much to carry out trade as to symbolize it for the astonishment of the masses, displaying the treasures of the world within ever more spectacular architectural settings. Like the pleasure gardens of the eighteenth century, the Expositions were varied, instructive, secular, and entertaining, and were frequented by all but the lowest classes. The number of exhibitors alone was staggering; some 50,000 firms displayed their goods at the 1867 Paris fair. The crowds were greater still. Ten million people attended the Centennial Exposition in Philadelphia in 1876. At the Panama-Pacific Exposition, 10 million visited the Palace of Fine Arts alone.

And how many people saw *The Birth of a Nation*? No hard figures exist; but by the end of 1917, gross box-office receipts from the United States and Canada probably amounted to $60 million, with a top ticket price of $2. We have no way of knowing how many people saw the movie more than once, nor can we guess how much money the theater-owners skimmed off the box office before they reported their receipts. But just to estimate the order of magnitude, we might reasonably say that as many as 30 million people might have watched *The Birth of a Nation*.

Griffith had created the first movie – the first spectacle of any kind – to surpass in popularity a World's Fair. It remained for him to make something that would function as a fair.

At the corner of Sunset and Hollywood in Los Angeles, in a kind of private estate that served as his studio, Griffith inaugurated the construction of his first folly for *Intolerance*: the walls of Babylon. Over the summer of 1915 they rose to a height of perhaps 150 feet, with battlements wide enough for a chariot to be driven along them. Griffith had not told his underlings that the various projects they were shooting were to be brought together into a single great scheme; and so his crew members, even more than the public at large, were puzzled to see Babylon surmounted with a large sign advertising *The Mother and the Law*.

To design the set, Griffith hired a theatrical draftsman named Walter L. Hall, whom he installed in a room built on stilts at one end of the lot. Hall could look out and see the set take shape, constructed by Griffith's master carpenter, Frank 'Huck' Wortman; then he would go back to sketching furiously in pencil on sheets of heavy cardboard. Karl Brown, who has given us the only account of Hall, describes an artist who was most likely academically trained, since he obsessed over the fundamentals of illusionism: linear perspective and infinitely precise draftsmanship. Brown reports that even though Hall worked without using a T-square, straight-edge, or compass, he could, on demand from Huck Wortman, add a scale line to the drawing, ticking off an inch free-hand.

Hall composed but did not invent. He based his drawings on existing pictures, most of which were supplied to him by Joseph Henabery, who served Griffith as an actor and assistant director. Using an invoice ledger as a scrapbook, Henabery eventually compiled a picture collection that weighed more than eight pounds. The art historian Bernard Hanson examined the scrapbook in the early 1970s and reported that most of the material in it had been clipped from books on Assyrio-Babylonian archaeology. Although the intertitles for the film would eventually insist on the historical accuracy of the scenes – while the souvenir programs distributed at larger theaters would include a bibliography, to assure the audience that 'great care' had been taken to make *Intolerance* 'as accurate as modern research and record render possible' – nobody thought to strive for a literal reconstruction. Hall's design for the Gate of Imgur Bel was based on an illustration of an artifact not in Babylon but in Khorsabad, built at least 175 years before the events shown in the film. When illustrations of genuine antiquities were lacking, the picture of a modern-day artist might do instead. *The Fall of Babylon* by Georges Rochegrosse – a painting exhibited in the 1891 Paris Salon and then installed in Louis Martin's Restaurant in New York – became a source of decorative details for the movie.

In general, Hall would choose details from the scrapbook and let his imagination do the rest. 'A partial remnant of a stairway at Persepolis became the entire great stairway to the great palace of Belshazzar,' Brown writes. Hall 'could look at a pictured fragment of a recently unearthed archaeological find and from it reconstruct the entire subject, whatever it might have been.' The throne of Belshazzar, notes Hanson, was a pastiche of furniture elements and decorations from three different sources. Another art historian who examined the scrapbook, Floyd W. Martin, has confirmed this procedure, pointing out that it was used for the costumes as well as for the sets and props.

While the walls of Babylon were under construction, Griffith busied himself elsewhere on the lot, shooting his French and Judean stories. What we now have of these sequences seems perfunctory. The French story concerns the love of two Huguenots, Prosper Latour (Eugene Pallette) and Brown Eyes (Margery Wilson), who have made the unfortunate mistake of scheduling their wedding for St. Bartholomew's day. While the Brown Eyes family happily makes plans, Catherine de Medici (Josephine Crowell) is hovering over her weakling son, Charles IX (Frank Bennett), urging him to sign the Huguenots' doom. On the fatal day, Prosper Latour fights his way through the streets of Paris to rescue Brown Eyes and her family, but all are cut down by the intolerant Catholic forces.

The Judean story, being familiar to most filmgoers, could be told even more economically. In fact, it wasn't told at all. Griffith chose to dramatize only those few episodes that fitted his theme: illustrations of the Pharisees' intolerance toward wine-bibbers, women taken in adultery, and anyone who did not join them in praying loudly in the street. As in the French and modern stories, the male lead (played by Howard Gaye) was threatened with a violent end.*

We cannot know, on the basis of the existing versions of *Intolerance*, how much of these sequences Griffith might have shot. Perhaps they were intended to be more fully realized; but I doubt it. In addition to showing different nations and periods, they represent contrasting modes of narrative, which Griffith may well have wanted to keep distinct. The Judean scenes are no more than a few moral emblems. The French story is a romance, consisting mostly of conventionalized love-play and

---

* Had Griffith wanted his Judean scenes to be dramatic rather than iconic, the precedents were available. As early as 1905, Gaumont had produced a *Life of Christ* (perhaps directed by Alice Guy) using 25 sets and 300 extras. The sets were based on pictures by James Jacques Joseph Tissot, first published in 1896–97 in the so-called *Tissot Bible*. Those same pictures served Griffith for *Intolerance*.

conventionalized courtly intrigue. The modern story is a fully developed drama about social problems, presented in a highly realistic manner – more realistic, perhaps, than many of today's viewers know.

The forces of intolerance in *The Mother and the Law* are sexually frustrated upper-class women who descend upon the slums to do good. Their principal victim is the Dear One (Mae Marsh), whose husband (Bobby Harron) has been framed for a crime and sent to jail. Upon entering the Dear One's wretched apartment, they find her somewhat the worse for having medicated herself against a cough. Shocked, they take away her baby, for the good of both the child and society at large, leaving the bereft mother to peer through windows at other, happier women.

To an audience in Griffith's time, this turn of events would have seemed fully as plausible as the bloody labor strike shown earlier in the film. In the last third of the nineteenth century and the beginning of the twentieth, members of private reform groups such as the Gerry Society took away children in great numbers from New York's Lower East Side. On the reformers' testimony, the families were ruled unfit – 'unfit' generally meaning they were immigrants from the less appreciated nations of Europe, who supported themselves in hand-to-mouth trades. The children, declared to be orphans, were then hauled away. Historians estimate that as many as half of the children in New York City orphanages at the beginning of the twentieth century had at least one living parent.

So the modern story in *Intolerance* is less melodramatic than it might appear. It is also lovingly dramatized by Griffith and played with extraordinary sensitivity and depth by all the actors, especially Mae Marsh. This is Griffith in his most serious and naturalistic mode, as seen before in *The Musketeers of Pig Alley* (1912) or the homecoming sequence of *The Birth of a Nation*. The French story is essentially a throwback to Griffith's many women-under-attack films – *An Unseen Enemy*, *The Girl and Her Trust* (both 1912) – and to the riproaring costume dramas of his youth, such as *The Count of Monte Cristo*. As for the Judean scenes, they seem to me ideographic, as if (like more than a few images from Griffith's earliest films) they were the texts of intertitles translated into pictorial form. They function on the same level as the single, repeated shot that links all the episodes of *Intolerance*: the living illustration of Whitman's line 'Out of the cradle endlessly rocking.'

Three stories, three narrative modes with which Griffith was long familiar. The Babylonian story, too, would be distinct in style. It was to be the epic component of *Intolerance*, full of great crowds, mighty battles, heroic characters, and astonishing scenery – much like the grandest sequences of *Judith of Bethulia* (1914) and *The Birth of a Nation*. Perhaps *Intolerance*, in representing only a few of the most significant civilizations, would fall short of a World's Fair; but as a summation of Griffith's art (meaning, of course, the whole art of the motion picture), it still might be encyclopedic.

The Babylonian section, which completes the cinematic compendium, resembles the other three in being a story of self-righteous hypocrites attempting to suppress love. The intolerant villain in this case is the High Priest of Bel (Tully Marshall), who is outraged that Belshazzar (Alfred Paget) and his Princess Beloved (Seena Owen) should have introduced to Babylon the worship of Ishtar, goddess of love. Jealous of his prerogatives, the High Priest conspires to betray Babylon to the forces of Cyrus the Great. Since he does so while the royals are lost in each other and the lavish pleasures of their court, the mission of foiling the plot falls to an alert peasant, the strapping, onion-gnawing Mountain Girl (Constance Talmadge), who despite her rough ways feels a selfless love for Belshazzar.

Had Griffith been designing a World's Fair and not a movie, his Babylonian Pavilion, like the other three, would have needed to satisfy architecture's minimum requirement: standing up. A self-evident plan would have been required as well, so visitors could find their way out when they'd had enough; and a certain amount of space would have been left between pavilions, so their facades might be appreciated. But in a movie, the attractions were brought together in time, rather than separated in space; the spectators had to be led by the hand, rather than being left free to wander.

Most important of all: the stories, taken individually, didn't need to hold up. Griffith cut freely among them, expecting the images to support each other, like sheets of paper whirled together by a stiff wind. In some cases the alternation has a thematic force, as when he cuts from a scene of modern-day prudery to a conflation of two biblical scenes: the marriage at Cana and the woman taken in adultery. But the film's coherence is ultimately a matter of kinesthetic power, generated by the rhythm of Griffith's editing. All the climaxes happen at once: Prosper Latour battles his way toward Brown Eyes while Mountain Girl drives her chariot furiously toward a last-minute rescue, as the Dear One races to save The Boy from the gallows.

Like exotic artifacts exhibited at a World's Fair in tribute to colonial might; like a fair's historicized architecture, built to put the glories of the past at the service of progress, the Old World figures in *Intolerance* fail in their rescue attempts and die. They perish so that the audience may rejoice more fully as the New World figures triumph over intolerance and resume their love. As for the fourth story: it provides the film with both an execution *and* a happy ending, despite its failure to contribute to the chase sequence.

Perhaps the images might form a self-supporting structure; but the Babylon set would not. The walls were completed by early fall 1915, just as the Santa Ana winds began to howl. No sooner did the walls of Babylon rise than they came close to blowing down. Workmen, including Bitzer and Brown, had to moor them with ship's ropes to railroad ties driven into the ground – and even then the walls were shaken so badly that shooting on them was perilous. When Griffith wanted a chariot to race along the rampart, perhaps 150 feet above the ground, Bitzer, Brown, Huck Wortman, and the horses all trembled as the walls of Babylon swayed. But the structure held; and since there had been no casualties, Griffith ordered a second take.

The siege towers that had been built for the Persian army turned out to be impossibly heavy. Griffith brought in elephants to push them. He'd wanted elephants anyway; Pastrone had had elephants in *Cabiria*. The filmmakers, being inexperienced as zookeepers, did not realize at first that they'd acquired both males and females. They learned quickly, on the job, to separate the unruly beasts. Then Griffith decided it would be exciting to make an 80-foot-high tower crash directly toward the viewer. Deputed to get the shot, Karl Brown gamely stood his ground, though the rate at which he cranked the camera went up as the tower came down. Extras were knocked unconscious when real rocks were really thrown from the heights of Babylon. For a night shot, Billy Bitzer rigged the entire set with magnesium flares and managed not to burn it down. Griffith continued for weeks to mass his forces around the walls, making up most of the action as he went along. By early winter, he was done – and so began construction of the second Babylon set.

This was Belshazzar's Court, and it was to be even bigger than the Walls of Babylon. Léon Barsacq estimates the towers this time grew to a height of 165 feet. From the foreground rose a staircase perhaps 60 feet wide – spacious enough to accommodate a ceremonial procession of Babylonian chorus girls, organized in ten files. The steps led up to a platform some 300 feet deep, where Belshazzar and the Princess Beloved might enjoy their feast. On either side rose bulging columns, each supporting a square entablature large enough for eight men to stand along its side, each entablature in its turn supporting a rearing plaster elephant. (Griffith could not document the use of elephants as a decorative motif in Babylon; but *Cabiria* had a set in which larger-than-life gilt elephants bore capitals on their backs to support the roof. That was evidence enough.) Plaster lions lined the sides of the great stair and sat guarding the base of the columns; more lions, along with winged, hawk-faced gods, were stenciled onto the facades; to one side, the statue of an immense, seated Ishtar suckled the life-size figure of a man.

While this second great folly was under construction, Griffith shot scenes of the Persian army on the march. Each day, as many as 3000 extras were put into costume and make-up at the studio and then mustered onto Pacific Electric's streetcars. Under the supervision of Griffith's assistant directors – which in this case probably included Erich Stroheim, W.S. Van Dyke, and George Siegmann – the extras rode toward the coast on the Watts–San Pedro line, until they came to a freshwater pond called the Dominguez Slough, which now was doubling as the Euphrates. There the Persians marched for weeks; but still the set was not finished, and so the production came to a temporary halt. While Huck Wortman's carpenters labored, Karl Brown went looking for 'Oriental music' to inspire Griffith for the scenes to come. He returned with a recording of the 'Bacchanale' from *Samson and Delilah* by Saint-Saëns.

It may have been spring before the set was ready – a year after Griffith had begun expanding *The Mother and the Law* into *Intolerance*, almost a year and a half since he'd set to work on his drama of strikers and slums and heartless do-gooders. Having begun at present-day ground level with company-town cottages and tenement alleys, he was finishing in Belshazzar's Court, viewed (among other angles) from on high, in a shot that would bring the audience swooping down into the great set. Allan Dwan (another of Griffith's assistants) claimed he had rigged the equipment that made the shot possible: an open elevator, mounted on a car that ran along narrow-gauge railroad tracks. Karl Brown claimed, with equal plausibility, that the device was built by theatrical artists. Machinery of this sort was used all the time in operas and other large-scale spectacles. 'Having all this open space to work in, without the need for concealing anything from an audience, and with plenty of counterweights to balance everything out, they found it all so easy that they marveled we should think it so marvelous' (p. 169).

By the end of spring 1916, principal photography was completed. Some accounts claim the first cut ran for eight hours and that Griffith hoped to show the film on two evenings; but if that was his plan, he didn't stick to it for long. Sometime in June, he showed a preliminary version of the film to Anita Loos, who was to write the intertitles; and on June 24, he registered his copyright by depositing a shot sequence in the Library of Congress. The copyright deposit, according to film historian Russell Merritt, suggests a rough cut of no more than twelve or thirteen reels, yielding about the same three-hour length as the first-run version of *The Birth of a Nation*.

On August 6, Griffith held a sneak preview of the film in Riverside, California, where he also had previewed *The Clansman*. The announcements, from the 'Italian Feature Co.,' promised

The $500,000 Spectacle

The Downfall of All Nations or Hatred the Oppressor

In Eleven Reels

Greater Than 'The Clansman,' 'Caberia' And 'Ben-Hur' Combined

I know of no record of the audience's response; but Joseph Henabery, who accompanied Griffith to the screening with Lillian Gish, Mae Marsh, and Bobby Harron, confessed the next day that he'd found the picture confusing.

On September 5, 1916, Griffith returned to New York for the premiere of *Intolerance: A Sun Play of the Ages, in a Prologue and Two Acts*. Again the premiere was held at the Liberty Theatre, on 42nd Street between Seventh and Eighth Avenues – across the street from the Ziegfeld Follies, around the corner and up the block from the Metropolitan Opera House. This time he was presenting a film that had cost $385,906 to produce, excluding projection prints, advertising, and promotion – almost four times the cost of *The Birth of a Nation* – and this time a large portion of the money was his own: $126,750. Unfortunately for Griffith, the reception was less rapturous than before.

'Unprecedented and indescribable splendor of pageantry,' wrote Alexander Woolcott in *The New York Times*, 'is combined with grotesque incoherence of design and utter fatuity of thought to make the long-awaited new Griffith picture at the Liberty an extraordinary mixture of good and bad' (Schickel, p. 332). Despite such notices, *Intolerance* did almost as well at the box office as had *The Birth of a Nation*, for the first three or four months. Then first-run business fell off; the broader public, who had flocked to see *The Birth of a Nation* in second-run houses and small theaters all over the country, showed too little curiosity for the picture to cover its costs. Griffith had to dig into his own pocket and lend $139,000 to his D.W.G. Corporation. In 1915, he'd received $250,431 in personal income, almost all of it from *The Birth of a Nation*. From 1915 through 1916, he'd spent $265,750 in personal wealth to make *Intolerance*.

The picture was a failure. But was it as huge a failure as people began to think?

Well into the 1980s, when Richard Schickel put the legend to rest, people imagined that Griffith ruined himself with *Intolerance*. He went to the grave paying off the crazy film – though somehow, three years after its release, he contrived to purchase as his studio the 28-acre Flagler estate on Long Island Sound. And his career never recovered – though he somehow managed to make *Hearts of the World* (1918), *Broken Blossoms* (1919), *Way Down East* (1920), and *Orphans of the Storm* (1921), and to collaborate in founding United Artists. It is easier to pick apart the tragic myth of *Intolerance* than to figure out why it was believed so fervently and for so long.

What reasons do people give for the picture's failure? Legend has it that *Intolerance* was impossibly unwieldy to make. But if we recall that Griffith was inventing Hollywood methods as he went along, the most striking feature of the production was its efficiency. Yes, entire armies were mustered, but they were transported to their location by public streetcar. People were injured, but in fewer numbers than at conventional industrial sites. Reels of footage piled up to the ceiling, but only for the sections of the picture for which they would be needed, and not for the Judean and French stories.

When we turn from the process to the product, the stated reasons for failure again fall strangely beside the point. Audiences, confronted with four intercut stories, supposedly found the film hard to follow. This is a surprising allegation, considering the frequent complaints that the picture was heavy-handed. Perhaps the theme of *Intolerance* was in fact too *easy* to grasp.

Those who were hoping for another tribute to white supremacy in the vein of *The Birth of a Nation* might have felt cheated when instead they got an argument for sexual love and against religious authority. Such sentiments would have played badly in many quarters, especially outside the big cities. In 1916, half the population of the United States lived in small towns and rural areas, which was precisely the market *Intolerance* failed to penetrate. As for audiences in the cities – reviewers especially – they, too, often complained of the theme of *Intolerance*, though registering a different objection. As we have seen, they called it fatuous. But since the film was so much *less* fatuous than *The Birth of a Nation*, perhaps we should think of this response as critical displacement: the tendency to save up a grudge against one work of a filmmaker and then pay it off against the next.

No doubt the great expectations attending *Intolerance* gave rise to the myth of a great failure; yet even that explanation falls short. Certainly *Intolerance* was undone by its own publicists, who planted the report that the production had cost $2 million. And yet, though people believed such a huge sum was at stake, they might have guessed the film would recoup some part of its cost. *Intolerance* ran for 22 weeks at the Liberty – only half as long as *The Birth of a Nation*, but long enough to pay for *something*.

No single explanation seems to be enough – though the presence of so many is suggestive. (One more: *Intolerance* concluded with an untimely message of pacifism, put on the screen only half a year before the United States entered World War I. And another, from Griffith's star Lillian Gish: Griffith should have promoted his stars.) In their very multiplicity, these charges against the film hint at having been cobbled together after the fact. They may, in truth, have little to do with the public's reception of *Intolerance* in 1916. I think they are retrojections – a reading back into *Intolerance* of Griffith's real moment of failure, which hit him about ten years later.

In 1916 and immediately thereafter, people might have seen *Intolerance* as a disappointment but not as a famous disaster. In the first place, with America entering the war, most people had other things to think about than Griffith's career. As for those who were truly movie-mad, they had the responsibility of keeping up with the fresh productions coming out each week. They couldn't dwell on Griffith's problems, which in any case were still manageable.

Anyone who was interested might have learned that the London premiere of *Intolerance*, held on April 7, 1917, was a triumph for Griffith. (He attended the screening on the way to filming his wartime drama *Hearts of the World*.) Nor did the London engagement mark the end of the film's European career. Although the admiration of his fellow filmmakers could have done nothing to improve Griffith's business prospects, he might have been pleased had he known that Sergei Eisenstein was beginning to make *Intolerance* into a textbook in the Soviet Union; while in Denmark, the young Carl Dreyer was imitating *Intolerance* in *Leaves from Satan's Book*, a film he shot in 1919 on the very loose basis of Marie Corelli's novel *The Sorrows of Satan*.

And even as the fame and influence of *Intolerance* spread in Europe, parts of the picture gained new life in America. In 1919, Griffith prepared the way for his new feature, *Broken Blossoms*, by hiring the George M. Cohan Theatre in New York and presenting revivals of his recent films. He showed a revised version of *Hearts of the World* and two features pieced together from *Intolerance*: *The Mother and the Law* (which at last was allowed to be itself) and *The Fall of Babylon*. Since *Broken Blossoms* opened to rapturous reviews and great commercial success, these satellites of *Intolerance* could not have radiated much of an aura of doom. If anything, they would have made Griffith's original calculation seem shrewd in retrospect: he'd created a road-show attraction that could throw off its own little system of features.

From 1916 through 1920, there could have been no legend of the fiasco of *Intolerance*. But in 1925–26, Griffith really did fail. The causes of that failure were too shabby for a man of his stature; and so a suitably grand downfall had to be devised. I believe this was the moment when Griffith and his admirers discovered *Intolerance* to have been the turning point of his career, and overreaching genius to have been his fatal flaw.

The events of 1925–26 were sadly lacking in drama. Like any pharmacist or dry cleaner who had borrowed too heavily while setting up a second shop, Griffith had overextended himself. His recent pictures – some worthier than others, but none as deliriously grand as *Intolerance* – had produced too little revenue for him to cover his debts; and he'd tied himself up worse by promising new pictures to both United Artists and Famous Players. To extricate himself, he had to sell his beautiful Flagler estate and abandon the attempt to remain independent of the recently instituted studio system. The man who had made *The Birth of a Nation* became a contract director for Famous Players.

His first movie for the company, *Sally of the Sawdust* (1925), was less than epochal; but at least it introduced W.C. Fields to the screen and turned a profit. The second contract picture, *That Royle Girl* (1926), was a washout, in part because Griffith doubled what had been a modest budget.

The third movie finished him. It was yet another version of Marie Corelli's *The Sorrows of Satan*, a novel that had become popular with a large and undiscerning audience upon its publication in 1895. By 1926, it was dripping with moss – but *The Sorrows of Satan* was supposed to be a prestige assignment (if only because Famous Players had been negotiating for the rights since the days when people took Corelli seriously), and so Griffith gave it his all. By the time he was done and the Famous Players executives had finished meddling with his work, the picture had cost $971,260, putting it $300,000 over budget. It opened to yawns. Adolph Zukor, as head of Famous Players, discreetly showed Griffith the door.

It was during this period that the more pitiable accounts of Griffith began to circulate – put about, interestingly enough, by his close associates. Gerrit Lloyd, a sometime journalist, sometime press agent who was in his circle, published a fan magazine article in September 1925 alerting the public to Griffith's many wounds. In June 1926, Lillian Gish told the press that 'this great artist' had been 'going through a most humiliating experience' as a result of 'selling himself to a film trust.' She reported that Griffith had told her, 'I have fifty bosses now, Lillian, but I am at least paying my debts.'

Was this also when he told her of his anguish over *Intolerance*? In her memoirs, published in 1969, Gish recalled getting a letter from Griffith after *Intolerance* opened, describing his wanderings through darkened theaters: 'I don't know where to go or where to turn since my great failure.' But writing at a distance of half a century, Gish might have got her chronology mixed up. In 1916–17, Griffith had neither the time nor the need for such moping. It sounds more like the behavior people observed in 1925–26 at the Famous Players studio in Astoria, New York. At some point, Griffith may well have sent a letter tagging *Intolerance* as 'my great failure'; but I believe he would have called it that (and invented the touching detail about barking his shins on empty theater seats) much later than 1917, around the time he persuaded Gish to recount his woes to the press.

While Griffith was going about in 1926 'like a hard-up, itinerant school teacher' (in the recollection of production designer Norman Bel Geddes), with his face set like 'a stone buddha'; while he was granting to the December 1926 *Photoplay* an interview that was at once self-aggrandizing and self-pitying; while he was leaving New York and moving back, now a lesser man, to Los Angeles and the scene of his bygone triumph, the year held one more significant event. The Film Arts Guild in New York presented a tenth anniversary reissue of *Intolerance*. How sad it must have seemed, to anyone who followed motion pictures. The man who had established the movies was now a relic – and here was the picture that had begun his ruination, so soon after his greatest success.

We find the legend codified in Terry Ramsaye's *A Million and One Nights* (published in 1926), a book that served for years as an indispensable history of the early motion picture. The 'screen masses' rejected 'the most venturesome experiment in all the history of film technique' because the masses lacked 'the deductive capacity for digesting historical experience.' The public 'went to *Intolerance* in just sufficient numbers to find out that it did not know what it was about. . . . *Intolerance* was a magnificent failure.'

The folly known as *Intolerance* – as distinct from the motion picture of the same name – appeared in 1926. Chronologically, it was the third of the follies considered in this book, following *L'Inhumaine* (1923) and *Greed* (1924). It made itself known contemporaneously with (and in contrast to) MGM's *Ben-Hur* (a big, costly film, but certainly not a folly) and only slightly preceded the appearance of *Metropolis* (1927). But the 1916 film known as *Intolerance* must hold our attention for just a while longer. We still need to ask whether anything that was put on screen contributed to the legend of failure.

One possible answer comes from Anita Loos, whose intertitles for *Intolerance* might be read as an implicit critique of the film – the first, and perhaps the sharpest. Despite her repeated use of the first-person plural – we are always watching *our* Sun Play of the Ages – Loos caught with uncanny accuracy the tone of an all-consuming *I*. This was the feature of the 1916 film with the most bearing on the legend of 1926. *Intolerance* is not just a cinematic World's Fair. It is a World's Fair that takes place within the mind of D.W. Griffith, who as a genius is singularly able to accommodate it.

Loos knew her man. She had worked with him on *The Birth of a Nation*, and she was perhaps the first to see a rough cut of *Intolerance*. Let us assume she conveyed the tone desired by Griffith, who approved her titles and also improved upon them, stamping each with his initials. He even said in public that the movie was to be understood as subjective: 'Events are not set forth in their historical sequence . . . but as they might flash across a mind seeking to parallel the life of the different ages.' Whose mind could that be, if not his?

Such an ambition might have presented itself to Griffith in the same way as the World's Fair: not as a model standing before him, waiting to be emulated, but as a limit to his field of vision, looming everywhere on the periphery of consciousness, framing the realm of the possible. And just as the Expositions were all-pervasive events, setting the highest example of cultural and commercial enterprise, so too was there an inescapable model of the world-encompassing artist. That figure was Richard Wagner, whose *Ring* cycle was first performed at Bayreuth in 1876, the year after Griffith's birth, and whose music was perhaps the single greatest artistic force in New York when the young Griffith first tried to make a place for himself in that city.

In the 1890s, just before Griffith came to New York, the conductor Anton Seidl had transformed the city's musical life with his tireless proselytizing for Wagner. Although the cult made its headquarters in the Metropolitan Opera House, its influence was surprisingly widespread. During the summer, at the Brighton Beach music pavilion in Brooklyn, Seidl conducted 'Wagner Nights' for audiences of 3000. According to the musicologist Joseph Horowitz, these events, though popular, were also serious and enthusiastic in mood – even worshipful – with little of the seeing-and-being-seen that characterized other forms of concert-going.

By 1903, Wagnerism in New York was even more common, though by then it had taken on a near-hysterical atmosphere. With Seidl dead, a new manager of the Metropolitan Opera proposed a stunt that would not have been attempted earlier: a staging of *Parsifal*. As all Wagnerites knew, the master himself had given explicit and repeated instructions that this sacred music-drama could be staged only at his Festival Playhouse in Bayreuth – a stipulation energetically enforced by his widow Cosima. In this case, she went so far as to have her attorneys petition the U.S. Circuit Court to grant an injunction against the Met's production. On November 24, 1903, the court refused to do so, a decision the newspapers treated as front-page news. When *Parsifal* had its Met premiere on December 24, the *Times* ran a review by Richard Aldrich, accompanied by two and a half pages of pictures, reports on who was in the audience and what they wore, tributes to the Met's manager, and half a page of musical notations of the opera's principal motifs. Griffith at the time was based in New York, acting in tab plays in the vaudeville houses and traveling through New England with touring companies. He was a man of the theater; he would have taken note of the biggest, most legit show in town.

Griffith probably had, at best, a superficial acquaintance with the operas. But he would have known about Wagner what everyone knew: that he was a revolutionary in art (if not in politics); a genius deeply in touch with the forces of both nature and the human heart; an artist who (despite much opposition) had created the biggest theatrical work ever conceived, for which he had united the heavens, the Earth, and the underworld within his own forehead. Griffith also would have known of Wagner as a sensualist, who in his art and his life had fearlessly expressed the liberating power of sexual love. This aspect of Wagner's reputation would have been of obvious relevance to the theme of *Intolerance*, as it was to Griffith himself – a man of strong and conflicted sexuality – who frequently could not keep his hands off his actresses and who (in 1916) became infatuated with one of the dancers hired for his Babylonian story, 14-year-old Carol Dempster.

Finally, Griffith would have known that Wagner's masterwork was performed in a theater of Wagner's own design, to which pilgrims journeyed in celebration of a festival Wagner had founded. A production at Bayreuth of the four music-dramas of *Der Ring des Nibelungen* was itself a kind of one-man World's Fair. It's unlikely that Griffith knew the details.* But he knew Wagner's image.

Griffith's own tastes in opera ran toward *Tosca* and *I Pagliacci*; he was known to croon melodies from both as he went about his business. Those works – like the works of any classical composer – would have done the job, had he merely wanted to demonstrate the high aspirations of his pictures and attract a sufficiently high-toned audience. But to project an image of greatness, he needed Wagner in particular.

Griffith drew on his music before *Intolerance*, in a gesture of no small import to the culture of moviegoing. In 1915, *Moving Picture World* published an article arguing that film accompanists should play popular favorites, since audiences were 'made up largely of people who are unable to appreciate classical music.' This sensible advice, which must have been a commonplace at the time, did not prevent Griffith from releasing *The Birth of a Nation* with an orchestral score he had supervised himself, mixing Civil War songs and 'Home Sweet Home' with snatches of Mozart, Schubert, Schumann, Tchaikovsky, Grieg, Mahler, and Wagner. Griffith even got into a row with his composer–arranger Joseph Carl Breil, who objected that the leitmotif the director demanded for the Ku Klux Klan sounded too much like 'The Ride of the Valkyries' and would provoke charges of plagiarism.

Years later, when the time came for him to work with Breil on the orchestral score for *Intolerance*, he still had Wagner in mind. Again he combined popular songs, such as Chauncy Olcott's 'My Wild Irish Rose,' with hymns ('A Mighty Fortress Is Our God') and excerpts from a wide range of classical sources. Among these were *Lakmé* by Delibes, Tchaikovsky's Symphony no. 6, Beethoven's *Pathétique* and *Appassionata* sonatas, 'Immenso Phtha' from Verdi's *Aïda*, and two sections of Wagner's *Ring*: 'The Ride of the Valkyries' (of course) and Siegfried's funeral march from *Götterdämmerung*. Gillian B. Anderson, the conductor who in the 1980s retrieved Breil's score from the Library of Congress and collaborated with The Museum of Modern Art in

---

* One detail he must have known: the number of nights in a *Ring* cycle. Could this have been his reason for choosing four as the number of stories in *Intolerance*?

assembling a scholarly reconstruction of *Intolerance*, has remarked that anyone might have used 'The Ride of the Valkyries.' But the funeral march, cued to accompany the death of Mountain Girl, was not at all standard issue. Its inclusion in the score hints at a more self-conscious use of Wagner's music.

Behind the folly of *Intolerance* looms not only the Panama-Pacific Exposition but also the shadow of Bayreuth, and the conflicting forces that found their illusory resolution in the *Ring*.

Wagner first proposed creating a festival in his autobiographical essay *A Communication to My Friends*, written in 1851 – a year before he completed the text of the *Ring*, two years before he composed the first notes of the score. Even if we take into account his uncanny ability to think in the long term – to make his works 'projects' in the literal sense – we still might wonder at the chronology. Before he'd truly begun the *Ring*, he was already specifying its mode of presentation.

We cannot know why the idea of a festival should have put itself forward with any urgency in 1851. But we do know that was also the year when London held the Crystal Palace Exposition. Wagner's festival and the World's Fairs were born simultaneously. It would be surprising if the creator of the one had not known that a German, Prince Albert, was responsible for the other; and Wagner surely knew that the town he ultimately chose for the festival, Bayreuth, was only 45 miles from Albert's birthplace in Coburg.

Although some of these details are of course mere coincidence, we still might describe Wagnerism in its highest form as a dialectical opposite of the Expositions. It cannot be coincidence that Wagner's patron Ludwig II should have wanted to build the festival theater within the Glass Palace in Munich; nor was it coincidence that Wagner reacted to this proposal with revulsion. His festival, like Albert's Exposition, would be the expression of an entire society – but a society transformed by art, not a money-enslaved society, not a society in which the powerful built their monuments upon the bodies of the suffering masses and called this triumph 'rationalism'. In his essays *Art and Revolution* and *The Work of Art of the Future*, both written in 1849, Wagner made clear his abhorrence of everything the Crystal Palace would stand for: progress in the gross material sense, the rule of productivity and efficiency, the conversion of art into an industrial commodity designed to gratify an elite. To this we might add the most obvious musical and theatrical equivalent of the World's Fairs, which was grand opera: that hodgepodge of showy set pieces, thrown together at great expense to amuse the rich and bored in those intervals when they weren't talking to each other.

The building that would house Wagner's festival would perhaps be a temporary structure (like the pavilions of an Exposition), but it would be simple and plain on the outside, not ostentatious like the Munich Palace or Garnier's Paris Opéra. Its world of wonders would be contained within, as the four music-dramas had taken shape within Wagner's consciousness. And in its scope, the *Ring* would surpass to some degree the ambitions of a World's Fair. 'My poem,' Wagner explained to Liszt, 'encompasses the beginning of the world and its destruction.'

.   The first Bayreuth festival opened as did an Exposition, with the participation of emperors, kings, and nobles, accompanied by artists and curiosity-seekers from across Europe and North America. Like an Exposition, it had its own guidebook: a brochure by Hans von Wolzogen listing the 90 leitmotifs of the *Ring*. ('A musical Baedeker,' wrote the critic Eduard Hanslick, 'without which no respectable tourist here dares to be seen' (Taylor, p. 422).) But perhaps the most telling parallel between Bayreuth and the World's Fairs lay in their character as private initiatives. Whether founded by an artist or a head of state, these were carefully planned, secular, entrepreneurial showplaces – outgrowths of the eighteenth-century amusement parks, and as such distinct from the religious, civic, and commercial agglomerations that were the medieval and Renaissance fairs.

We can say this much for Wagner's festival, compared to Albert's: it incorporated, explicitly and thematically, a sense of unease about its own contradictions. If the World's Fairs were outgoing, confident expressions of nineteenth-century capitalism, then the *Ring* is the inward-looking, pessimistic expression of that same society's doubts.

The *Ring* is about the crimes committed in realizing a very large, ambitious, costly building project. Although the building in the music-dramas is called Valhalla, we might just as well think of it as the Crystal Palace, the walls of Babylon, the Festival Playhouse at Bayreuth, or the *Ring* itself. The structure, as envisioned, is so glorious, so obviously right, as to seem to justify the means of its construction.

Mannes Ehre, ewige Macht
ragen zu endlosem Ruhm!

sings Wotan upon his first appearance in the *Ring*, as he dreams of Valhalla: 'Man's honor, everlasting strength, go endlessly on to fame!' But as we learn over the course of the next fifteen hours, the foundations are laid in injustice, the structure itself is too heavy, and the whole thing must ultimately fall.

That's one way to see it, anyway. Wagner began writing the text of the *Ring* at the time of his participation in the Dresden uprising of 1849, when he was spending much of his time in the company of Mikhail Bakunin and issuing unambiguous statements about his political goals:

From its root up will I destroy the order of things in which ye live, for it is sprung from sin ... I will destroy each phantom that has rule o'er men. I will destroy the dominion of one over many, of the dead o'er the living, of matter over spirit; I will break the power of the mighty, of law, of property. (Goldman and Sprinchorn, p. 72)

And so forth. But he completed the text of the *Ring* in exile, after the failure of the revolution (if we may call 'revolution' an effort to make the King of Prussia into a new German emperor). A work that had been inaugurated in a moment of political passion was completed as the 'purest' poetic form, that of timeless myth; an artist who had acknowledged society's divisions when he railed against 'the power of the mighty' went on to imagine he might speak for society as a whole (excepting, of course, unassimilable elements such as the Jews) under the patronage of the King of Bavaria.

In *The Perfect Wagnerite*, Shaw put forward the perfect historicist explanation of the *Ring*'s inconsistencies: 'Siegfried did not arrive and Bismarck did.' Wagner, having chained himself for a quarter of a century to an outmoded text, was finally reduced to writing grand opera after all. But the music-dramas, grand opera, and the Expositions were always part of the same world; the distinguishing feature of the *Ring* was not its distance from this world but its ability to make the modern age 'speak its most intimate language,' as Nietzsche wrote in *The Case of Wagner*, 'concealing neither its good nor its bad side, utterly free from shame or embarrassment,' in all its confusion.

Even in 1853, the *Ring* was a tohu-bohu pretending to be a world. One moment you imagine you're following a political allegory (even though it's not entirely clear which set of characters represents which class). The next moment, you're eavesdropping on a domestic argument between Wagner and his unhappy first wife, Minna; and after that you're plunged into a lengthy speculation on free will versus determinism. Intellectually, Valhalla turns out to be as jerrybuilt a structure as was ever slapped together, and has been called so many times. But the *Ring* derives its power precisely from Wagner's struggle to tug his incompatibilities into a single framework. Emotionally, artistically, the work comes together through Wagner's music.

The musical procedures Wagner had inherited were ideally suited to this job. As Charles Rosen argued in his book *The Classical Style*, the music of Haydn, Mozart, and Beethoven was essentially dramatic. It established conflicts, brought them to a state of high tension, and then resolved them. Wagner's innovation was to postpone the resolution indefinitely. He held more compositional elements in tension for a longer period than anyone had imagined possible, until the listener, yielding to the flow, came to feel the process of sustaining the tensions might be as satisfying as a resolution that never arrived.

In Wagner's music-dramas, the musical procedures pour uniformly over the text, covering the discrepancies between various levels of storytelling. But film editing, though potentially both a rhythmic and motivic art, is not music. The narrative bumps stick out in *Intolerance*, no matter how ingeniously Griffith cuts among his shots. Perhaps part of the problem lies in the specificity of the images: the revenge of Bazin's film realism upon Griffith's movie symbolism. 'Babylon' and 'France,' once established, stubbornly remain 'Babylon' and 'France,' refusing to become metaphorical. The viewer is also too keenly aware that these scenes from long ago, though pitched at a different level from the modern-day story, were shot at the same time and with the same crew. By juxtaposing one against the other, the intercutting merely aggravates the viewer's sense that they all should seem as realistic as *The Mother and the Law*.

Griffith's attempt at musical form tends to separate things, where Wagner's drew them together. Worse still, Griffith too plainly wants to achieve a resolution. The figures from the Old World must perish; the children of the New World must be saved; the warring nations must put down their weapons as the Vanquisher of *Intolerance* appears in glory over the battlefields of Europe. Although *Intolerance* is a long movie, you feel the rush toward a happy ending – a kind of forced optimism, which fails to convince where Wagner's pessimism had succeeded.

Not that this had much to do with commercial failure in 1916; but by 1926, the Wagnerian aura that hung about *Intolerance* would have supplied the pessimism Griffith had lacked. The picture must have been doomed from the moment its foundations were laid. Besides, Wagnerian ambitions were coming to seem as quaint as the World's Fairs themselves; both had been superseded by the mass-produced entertainment Griffith had himself established. Philadelphia's Sesqui-Centennial opened to disaster in 1926, and a writer in *The Nation* knew why: 'Today every child has seen Javanese and Ceylonese villages on the screen' (Harris, p. 24). Although the public's passion for Expositions would revive a few times more, movies were by far the more efficient means for providing exoticism and spectacle, magnificence and instruction, and could furnish them every day.

The society of World's Fairs and Wagner Nights had become a society of movies – but a society that also knew, on occasion, the dialectical opposite of movies, the folly. People would remember the moralized story of Griffith's 'betrayal' of the movies (as Terry Ramsaye called it), his impossible, extravagant attempt to make 'the life of the different ages' flash across his mind. Some filmmakers, instead of recoiling from his example, would feel moved to commit betrayals of their own. The urge might manifest itself even in those who were neither provincial nor autodidactic, those who felt an absolute ownership of their 'culture.'

When in 1971 he was denied the rights to film a version of *Remembrance of Things Past*, Luchino Visconti turned unhappily from that project, whose script already ran to 363 pages, and took up something explicitly crazy: *Ludwig*. Cobbling together a budget from four producers – one Italian, one French, and two German – he began shooting his story of the 'mad' king at the end of January 1972.

It's possible that other filmmakers might have wangled the rights to shoot in Ludwig II's folly-castles in Bavaria: Herrenchiemsee, Neuschwanstein, Linderhof. But only Visconti could have assembled his props and furnishings exclusively from Habsburg collections. Other filmmakers might have faithfully re-created a nineteenth-century circus when the script called for one, to stage a meeting between Ludwig and his cousin, Empress Elisabeth of Austria. Only Visconti would have insisted on moving his crew to Austria, so the re-creation might be realized near the imperial hunting lodge at Bad Ischl. This was realism as Ludwig himself had practiced it: the construction of an authentic, full-scale replica of an artistic vision, at whatever cost and at whatever pains.

At the heart of the film were a set of impossible loves: Ludwig's for his cousin Elisabeth and Richard Wagner, Visconti's for his star Helmut Berger. Visconti had met Berger a few years earlier in Kitzbühel and had been traveling with him since, finding a small role for him in an episode of the anthology film *Le Streghe* (*The Witches*, 1966) and then casting him as a principal in his 1969 feature *The Damned* (or, in Italy, *La Caduta degli dei*). Visconti poured money and devotion into Berger's career, as if reversing the relationship between Wagner and his beautiful young patron. For Wagner, Ludwig built Bayreuth (the most modest project of the king's architectural career). For Berger, Visconti made *Ludwig* (or, in France, *Le Crépuscule des dieux*), a project as lavish as Ludwig's castles – some of which Visconti paid to restore as part of the production.

The question of why the castles were built – why, for that matter, the film was made – haunts *Ludwig* from the opening shot, as the camera performs a slow, caressing pan of a baroque ceiling, then comes to rest on the face of the 18-year-old Ludwig on the day of his coronation. The young king was born to splendor; but extravagance would develop only in response to Wagner, a man whom Visconti was at pains to portray as earthbound, venal, almost brutally self-centered. His scenes of Wagner's family at home are nightmares of suffocation. What makes them all the more unbearable is the sense that Ludwig longs to participate in this heavy, bourgeois domesticity, though as monarch, patron, and homosexual he's shut out. As compensation, he has only the fantasies aroused by Wagner's music, which he realizes in structures such as the grotto at Linderhof: the inside of a skull, you'd think, where swans from *Lohengrin* float as captives in a pool.

The shooting of Ludwig's story, which itself grew progressively more grotesque, dragged on into June 1972. In July, not long after photography was completed, the exhausted Visconti suffered a stroke. He was in Rome; as soon as he was strong enough to be transferred from the city, his family and friends sent him to a clinic in Zurich, where he spent August and most of September. The thought of leaving *Ludwig* unfinished tormented him, so he pushed himself through physical therapy, meanwhile deciding on the music for the film, and at the end of September went to Villa Erba at Cernobbio, where he edited *Ludwig*. Even then, the battles did not end. He wanted a running time of about four hours, but the producers insisted the film had to come in at three.

Ludwig had its public premiere on January 18, 1973, in Bonn. Visconti was too weak to attend. He was supposed to stage *Tristan und Isolde* for Leonard Bernstein at the Vienna Staatsoper later that year and then to produce the *Ring* for La Scala. He found the strength to direct *Manon Lescaut* at the Spoleto Festival; but the Wagnerian engagements had to be canceled.

Visconti had said he was interested in Ludwig as a victim: an absolute monarch who lost out in every human relationship, became a prisoner of psychiatry, and died in shadowy circumstances while still a young man. His beautiful cousin Elisabeth (played by Romy Schneider) lent her own tragic allure to the story: in conversation, Visconti was known to dwell on her death by an assassin's hand, and the later suicide of her son Rudolf at Mayerling. About these fabulous, unhappy characters who had been enchanted by art, he made a fabulous work of art that was itself doomed. 'Interesting without ever being compelling, eye-filling but mind-starving,' wrote the reviewer for *Variety* on February 21, 1973 – a formula that has become standard in criticizing follies. 'Commercial outlook, even in the U.S. primary sophisticated market, is thin.' MGM demanded that Visconti cut the film by thirty minutes for the U.S. release – not that gross a presumption, considering his European distributors had also demanded further cuts. But a shorter *Ludwig* was still *Ludwig*. It faded quickly from release; and though a longer version, in a new print, caused a stir at the Venice festival in 1980, its commercial run in 1983 failed to duplicate the success of the earlier re-release of *The Leopard* (1963).

Perhaps this folly tells its own story at the moment when a lesser character, come to Ludwig's castle at Herrenchiemsee, is led along the great hall of mirrors. He walks and he walks, since the magnificence stretches on for 211 feet. He walks and marvels; but past a certain point in his walking, he has to throw back his head and laugh.

The Politics of Authorship

Erich Oswald Hans Carl Marie Stroheim von Nordenwald was born on September 22, 1885, in Vienna. His father, a count, bore the rank of colonel in the Imperial Dragoons. His mother, a baroness, was a lady-in-waiting to the same Empress Elisabeth who would one day figure in *Ludwig*.

As a youth, von Stroheim attended the Imperial Military Academy and received a commission in the cavalry, in which he served for seven years before being detailed to the Palace Guard. With the keen eye for detail that was later to distinguish him as a filmmaker, he witnessed the elegance of the Habsburg court and its corruption. Then, for reasons he found it ungentlemanly to discuss, he severed his ties with the Imperial service and embarked for America on a cattle boat. Upon arriving in the new country, he enlisted at once in the United States Cavalry. Later, he supported himself through a series of odd jobs in New York City – tour guide, flypaper salesman, singer in a beer garden – then took up arms again as a captain in the Mexican army during the years of Pancho Villa's insurgency.

Such is the account of the filmmaker's early career given by one of his biographers, Peter Noble, in 1950. It was a remarkably late date for anyone to have believed these tales; yet they continued to circulate well after Stroheim's death in 1957, until Denis Marion put them to rest in the winter 1961–62 issue of *Sight and Sound*.

Cinephiles have since learned that the filmmaker was indeed born in Vienna on September 22, 1885, as Erich Oswald Stroheim. His mother, Johanna Bondy, was a Jew from Prague. His father Benno, a Jew from Silesia, was a merchant in felt, straw, and feathers who later became owner of a small factory that made hats. As a youth, Stroheim worked as a supervisor in the factory. He also served in the army; but he did so as a conscript, held the rank of private, and apparently deserted before his year was up. The ship on which he sailed for America was not a cattle boat but the *Prince Friedrich Wilhelm*, from which Stroheim disembarked at Ellis Island on November 25, 1909.

The list of odd jobs may be true. It's also true that Stroheim performed some military service in America: during 1911, he made a few dollars as a private in the New York National Guard. The fabulations he fed to Peter Noble begin to tally with fact only around 1912, the year Stroheim entered into an unhappy marriage in San Francisco. The subsequent divorce, involving charges of sadism and playwrighting, caused him to continue his varied activities at a resort hotel at Lake Tahoe, where in addition to performing menial chores he gained the attention of a wealthy married woman, who agreed to pay for a production of his play. It failed; but since the scene of this failure was Los Angeles, Stroheim took the opportunity to introduce himself, 'von' and all, to D.W. Griffith, who seems to have used him as a horse wrangler and extra for *The Birth of a Nation*. So began a famously troubled career in motion pictures.

Stroheim worked as one of the many assistant directors on *Intolerance*, in which picture he also got to play a Pharisee. But it was only with the entry of the United States into World War I that Stroheim found his *métier*, embodying a succession of dastardly Prussian officers. He even got to play one for Griffith, who cast him as a Hun (though not the leading Hun) in *Hearts of the World*. To his chagrin, Stroheim spent most of his time off-camera, mustering the extras.

He was later fond of saying he had 'graduated from the D.W. Griffith school.' We might say he passed his finals when he directed the battle scenes for *The Heart of Humanity*, a knock-off of *Hearts of the World* made in 1918 for Universal. This assignment gave him access not only to Universal City but also (with much pushing) to the studio's boss, Carl Laemmle.

Did Stroheim let Laemmle know he was Jewish? The secret, had it been imparted, could only have improved his chances. Laemmle was fabled for his nepotism, 'family' in his case meaning almost anyone who came from Württemberg; he might have warmed to a fellow Jew. But Stroheim seems to have kept the secret even with Laemmle, to judge from the way everyone continued to believe the 'von.'* Perhaps it was enough for him to address Laemmle in German; or perhaps he found that by maintaining his Palace Guard imposture, he could convince 'Uncle Carl' that here was a man who combined superior breeding with an ability to get things done.

42 * Years later, Orson Welles claimed that he, for one, had seen through Stroheim. Welles also used to do a mind-reading act.

And, of course, he saved the studio money. According to film historian Thomas Schatz, Universal at that time maintained a policy of avoiding costly items such as stars and feature films. It committed itself instead to the efficient manufacture of five-reel programmers, newsreels, and serials, destined primarily for neighborhood and small-town theaters. We may imagine Laemmle's delight when he learned that this charming German fellow would direct, for no money, an original script he would give Universal for free. Stroheim required nothing but a modest salary of $200 a week in exchange for playing the lead.

The picture Laemmle got for this deal was *Blind Husbands*: eight reels of eyebrow-raising trans-Atlantic dalliance. Having been defeated in World War I, the Hun now returned to the screen to seduce American women, and no doubt give American men a few lessons in sophisticated cold-bloodedness. *Blind Husbands* proved to be a winning mixture of pleasures for the audience: the thrill of abasement before a 'genius' (as the advertisements called Stroheim); the thrill of power at seeing that genius crushed in the final reel. According to Richard Koszarski's authoritative biography of Stroheim, the picture made $328,000 during its first year of release – six times the profit of the average Universal feature. It also gave Laemmle the two things he least wanted: a star, and a precedent for making more first-run films.

Stroheim followed *Blind Husbands* with *The Devil's Pass Key* (1920), which confirmed his success and added to it a reputation for formal innovation. (Much was made at the time of the picture's expressive use of color.) Then, in 1920, he started production on *Foolish Wives*.

Had Stroheim not gone on to make *Greed*, *Foolish Wives* might be known as his great folly. It was the picture on which he spent most lavishly, the one for which he constructed his equivalent of Babylon on the Universal lot. Unlike Griffith, Wotan, or the designers of World's Fairs, he did not make a palace. Stroheim built a casino.

The most significant exterior scenes of *Foolish Wives* take place on a full-scale, perfectly detailed replica of a street in Monte Carlo. The opening shot (at least in the version that has come down to us) is of a roulette wheel; and though the plot, once more, has to do with the seduction of an American wife, much of its working out is concerned with ways to toss around unearned money. Chief among these devices is counterfeiting. The film's trio of villains, of whom Stroheim's character is the centerpiece, maintain themselves in conspicuous luxury by passing funny money at the gambling tables. Of course, the villains' identities are as fraudulent as their banknotes, giving rise to a remarkable piece of self-portraiture. Stroheim plays 'Count Karamzin,' a man who lives by his wits and who therefore finds it useful to pose as an officer and an aristocrat.

Since the audience did not know this was in essence Stroheim's own situation, the choice of role may be something less than confessional. Even so, viewers would have required no great leap of the imagination to realize that Stroheim himself was the subject of *Foolish Wives*. When his Karamzin, sitting on the terrace of the Hôtel de Paris, begins to woo the neglected wife of an American diplomat, he does so by pointing out an amusing passage in the book she's been reading: *Foolish Wives*, by Erich von Stroheim. It's as if she's being offered a guided tour of a fraudulent world, conducted by the fraud who truly created it.

Like Griffith in *Intolerance*, Stroheim wanted the audience to feel his presence everywhere in the film. But *Foolish Wives* lacks the didacticism and moral fervor of the Master (as Stroheim liked to call him). Self-representation in *Foolish Wives* was an exercise in irony – a high-stakes game, but a game nonetheless.

As his bets on the production mounted, Universal made the most of the situation by boasting of its own extravagance. Laemmle took out advertisements – 'He's going to make you <u>hate him</u>! even if it takes a million dollars of our money to do it!' – and put up billboards to help the public keep track of the production: 'To date, $423,000 has been spent on von $troheim's *Foolish Wives*.' Eventually the expense rose to the level predicted, and Universal duly advertised 'the first million-dollar picture,' a claim that somehow was not contradicted by the belief that *Intolerance* had cost two million.

The premiere was held at New York's Central Theatre on January 11, 1922. 'An insult to every American,' wrote the reviewer in *Photoplay*. There was higher praise, too; but *Foolish Wives* nevertheless faltered at the box office, eventually grossing only $869,285. This was a lot of money, of course; but Stroheim had spent much more.

He had suffered the first setback in his career as actor–writer–director. To him, and to generations of film historians, it was also the first catastrophe inflicted upon him by his legendary antagonist, Irving Thalberg. The story of *Foolish Wives*, and of the subsequent catastrophe of *Greed*, is usually told in terms of the clash between these two incompatible figures: Stroheim the artist, who needed his freedom to create, and Thalberg the corporate executive, who needed to impose the order of his own work-in-progress, the studio system. There is evidence – as Jonathan Rosenbaum points out in his invaluable monograph on *Greed* – that the parties to this struggle eventually came to act out their roles, as if collaborating on the creation of the legend. But by that point, two and a half years after the release of *Foolish Wives*, self-representation was no longer a game to Stroheim. He had become as earnest as Griffith.

We will get to that story. But to make sense of it, let us first consider a relationship even stormier than the one between Stroheim and Thalberg: the one between Stroheim and his public.

'An insult to every American.' If we take this comment from *Photoplay* seriously, we begin to understand how the public had changed between the release of *Blind Husbands* in 1919 and *Foolish Wives* in 1922. The first emerged during a moment of upheaval; the second, in the midst of reaction.

In the year *Blind Husbands* was released, America was undergoing a postwar economic crisis, with prices rising steeply (they doubled between 1915 and 1920) and unemployment peaking at 19 percent. Unions called 3600 industrial strikes in 1919, involving 4 million workers. In Seattle, one of these actions turned into a general strike – the first in U.S. history – which the city's mayor described as the initial step toward 'an attempted revolution.' Although the strongest and most visible of the nation's radical organizations, the homegrown Industrial Workers of the World, received credit and blame for the Seattle strike, the victory of Bolshevism in Russia also led to the founding in 1919 of two American communist parties.

As if this weren't enough to give the impression of all hell breaking loose, 1919 saw the eruption of race riots throughout the country, the worst of them in Chicago, as white workers took revenge on the blacks who had moved into factory jobs. Blacks fought back. In New York, Marcus Garvey solidified America's first major black nationalist movement by establishing his Black Star shipping line. (The following year, 25,000 people gathered at Madison Square Garden for the convention of his United Negro Improvement Association.) Nor was black militancy confined to the North. Between 1917 and 1919, membership in the National Association for the Advancement of Colored People jumped from just over 9000 to more than 90,000, with most of the growth taking place in the South.

As for the nation's largest group of disenfranchised citizens, they were making themselves highly visible in the year of *Blind Husbands*. The agitation for women's suffrage reached its climax that year, followed in 1920 by ratification of the Nineteenth Amendment.

In her history of this period, Lynn Dumenil points out that the war did not create the forces that broke loose in 1919. But the war did help set them free within an America that was newly urban, newly industrial, and just beginning to recognize itself as a world power. For a moment, the country's elites were caught by surprise, as were the more conservative segments of the public at large. Then the lid clamped down.

Attorney General A. Mitchell Palmer conducted his notorious political raids in 1919–20, culminating in the arrest of 10,000 people. State governments collaborated with employers in busting unions; membership dropped from 5 million in 1920 to 3.6 million in 1923. Immigrants – the bearers of socialism and many other unwholesome traits – were restricted from entering the country, beginning with the passage of a quota act in 1921. (The final National Origins Act was passed into law three years later.) The Ku Klux Klan reasserted itself, hiring specialists in public relations to organize a recruitment drive. From 1920 through 1925, the Klan attracted perhaps 5 million new members, becoming a presence in cities in the North and West (including Los Angeles) and giving women a nativist, conservative outlet for their votes through its auxiliary, Women of the Ku Klux Klan.

Progressivism and radicalism did not die out easily. The 1921 trial and conviction of the anarchists Nicola Sacco and Bartolomeo Vanzetti on charges of bank robbery and murder gave the left a cause to rally around. The 1922 elections brought many progressives into public office and saw the defeat of many conservatives. But Sacco and Vanzetti were ultimately doomed; the elections of 1922 were reversed by those of 1924. By the time *Foolish Wives* opened, the country's dominant ideology was the newly coined 'Americanism'; its president, Warren G. Harding, was promising a return to 'normalcy'; its leading corporate voice, *The Wall Street Journal*, was satisfied that 'Never before, here or anywhere else, has a government been so completely fused with business.'

Business – meaning the managers of corporations – now began to take control of one of the more slippery concepts in politics: that of the 'progressive.' Before the war, the term generally had belonged to those people who sought to limit the encroachments of corporate power, acting in the name of the public good. This good could be thought of as real property: a *res publica*, or common wealth. Progressives in this sense continued to be a force in the early 1920s, led by figures such as Robert La Follette. But after 1919, corporate managers, through their publicists and lobbyists, increasingly claimed that *they* were the true progressives. They did not necessarily use the name; but as Dumenil observes, they took pains to describe themselves as forward-looking, modern, dedicated to 'service.' Those who wanted to advance the public good were therefore advised to allow corporate managers to do as they pleased. In fact, 'the public good,' in the sense of common wealth, began to be defined out of existence; society amounted to nothing but an agglomeration of private interests. In the celebrated dictum of President Calvin Coolidge, 'The business of America is business.'

For Hollywood, the wave of postwar reaction struck in the form of the Fatty Arbuckle scandal. In 1921, a young woman named Virginia Rappe went to a party attended by Arbuckle and came out dead. The district attorney, acting on a combination of shaky evidence and political ambition, charged Arbuckle with manslaughter. An uproar ensued, in which editorialists railed against the loose morals practiced and promoted by filmmakers, Arbuckle lost his career as a star comedian, and Hollywood producers founded an office for self-censorship.

Foolish Wives had the bad luck to open on the same day as Arbuckle's much-publicized second trial, a coincidence that reinforced the impression of the film's immorality. It didn't matter that Stroheim's Karamzin came to a bad end and was stuffed down a sewer, or that his main antagonist, the American diplomat, at last showed himself to be manly and wise. The more conventional audience first had to endure nine reels of an arrogant foreigner's smirking and lip-smacking, as he effortlessly led astray an American wife while mocking her husband's devotion to the duty of every American: business. Conservative moviegoers could also object to Stroheim's matter-of-fact treatment of soldiers maimed in the recent war – a frequent presence in *Foolish Wives*. And Stroheim himself may have seemed politically suspect, since he suggested there might be something fraudulent about expatriate Russian aristocrats who had lost everything – everything – to the Revolution.

Yet even in 1922, some Americans could enjoy *Foolish Wives*. They were too sparse in number to make Stroheim's bet pay off, but they existed. In fact, they allowed the picture to rank ninth at the American box office in 1922, according to one estimate cited by Koszarski. Given the climate into which the film was released, this degree of success was remarkable.

For shorthand, we might speak of an audience of Stroheim followers. To understand their relationship to the larger audience – and to take the full measure of Stroheim's audacity in following *Foolish Wives* with *Greed* – we will need to think for a moment about *where* the audience watched its movies. For that matter, we will need to consider the kinds of places where people gather in Stroheim's films.

The Monte Carlo street that Stroheim built for *Foolish Wives* is a good place for holding a parade. You might even say it has a parade perpetually in progress. The avenue is broad, the shady sidewalks ample, and Stroheim crowds both with a citizenry engaged full-time in creating open-air spectacles, formal and informal alike. One of the most notable features of *Greed*, by contrast, is its lack of any such civic space. The characters go to places of public diversion – a cliff-side beer garden, an amusement park, a vaudeville theater – but they are all privately owned. In fact, *Greed* specifies in each case that money must be paid before any fun can be had.

This was another characteristic of the America for which and about which Stroheim made *Greed*: its sense of public space was shrinking. We might even interpret in this context the loss of interest in World's Fairs. Although the fairs were privately managed, from 1876 to 1915 they left behind great public amenities: park systems and civic museums. The 1893 fair in particular sparked an entire City Beautiful movement, which transformed not only Chicago but large parts of many other cities. The 1920s saw a waning in this drive to create civic spaces; at the same time, the fairs themselves waned temporarily. (It's telling that they gained strength again in the 1930s, as the federal government tried to counteract the Depression by launching a major new series of public works.)

But instead of looking ahead to the 1930s, let's look back again. If we recall how follies, amusement parks, and World's Fairs developed, it becomes apparent that the communal space of the medieval and Renaissance fairs was superseded over the centuries by privately managed spaces, conceived not for participation but for spectatorship. This long-term displacement of public by private space was merely continued and intensified in the 1920s. The 'public' places frequented by the characters in *Greed*, such as the vaudeville theater, played their role in this development. In general, that role became larger as these places filled up with the middle class.

Consider the history of vaudeville. In the years after the Civil War, American variety shows were principally played in male-only beer halls (where the most eagerly awaited part of the production was the 'afterpiece,' or dirty-joke pantomime), and also in the relatively open settings of barns, livery stables, and markets. Enterprising showmen of that period also built 'museums of curiosities' – freak shows – where jugglers, acrobats, and comedians would appear in alternation with Jo-Jo the Dog-Faced Boy and the unfortunate Bertha Mills, whose feet were 19 inches long.

We should not be surprised to learn that acts traveled back and forth from 'museums' and beer halls to the midways of World's Fairs. Nor is it startling that one of the performers, Tony Pastor, should have had the clever idea of opening the first clean variety show in the United States. He launched his enterprise in New York City in October 1881, reasoning that he could make more money if women as well as men could attend. He therefore eliminated the freaks and afterpieces and presented nothing more shocking than Ferguson and Mack's knockabout Irish comedy; blackface comics Lester and Allen; Lillie Western, who dressed in trousers and played 'Wedding Bells' on the concertina; and Ella Wesner, a male impersonator who performed English music-hall songs, monologues, and comic turns.

Others followed where Pastor had led. In Boston in 1885, Edward Franklin Albee and Benjamin Franklin Keith – circus men by training – started down a path that would lead to their ownership of a nationwide circuit of clean vaudeville houses, as they presented a cut-price, cut-script, pirated version of *The Mikado*. In 1893, Koster and Bial opened a splendid vaudeville house on 34th Street in New York. (It soon became the site of the first exhibition of projected motion pictures in the United States.) Most glorious of all, Florenz Ziegfeld, Jr. launched his 'Follies' in 1907 on the roof garden of the New York Theatre. With Ziegfeld, vaudeville became an entertainment not just for the middle class but for its most affluent, sophisticated members. He turned his roof garden into a replica of a Parisian café and mounted, at breakneck pace, a succession of topical skits, dance numbers, and specialty acts, including a parody of Richard Strauss's *Salome*, which only recently had received its scandalous American premiere at the Metropolitan Opera.

Operatic parody was a recurring feature of vaudeville in its cleaned-up phase. This, too, may be significant, since opera itself had undergone a transition into the realm of the middle class. The only difference was that it traveled from the opposite direction.

According to Donald Jay Grout, the immediate predecessors of opera were two forms of courtly entertainment: the ballet (a set of dances performed by the members of the court, derived from the masquerades of carnival) and the *intermedio* (a musical number inserted into a secular drama). Out of these spectacles came the sixteenth-century pastorale (a courtly drama based on classical sources, sung in its entirety) and then opera.

Now, courts are elite places, but they are anything but private. The entertainments enjoyed there, along with those mounted in other spaces under the sponsorship of the court, had a civic aspect and could reach many people who were not blessed by noble birth. In the case of opera, the demand for this new entertainment grew rapidly among the wider public, leading in 1637 to the inauguration, in Venice, of the first opera house open to the general public. Grout says that by the last years of the seventeenth century, no fewer than six opera troupes were playing to the 125,000 citizens of Venice. These patrons were an urban audience made up in large part of merchants, bankers, affluent tradespeople dealing in luxury goods: a middle class. Their taste in entertainment should not surprise us. As Grout writes:

The Aristotelian unities gave way before a bewildering succession of scenes, sometimes as many as fifteen or twenty in a single act, full of strong feeling and suspense, abounding in sharp contrasts and effects of all kinds. Lavish scenic backgrounds added to the spectacle. Pastoral idylls, dreams, oracles, incantations, spectral apparitions, descents of gods, shipwrecks, sieges, and battles filled the stage. (Grout, p. 88)

These extravagances would multiply during the period of baroque opera, only to be pruned back during the period of the refined, regulated *opera seria*. But the overall evolution of opera was in the direction of grandeur, variety, and ostentation, presented for a larger and larger audience of the middle class.

This development reached its peak in Paris with grand opera, the style established in the 1830s by Giacomo Meyerbeer's *Robert le Diable* and *Les Huguenots*. Grout compares grand opera to the historical novels of Sir Walter Scott and Alexandre Dumas *père* and the romantic dramas of Victor Hugo: middle-class literature *par excellence*. No wonder. The Paris Opéra enjoyed little support from the government. It depended on box-office receipts from upper-middle-class customers, whom it strove to please.

Imagine the convergence of the two lines of development we have been tracing, one spreading downward from the Italian courts to the Paris Opéra, the second rising from the beer halls of post-Civil War America to the roof garden of the New York Theatre. They meet in the movie palaces, amid the middle class of the 1920s.

The triumph of this new form of private space, conceived *as if* it were public, was another characteristic of the decade. Relatively few of these grand theaters existed when the 1920s began, as Koszarski notes, nor did the movie industry yet gear itself to them. But by the decade's end, the dominant features of American movie culture – in the landscape of cities and in the minds of industry executives – were named Roxy, Tivoli, Capitol, Olympic, Paradise.

These were the movie industry's equivalents to the fairgrounds of Expositions; but unlike World's Fairs, they were open for business every day of the week, in every major city at once. Writing of the movie palaces, historian Ben Hall has remarked that 'The United States in the twenties was dotted with a thousand Xanadus' (Koszarski, *An Evening's Entertainment*, p. 20). Some recalled the exoticism of eighteenth-century follies, taking the form of Chinese pagodas, Egyptian temples, Aztec monuments. More often, the movie palaces were as eclectic as fairground architecture, tossing together Moorish arches with Renaissance grillwork, Gothic niches, and engaged classical columns, all under a ceiling that sparkled like the sky at ten minutes past dusk. The patron's entrance to this wonderland led in a ceremonial procession through lobbies that became progressively more exalted, until a uniformed usher would show the way into the auditorium's splendor. The room shook from the blasts of the Wurlitzer organ. An orchestra played selections of popular tunes and light classical music. Dancers, comedians, slide shows – even dramatic 'prologues' with full costumes and sets – crossed the stage. In the midst of it all, one might watch a motion picture.

This was a long way from the nickelodeons of the century's early years, where the audience had been dominated by immigrants and the working class. As many film historians have argued, the increasing emphasis on the production of features beginning around 1909, along with the steady upgrading of urban theaters, helped to convert moviegoing into a middle-class pastime. The 1920s witnessed a great expansion in this audience – in filmgoing generally, but most tellingly among white-collar workers, small-scale entrepreneurs, and their families in the large cities. Through the magic of oversimplification, we may observe that this change, too, was merely one more moment in the *embourgeoisement* of forms of entertainment, and of the creation of 'public' spaces that actually were private.*

With the aid of this caricature, we may perhaps recognize the more prominent features of the audience that rejected *Foolish Wives* – the same audience that by the mid-1920s remembered *Intolerance* as having been nothing but a crazy failure. Trusting in the progressive spirit of its corporate bosses, proud of its Americanism, eager to be diverted by novelties and eclectic ostentation – 'causes without effects,' as Richard Wagner said of grand opera – the middle-class audience of the movie palaces wanted nothing from the screen but gratification, and plenty of it.

But there was also the audience that welcomed *Foolish Wives*. If we want to understand their response to Stroheim, we might continue this

---

* Did Walter L. Hall, designer of the Babylonian set for *Intolerance*, play a role in these developments? My research shows that immediately before going to work for Griffith, Hall was employed by the Edward H. Flagg Scenic Company in Los Angeles, a firm that produced settings, props, and other theatrical equipment and also engaged in the planning and design of theaters. Perhaps Hall came to Griffith's attention for having drawn some theater's exotic, antiquarian decor.

line of argument by comparing them to the audience – more properly, audiences – that in earlier years had gathered around Wagner.

Joseph Horowitz notes that Wagner's disparate followers included Christians and neopagans, pessimists and meliorists, Romantics and modernists. What held them together – apart from the shared experience of emotional release afforded by Wagner's music-dramas – was a conviction that they were challenging the status quo. In a society where commerce dominated all human relations, including the sexual and the artistic, Wagnerism sounded the cry for a truer, deeper life. What's more, there was nothing nostalgic about this protest. Wagnerites were devoted to the most stirring art of the present moment – indeed, to the art of the future. They, too, were progressives.

It would be easy to sneer at such aspirations – to say the Wagnerites were middle-class people who had risen in confused rebellion against themselves. Of course they were; and the terms of their revolt were not always useful. Longing to be a public and not just a class, some of them (including Wagner) became caught up in the ruinous ideologies of nationalism and race; others, in equally vaporous notions of spiritual community. But at least the Wagnerites were sufficiently self-aware, compared to the audience for grand opera, to feel unease about the modern world and their place in it; at least they could identify the need for some form of public life that was not driven by getting and spending. And in their allegiance to Wagner himself, they were perhaps making an imaginative leap, rather than indulging in mere hero-worship.

In a society given over to private moneyed interests, the Wagnerites hoped to reestablish public space through a paradoxical strategy: by intensifying the private into the individual. Bayreuth was the Opéra swallowed whole by one man. Only a great artist such as Wagner could have pulled off the trick. But through him, everyone could share in an experience that both encompassed the world and redeemed it from venality.

Stroheim's audience cannot be identified as well as Wagner's. Although historians can trace, more or less, who went to Bayreuth or to Seidl's productions at the Metropolitan Opera, we can't specify who bought tickets in Des Moines to see Stroheim's pictures. And yet, if we peer into a nonexistent book called *Foolish Wives*, as it is offered to us within the movie, we read the characteristic sentiments of the Wagnerite. The crass demands of modern society have turned American men into debased creatures: blind to beauty, deaf to courtesy, conscious of nothing but the struggle for money. To enjoy Stroheim's performance in *Foolish Wives* was to admit, if only until the last reel, that there might be some truth in this criticism.

An appreciation of *Foolish Wives* also marked one as having progressive tastes: up to date, but not avant-garde. This trait, too, recalled Wagnerism, which in America had been part of the genteel tradition. In the late nineteenth century and the early years of the twentieth, the music-dramas were understood to be advanced but not shocking or unhealthy (unlike, say, Strauss's *Salome*). In the same way, *Foolish Wives* was modern but not modernist, especially when compared with productions of the moment such as Dadaist outrages, the German Expressionist film *The Cabinet of Dr. Caligari* (Robert Wiene, 1920), and the recently serialized *Ulysses*.

Finally, to admire Stroheim's achievement as a writer–director–actor was to trust in the power of the individual artist to swallow, rather than to be swallowed up. Like Wagner – or Griffith – Stroheim could contain a world within himself, and do it not merely for the sake of pride but to reconnect the public to the deep impulses of art. Stroheim promised to subsume an entire corporate system within himself, and by making it individual return it to the public. For our sake, he spent a million dollars of Universal's money.

But *Foolish Wives* was still something that could conceivably be shown in a movie palace, where the unstable audience of Stroheim followers might overlap with a crowd of mere curiosity-seekers. Like *Intolerance*, it proposed an alternative line of development *within* the movies. (We might compare this with the way Wagner's music-dramas can be removed from Bayreuth and put into normal opera houses, where today they coexist quite comfortably with even the works of Meyerbeer.) *Greed* was different. It is perhaps best understood not as a motion picture but as an act of sabotage – the flinging of something unassimilable into the machinery.

Nothing about the film's paraphrasable content or form was inherently radical; but the act of making a film with that form and content amounted to political revolt. In effect, Stroheim had broken with the movies; *Greed* simply did not fit into any category available in the early 1920s. Other dramas of working-class life were being made (think of *The Mother and the Law*), but none of them threatened to drag on for eight hours. Very long films were being made, too: Henri Diamant-Berger's lavish, twelve-hour *Les Trois Mousquetaires* (1921–22), which celebrated its premiere on three consecutive nights at the Trocadéro in Paris, or Fritz Lang's two-part, four-hour crime thriller *Dr. Mabuse, der Spieler* (1922), compounded of occultism, documentary observation, and political paranoia. In Europe, there was even room for the occasional oddball – notably Abel Gance's nine-hour *La Roue* (1922), which caused a sensation by narrating a melodramatic, ripely 'literary' story through bravura avant-garde gestures. The two-part *Foolish Wives* might have made sense among these superproductions; but not *Greed*.

Monumentally long but unrelievedly grubby, *Greed* was the great anti-folly. By the mere fact of its having been made, the film said 'no' – no to the system of film production in which Stroheim was working, no to the entire social and political system in which Thalberg's methods made sense. By creating *Greed*, Stroheim was demanding a world in which *Greed* would not be impossible.

Greed was the anti-folly in another sense as well. It marked Stroheim's temporary break with the Romantic notion of the author. Having followed the world-encompassing strategies of Wagner and Griffith, he now gave them another paradoxical twist. In *Greed*, Stroheim reestablished a sense of public space by *removing* himself from the world he created.

The source for *Greed* was a popular novel by Frank Norris, *McTeague*, published in 1899. Since the title character was a fraud, Stroheim again had an opportunity for self-portraiture. But a title character need not be central. The most striking feature of *Greed* was its refusal to fix the narrative on any one character.

That, at least, was Stroheim's intention, as we may reconstruct it from the extant copy of his script. The *Greed* that eventually reached theaters, in a cut imposed by the studio, is a different story.

As we have received it from MGM, *Greed* is essentially a three-character film. Bearish, simple Mac (Gibson Gowland) works on Polk Street in San Francisco, where he practices dentistry without benefit of a license. One day, his sharp-dressing buddy Marcus (Jean Hersholt) brings in Trina (ZaSu Pitts), his cousin and 'sweetie,' who needs to have three teeth pulled. Mac falls for her dark, frail, nervous beauty. When he confesses his feelings to his buddy, Marcus rises to the moral challenge by grandly declaring that Mac can have her. At this point, Trina herself has not been consulted; but after a struggle she yields to Mac's animal force. For a moment, everyone seems content. But on the evening of the engagement party, Trina has a fatal stroke of luck: she wins $5000 in a lottery.

The money changes everything. Trina feels more passion for her winnings than for Mac; and Marcus believes he's lost not only his girlfriend but also a small fortune. The rest of the film is a downward spiral of betrayal, mania, drunkenness, domestic violence, and murder, culminating (for no plausible reason) on the salt flats of Death Valley, where the evils of greed are represented as if on a mythic scale.

This story was indeed part of Stroheim's script. There was also a lot more. As Jonathan Rosenbaum has demonstrated, Stroheim retained two subplots from Norris's novel, each of which focused on the fortunes of a different couple. Instead of following three characters, the audience would have needed to track at least seven; and Stroheim was in no hurry to bring them together into a plot. For example, his film included a very long sequence – excised from the studio version – in which he followed the seven characters through a typical Saturday, casually cross-cutting among their comings and goings.

As Stroheim told an interviewer while he was shooting *Greed*, 'Plot is a pattern, the mechanism by which infantile minds are intrigued. . . . But life, raw, immense, swirling, has no plot.' In the Saturday sequence, as elsewhere, Stroheim seems to have attempted to present the swirl and not the pattern. 'Practically nothing of any narrative consequence happens' in the Saturday sequence, Rosenbaum observes (pp. 28–9). Its method of exposition 'suggests something quite radical for film, and not only for that period; it might even seem a bit over-extended in an Antonioni film of the 60s.'

So, even though certain elements of Mac's character might remind us of Stroheim – the false credentials, the wife-beating – we cannot put him in a privileged position within the film, let alone make him the stand-in for an all-controlling filmmaker. If we insist on reading Stroheim into *Greed*, we will need to think in terms of autobiography rather than self-portraiture – and then discover in turn the limits of that interpretation.

As Rosenbaum notes, *McTeague* is set in the 1890s, whereas *Greed* begins in 1908. This updating makes the film's action contemporaneous with Stroheim's first rough years in New York and San Francisco. When he went on location for the film, Stroheim was revisiting settings he knew only too well: boarding houses that had been wallpapered into a form of respectability, second-floor offices that looked out onto grimy Polk Street, saloons crowded with jobless men cadging drinks, railroad depots that delivered passengers into industrial no-man's-lands. We are a long way from the Europe of *Foolish Wives*, in an America of low, narrow buildings made of unfinished wood planks. No boulevards, parks, or parade grounds exist here; only when a space is unwanted is it left available to the public, so that poor lovers do their courting over open sewers. 'Iris in,' says the script, 'on a medium shot of a dead rat and other sewage floating by in the water.'

Stroheim knew this America more intimately than had Frank Norris, a millionaire's son, who wrote *McTeague* while studying at Berkeley and Harvard, and whose research trips onto Polk Street amounted to literary slumming. But then, it was no distinction for Stroheim to have known this America. Millions did. If the updating to 1908 introduced a degree of autobiographical feeling for Stroheim – and I'm sure it did – this was the autobiography of someone who keenly remembered being a nobody.

It proved to be an arduous task, filming the raw swirl of nobody's America. Stroheim moved into the St. Francis Hotel in San Francisco early in 1923 and began writing the script, or rather talking it out in sessions that could last for eighteen hours. Shooting began on March 13 and was interrupted soon after, when Stroheim collapsed from the overwork to which he'd already subjected himself. But he recovered quickly enough, and by the end of July the San Francisco shooting was done, despite the delays caused by Stroheim's methods. He talked the actors through the most minute details of their performances, made them live in the same shabby places where their characters lived, and demanded take after take. Some of the repetition was caused by Stroheim's experiments with the lighting, which he kept as natural as possible; some, by his wanting to cover the scenes from every possible angle. When certain angles proved physically impossible, he would order a wall torn out of the set – no small matter, since he was filming on location, in ordinary buildings.

For the conclusion of *Greed*, Stroheim was determined to shoot in the authentic Death Valley, just as he'd insisted on the authentic Polk Street and Oakland. The company reached the desert during the fiercest heat of summer. Jean Hersholt recalled that

out of 41 men, 14 fell ill and had to be sent back. When the picture was finished I had lost 27 pounds and was ill in hospital, delirious with fever. . . . Every day Gibson Gowland and myself would crawl across those miles of sunbaked salt . . . Stroheim yelled at us, 'Fight, fight! Try to hate each other as you both hate me!' (Koszarski, *The Man You Loved to Hate*, pp. 136–8).

Still the ordeal wasn't finished. On September 13 the company moved on to Placer County in northern California, to the authentic site of the Big Dipper mine. Stroheim was not content merely to go underground; he had to shoot 3000 feet down a mineshaft.

The production wrapped on October 6, 1923. Koszarski gives the summary: 198 shooting days and 446,103 feet of negative. Out of this mountain of footage, Stroheim carved a rough cut by early 1924. By March 1924 – a year after shooting began – he had trimmed the film to perhaps 22 reels, which might have taken anywhere from six to eight hours to watch, depending on projection speed.

On April 10, 1924, the studio for which Stroheim was making *Greed*, the Goldwyn Company, was merged with Metro Pictures Corporation, giving rise to Metro-Goldwyn-Mayer. At that point, Stroheim, *Greed*, and the concept of the cinematic author all fell definitively into the hands of Irving Thalberg, who had been installed as the new company's head of production.

Thalberg and Stroheim were already bitter opponents, having fought over *Foolish Wives*. Their struggle over *Greed* raised their antagonism to the level of myth. Perhaps we may indulge in one more telling of the tale.

The first thing one notices about Thalberg and Stroheim is that they were dangerously alike.

Thalberg, too, came from a German Jewish merchant family, though he did not think to conceal the fact. His father, William, was an importer of lace. His mother, Henrietta Heyman, belonged to a family that had founded a New York department store. The Thalbergs were sufficiently steeped in German culture for Irving to have been force-fed Hegel and Schopenhauer during his childhood in Brooklyn. (I suspect there was Wagner, too.) But the Thalbergs were not prosperous enough to send their son to college. After graduating from high school, he went to work as a secretary, took business courses in the evenings, and wrote advertisements for the *Brooklyn Eagle*: a succession of odd (though not colorful) jobs around New York. A weak heart would have ruled out any stints with the army, Mexican or otherwise. The presence of his family (his mother especially) made it unnecessary for him to develop Stroheim's air of proud isolation.

It was through his family, most likely, that Thalberg found a job in Universal's New York office. He began in 1918 as a $25-a-week secretary and soon became Laemmle's personal assistant. In spring 1920, he relocated to Los Angeles to serve as Laemmle's eyes and ears. He was 20 years old.

Within months, Thalberg took stock of Universal City, shouldered aside the other executives, and became the studio's sole head of production, at a salary of $90 a week. The studio system – the concentration of decision-making in the hands of a producer – began at this moment, while Stroheim was gaily pouring money into *Foolish Wives*.

At the time, Universal's first-run features, known in the trade as 'Jewels,' numbered only half a dozen out of the hundreds of pictures the company made each year. As Thomas Schatz notes, the Universal executives and the directors in charge of the Jewels assumed these exceptional productions were just that. They were made 'outside the system' and frequently took shape off the lot. In a first attempt to regulate this anomaly and its most unruly figure, Thalberg summoned Stroheim to discuss the budget and schedule for *Foolish Wives*. The famous filmmaker, 35 years old and with a bearing both military and aristocratic to maintain, would not stoop to explain himself to a sickly, unknown Brooklyn lad of 20. The lad shut down the production.

Stroheim responded with a tactical retreat and a diplomatic initiative. First he appeared to give in to Thalberg, so *Foolish Wives* could proceed; then he went over the lad's head to the accommodating Laemmle. Before Thalberg could assert himself a second time, Stroheim had spent $1.1 million on *Foolish Wives* (on an initial budget of $250,000) and was ready to hand Universal a version that filled 20 reels, suitable for showing at special prices as a two-part motion picture event. Thalberg replied that an event was not necessary; a feature film would do. When Stroheim refused to shorten the film, Thalberg locked him out of the editing room and cut the picture himself, making a fourteen-reel version for the first run and a ten-reel version for general release. By this point, given the public's mood, Thalberg was also cutting the company's losses.

Little wonder that when Stroheim started his next picture, *The Merry-Go-Round*, he could no longer appeal to Laemmle's good nature. Rather than put himself under Thalberg's control, Stroheim walked off the Universal lot.* He had found more congenial circumstances at the Goldwyn Company, with which he signed a contract in December 1922.

The studio's anarchy must have seemed promising. By this time, Samuel Goldwyn himself was gone, having spent heavily on hiring 'Eminent Authors' such as Maurice Maeterlinck, for which efforts the stockholders had voted him out. The studio had passed into the hands of Frank Godsol and Abe Lehr; but the high-rolling continued, unchecked by anyone with Goldwyn's experience in hedging bets. Godsol and Lehr were busily acquiring properties such as *Ben-Hur* and the directors to go with them.

Perhaps they thought the terms they offered Stroheim were shrewd. For each of the three films he was to direct, they specified the budget ($175,000, unless more was explicitly authorized), the length (4500–8500 feet, or between five and nine reels), and the production schedule (fourteen weeks from the first day of shooting to the presentation of a work print). Stroheim would have to make two films before he got to

* An unhappy circumstance for the thesis of this book. *The Merry-Go-Round* concerns a Viennese aristocrat who indulges in a romance at a fairground.

star in the third; and any budget overruns would come out of his share of the profits.

But the tough image the Goldwyn Company wanted to project must have melted into airy nothing when Stroheim read one further clause: 'None of the said pictures shall be of a morbid, gruesome or offensive character.' If Godsol and Lehr meant what they said, why on earth would they hire *him*? He signed cheerfully and set to work on *Greed*.

To make this morbid, gruesome, offensive picture, Stroheim labored for 64 weeks, spent $585,250 ($238,250 above the authorized budget), and came up with a cut that was three times longer than the contract stipulated. Perhaps he might have persuaded Godsol and Lehr to release something resembling this *Greed*; but then Thalberg unexpectedly reappeared. Alarmed, Stroheim shipped the picture to his friend and fellow-director Rex Ingram in New York, who began to supervise a further cut of perhaps fifteen to eighteen reels. But Stroheim was expecting little sympathy, and he got none, either from Thalberg or from his boss, Louis B. Mayer.

An interview in *Picture Play*, published in the June 1924 issue, may reveal something about Stroheim's frame of mind during the crisis. The words might or might not be his – you can never tell with movie magazines – but the attitudes conveyed seem credible.

The public, he said, must know that what they see in his film is 'as reliable as the National Geographic Magazine or the Encyclopaedia Britannica.'

[Audiences] think von Stroheim will stand up and fight for correctness of detail; that he is willing to suffer the consequences; that he is willing to go to damnation for his convictions. And he is. Because everything he puts before the eyes of an audience must be the thing itself – the real thing.

We hear a man who was besieged and losing confidence that he could hold out. But, more than that, we hear the man's testimony about what he thought he was defending. Self-representation was no longer the ironic game it had been in *Foolish Wives*. Nothing less than reality was at stake.

The world of *Greed* had to seem so real that it might have existed on its own, as if it needed no filmmaker. (Who is the author of an encyclopedia? Where is its 'I'?) Yet, strangely enough, this self-obliteration was the sole guarantor of the filmmaker's good name. The more fully he effaced himself from the debased world of *Greed*, the better he would affirm the enviable character of von Stroheim, artist and aristocrat; the more fully he affirmed that character, the more he needed to build up the illusion that *Greed* showed an autonomous, 'real' world.

Even in the studio cut of *Greed*, evidence remains of a clockwork mechanism built into the film. The picture begins not with individual characters or even social settings but with machinery: the equipment of gold-mining. We see steam-driven pistons crushing rocks into ore-laden mud. At the end, we also see how this gold is returned to the earth, as Trina's coins, now blood-spattered, lie on the salt flats, waiting to be crusted over. Mineral to mineral; dust to dust. The final image, the most extreme of long shots, shows that Mac, too, has become no more than a speck that soon will be absorbed into the indifferent landscape.

Given the film's reputation for naturalism, which Stroheim himself helped to promote, we might be tempted to think of *Greed* as a mountain of grubby details, beneath which the characters are progressively buried. Yet *Greed* also has its nonmechanistic side, set loose in moments of satire and fantasy. Expressionistic images sometimes interrupt the narrative: a shot of elongated, emaciated arms reaching into a pile of gold; an image of a character writhing in the grip of a giant's hand. At other times, Stroheim found ways to step back from naturalism while staying within the narrative frame: on the wedding night, and again on the night when he murders Trina, Mac pulls shut a room partition, as if drawing a curtain across the proscenium of a stage. Perhaps most important of all, Stroheim cast a comic actress to play Trina. Far more than Gowland or Hersholt, ZaSu Pitts is at the heart of the release version of *Greed*, giving a performance that is all the more engrossing for being highly stylized. With a sly tilt to the right side of her mouth, a shrewd squint, and a too-dainty posing of her arms, she turns Trina into the allegorical figure called for by the title. Pitts is only as 'natural' as she must be to stand up to the camera's proximity. Otherwise, she may be said to deliver a brilliant *commedia dell'arte* performance, realized without a mask.

In speaking of the film, Stroheim might have emphasized this aspect of *Greed*. Instead, he and the defenders who followed him concentrated on the grind of 'reality.' Perhaps they were just letting the clockwork run down. After Louis B. Mayer seized the film and had it cut to ten reels, Stroheim told everyone that MGM had burned the original negative to extract the few cents' worth of silver in the emulsion – as if the physical artifact of *Greed* were doomed to return to the elements, like the gold within the story.

But I also think 'reality' served as a shield for the filmmaker's identity, especially once MGM threatened to take control. What might happen if

Thalberg cut *Greed* into a conventional story? People would recognize it as a fiction – something that may be believed provisionally but is not to be thought of as fact. And once people were allowed to doubt the veracity of the world they were being shown, what was to stop them from questioning the veracity of 'von Stroheim'? To preserve the fiction of his identity, Stroheim had to insist on the authenticity of a fiction.

The ultimate expression of this duality was the claim that Stroheim had subordinated himself completely to Norris's text. Rosenbaum cites a few instances of this legend. Here, for example, is an excerpt from the afterword to an edition of Norris's novel: '[Stroheim] is said to have followed *McTeague* page by page, never missing a paragraph. We'll never know because the uncut *Greed*, greatest of all movies, is lost forever.' ('By definition,' Rosenbaum adds tartly, 'it would appear that the "greatest of all movies" would have to be unseeable as well as "lost forever" in order to keep the myth firmly intact' (pp. 9–10).) There is also this, from a history of Metro-Goldwyn-Mayer broadcast on American television in 1992: 'Stroheim was determined to film each and every page of the novel from cover to cover. . . . He began on page one and went right through the book.' This legend crops up even in reference works, such as the English edition of Georges Sadoul's *Dictionary of Films* ('Stroheim's original script followed the novel in every detail') and Ephraim Katz's *Film Encyclopedia* ('an obsessive commitment to a literal transcription of every detail in the author's book').

The improbability of this procedure is perhaps less impressive than the notion that mechanistic fidelity would be a virtue. We seem to have returned to Bazin's theory of film as related to the embalmer's art, or John Szarkowski's insistence on the fundamental objectivity of the camera, 'the pencil of nature.' If we are satisfied to know that in photography the physical world reproduces itself, allowing us to see 'the thing itself,' then we might also be reassured to think a novel had been transubstantiated into film, in its entirety and without human interference.

This idea, however strange, has also been strangely persistent. It may, in fact, be the principal legacy of *Greed*. The version released by MGM on December 4, 1924 – to commercial disaster – has been sought out by relatively few people. The film envisioned by Stroheim can't be seen at all. *Greed* therefore exists primarily as an idea about filmmaking, which has passed among directors and writers, critics and moviegoers, for three-quarters of a century. A reputation for exhaustive veracity – whether to physical detail or to the book – is a large part of this legend. With it comes another idea, which is even stranger considering

Stroheim's efforts to efface himself from *Greed*. The film, or its legend, is central to the idea of Stroheim as an author.

Before putting that idea to the test, perhaps we should consider the revival of interest in Stroheim that took place around the same time as the word 'author' began to go into polemical use.

During the 1930s and 1940s, Stroheim was known primarily as an actor, most notably for his performance in Jean Renoir's *La Grande Illusion* (1937). Then, beginning in the late 1940s, Stroheim the director began to be talked of again. When Henri Langlois began to present retrospectives at the Cinémathèque Française, he devoted one of the first to Stroheim's films, as both actor and director. In 1950, Langlois even persuaded Stroheim to watch the MGM *Greed* at the Cinémathèque, an event that genuinely moved many film enthusiasts. Around this same time, Langlois and his colleague Lotte Eisner began to work with Stroheim on a restoration of *The Wedding March* (1928), which was given its premiere in February 1954 at the São Paulo Film Festival.

This revival was not confined to the Cinémathèque. In 1950, Billy Wilder offered a cruel reminder of Stroheim's past by casting him in *Sunset Boulevard* as Max von Mayerling – once a great director of silent films, now the butler to a madwoman. In 1952, *Greed* appeared prominently on a Belgian festival's poll of favorite films (Luchino Visconti, Orson Welles, and Billy Wilder all mentioned it) and in the *Sight and Sound* critics' poll of all-time greatest films.

Of course, none of these people had seen Stroheim's *Greed*; they knew only the MGM version. But that was all the more reason to proclaim the greatness of the dismembered torso. Stroheim was (to quote the title of Peter Noble's 1950 biography) 'the Hollywood Scapegoat.' As the legendary opponent of Thalberg, he exemplified the individual's struggle for self-expression within an industrial system. He also fitted in nicely with certain other polemics of the moment. As a Hollywood director who had returned to Europe, he served as a bridge figure for certain French and Italian filmmakers who wanted to pursue art and directorial autonomy. He could also be seen as a forerunner of those people – including Welles, Chaplin, and the victims of the blacklist – who became expatriates from America in the 1950s.

For all these reasons, Stroheim was a key figure in the *politique des auteurs* promoted by *Cahiers du Cinéma*. By common consent, the founding document of this *politique* was the essay 'Une Certaine Tendance du cinéma français,' written by Cinémathèque denizen François Truffaut while *The Wedding March* was being restored, and published in the January 1954 issue of *Cahiers*. From there, thanks to Andrew Sarris, auteurism spread in 1963 to the pages of *Film Culture* (becoming a 'theory' along the way) and on to film societies, art houses, popular magazines, and finally to colleges and film schools, where a generation that included Francis Coppola and Martin Scorsese learned to believe in the auteur.

The diffusion of the theory – or *politique*, if you prefer – no doubt owed less to the essay itself than to the filmmaking careers subsequently enjoyed by Truffaut and his *Cahiers* colleagues, especially Jean-Luc Godard and Eric Rohmer. Even so, 'Une Certaine Tendance du cinéma français' holds a sufficiently important place within film history that we might want to know how Stroheim figures in it, particularly as regards his self-effacing authorship of *Greed*.

Those who know of Truffaut's essay only through its consequences, or are familiar with the title but little more, might be surprised to learn that this article neither defines the concept of an auteur nor reevaluates any Hollywood productions. Nor is Stroheim directly addressed in the piece. Since he was not a French filmmaker, his career was outside the scope of the essay; and yet his presence may be intuited everywhere. Among its other peculiarities, 'Une Certaine Tendance du cinéma français' concentrates on an issue central to the legend of *Greed*: the fidelity of a film to a novel.

To be enjoyed to its fullest, the essay should perhaps be read as it was originally presented in *Cahiers*.

At the top of the first page stands the title, as bland as Thursday afternoon, flanked by a photograph of screenwriter Jean Aurenche. A pleasant-looking man, you might think; very middle-aged, very clean. No doubt the article will consist of judicious praises of his work. Nothing you read in the first paragraphs disappoints this expectation.

The purpose of the essay, writes Truffaut with becoming modesty, is to sketch the limits of that branch of the national cinema known as psychological realism. Out of a hundred French films released each year, only ten or twelve merit the attention of critics and cinephiles and therefore of *Cahiers*. It is universally understood that these ten or twelve, exemplars of the recently named 'tradition of quality,' belong to the school of psychological realism, among whose leading figures are Aurenche and Pierre Bost, specialists in adapting novels for the screen.

The great merit of these writers, everyone agrees, is their perfect fidelity to the original text. You nod; you turn the page. All at once, the mild Truffaut grows fangs.

Aurenche and Bost are *not* faithful to their texts! They betray most grievously the spirit of Georges Bernanos's novel *Le Journal d'un curé de campagne*. A detailed analysis follows, proving not only that the screenwriters diverge from their source but that they do so deliberately, gratuitously, programmatically. In plain fact, writes Truffaut, his tone rising toward that of the Holy Office, Aurenche and Bost show 'a very marked taste for profanation and blasphemy.'

By the way: their script was never produced. As Truffaut acknowledges almost parenthetically, he is protesting against a phantom film. Or rather, he's hit upon an elaborate strategy for praising a real one. To point out the merits of Robert Bresson's 1951 *Le Journal d'un curé de campagne*, Truffaut has chosen to deride a whole set of other productions. These are so meretricious that he can address them simply by talking about their scripts. The directors (such as Claude Autant-Lara) are hardly worth naming, as demonstrated by the fact that their pictures don't even need to be made to be insulted.

Having reached this pitch, Truffaut abruptly drops the role of Inquisitor. He admits, despite all the fuss he's made, that he doesn't much care whether Aurenche believes in the doctrines of the Church. The issue is simply one of honesty. Aurenche holds anticlerical convictions, as can be confirmed by examining both his scripts and his biography. (He is, Truffaut notes, a former associate of Surrealists and anarchists.) If Aurenche were to live in harmony with his principles, he would not adapt any book that showed a priest in a sympathetic light. But since films about clergymen happen to be in fashion, Aurenche takes the jobs that are offered him and works in a few nudges and winks for his buddies. He doesn't practice the art of film; he practices the art of putting one over on the producers, and on the public, too.

As a subhead announces, 'The Mask Is Removed.' Because Aurenche and Bost think of themselves as literary men and believe in the innate superiority of literature to film, they feel lowered by their work. The resulting self-contempt spills over into an explicit scorn for movies and the people who watch them. Hence a telltale feature of psychological realism: out of all the literary subjects its practitioners might choose to adapt, they invariably select stories about blocked impulses. (You remark, in passing, that the issue of fidelity to the source has dropped away. Like the question of respect for the Catholic faith, it apparently was beside the point, though useful for making a to-do.) 'In films of psychological realism, all beings are vile – but so great is the authors' desire to show their superiority to the characters, that those who by chance aren't nasty are (still better) infinitely grotesque.'

And yet, Truffaut writes, 'I know a handful of men in France who would be INCAPABLE of conceiving' of 'these abject characters who speak abject phrases.' The pages open to show photographs of Jean Cocteau, Abel Gance, Max Ophuls, Jean Renoir, each appearing above a caption that begins with the same two words. These French men of cinema, who 'by a curious coincidence' write their own dialogue and sometimes their own stories, are 'The authors.'

The word has finally been pronounced. With that, Truffaut races toward the finish, praising the French authors (mostly through captions under their photographs) while condemning the psychological realists for having created 'an antibourgeois cinema made by the bourgeois, for the bourgeois.' No wonder 'working people hardly appreciate this form of cinema, even when it tries to get close to them. . . . It is apparent that the general audience prefers naive little foreign films [including Hollywood productions] that show people "as they should be" and not as Aurenche and Bost believe they are.'

As if to seal the argument, Truffaut appends one more photograph: a film still, showing a funeral wagon that is no doubt carrying Aurenche and Bost to their deserved place. The caption: 'This hearse, dear to our overabundance of filmmakers who enjoy burials, does not come from any of their films . . . but from *Miracle in Milan*, because certain Italians, too . . . But that's another story.'

A remarkable performance: neither consistent in its terms nor clear in its implications, but infinitely generative, as the coming years would show. What would happen if we took its arguments seriously?

We might then find that the perpetrators of psychological realism have an unnamed companion in the hearse. The author of *Greed* haunts the essay like a guilty conscience. Though Stroheim was said to have been faithful to *McTeague*, he, too, departed in many ways from his source, as may be determined by examining the script for *his* phantom film. Though Stroheim was unquestionably a 'man of the cinema,' his manner of addressing the audience was as duplicitous as that of Aurenche and Bost; we might say he spent his entire career 'putting one over' on the producers and the public. His characters in *Greed* are surely as abject (nasty, infinitely grotesque) as any to be found in the cinema of psychological realism. And though 2000 people might have shown up for a one-night-only festival screening in São Paulo, the general public had unquestionably rejected whatever was left of *Greed*, just as it yawned at the tradition of quality.

But of course the essay can't be pinned down to mere propositions. Truffaut did not make arguments. He struck poses and abandoned them, as if attempting to transmit his intentions semaphorically – that is, by motion pictures, which might impart their dynamism to a sympathetic reader. To understand him, we need to follow his line of movement. If we do, we discover in it one of the most characteristic gestures of auteurist criticism: the translation of a film's explicit subject matter into a representation of the processes of filmmaking and of the filmmaker's life.

Truffaut did not discover such metaphors only in the works of authors. Even a film of psychological realism might carry an unintended confession of the sins of Aurenche and Bost. But an attempt to perform such a metaphorical transformation of *Greed* will reveal once again that the film confounds auteurist thinking.

Greed may perhaps be interpreted as Stroheim's embittered response to Thalberg, and more generally to the system of regimented commerce he enforced. Here the dates of production are of some interest. Stroheim spoke of *McTeague* as early as January 1920, when he as yet had no feelings to express about Irving Thalberg; but three eventful years separated the intent from the act of creation. When he began to work on *Greed* early in 1923, Stroheim did so in the context of his humiliation over *Foolish Wives*. And yet, unless unlicensed dentistry is somehow comparable to cinema, nothing in *Greed* specifically evokes the filmmaker's struggle. We enter a world that excludes both the cruel glamour of 'von' and the artistry of Stroheim – a world so devoid of personality that the only 'performer' in it is a mechanical player piano. The auteurist theme of an individual in tension with society – a creator with a system of production – would be laughable here, because *Greed* admits neither creators nor individuals. The film's theme might even be summed up as the loss of self; its main action, the draining away of whatever small decency had animated Mac, Trina, and Marcus.

Besides, why couldn't Thalberg, too, be defined as an auteur? At the beginning of the video series he made in the 1990s, *Histoire(s) du cinéma*, Jean-Luc Godard sardonically made just that proposal. Like all of Godard's ironies, it is worth taking at face value – especially in this context.

Stroheim expressed his authorial ambitions by making bigger and bigger films. So did Thalberg. He quarreled with Carl Laemmle and left Universal over just that issue; and for MGM, his first great hits were films on which he risked large sums. *Ben-Hur*, which he inherited with the Metro studio, was in disastrous shape when Thalberg took over. Instead of cutting his losses, he spent lavishly on the picture and in December 1925 released a film that lost money for MGM but helped establish the new studio's reputation. That same year, Thalberg ordered large-scale reshooting on King Vidor's World War I drama *The Big*

Parade, a decision that delayed release of the picture and caused a 20 percent budget overrun. Very Stroheim-like – except that *The Big Parade* was a huge hit.

Did Stroheim paradoxically confirm his authorship by removing himself from *Greed*? Thalberg did something similar in virtually all his pictures. He never took an on-screen credit, thereby making himself famous for self-effacement. Did Stroheim cast a cold eye on his characters? So did Thalberg at times. Karl Dane's continual tobacco-spitting as one of the doughboys in *The Big Parade* is at least as naturalistic, and stomach-turning, as Jean Hersholt's nose-picking in *Greed*.

One difficulty remains: Thalberg served the public of the movie palaces. In fact, MGM was created by movie palaces; an exhibitor, the Loew's chain, formed the studio to provide suitable products for its theaters. Unfortunately, Truffaut's definition of authorship will not disallow Thalberg on these grounds. The essay objects to an antibourgeois cinema made by the bourgeois, for the bourgeois. Presumably, the objection would vanish if the cinema, like Thalberg's, were forthrightly probourgeois – a reading that is perhaps confirmed by Truffaut's own later films.

Of course, none of this matters. For more than seventy years, people have spoken of *Greed* as if it were the highest form of Stroheim's art, instead of the most anomalous; and the mistake may have been a good thing. The legend of *Greed*, unexamined, has taken pride of place among the myths of glorious cinematic failures, spurring a succession of younger filmmakers to action. Perhaps that's another meaning of the picture of the hearse at the end of 'Une Certaine Tendance.' To judge from Truffaut's unrestrained insolence, we might imagine he was writing not an essay but a revenge drama, starring himself as the fearless, scornful Siegfried. Soon he would reforge the shattered sword of Stroheim; soon he would dispatch Aurenche and Bost and all the enemies of cinema. And so, in fact, he did.

But *Greed* has also been a lost opportunity. Panicked by Thalberg's return, under terrible pressure, Stroheim himself initiated the failure by falling back on the use of conventional terms to defend this most unconventional project. His most distinctive achievement in *Greed* was to have established an expressionistic, satirical tone without imposing an authorial 'I'; yet he spoke instead about objectivity and the individual's struggle against assembly-line society. In so doing, he obscured not only the nature of the film but also the radicalism of his gesture in making it.

By an act of sabotage, Stroheim had in effect tried to break the system of production. In his defiance, he might be compared to those contemporaneous Dadaists whose 'artworks' included the disruption of church services and the armed hijacking of freighters. Yet this comparison works only up to a point. *Greed*, too, was a disruption, but it did not emerge from an avant-garde – that is, from a small group of artists who had embraced their status as outsiders, if only provisionally. *Greed* was a direct assault on the means of production, carried out with full publicity by a world-famous figure. We might do better to say that Stroheim's 'no' was an act of latter-day Nihilism. This comparison comes closer; but it, too, falls short. Unlike the Nihilists, Stroheim nearly succeeded. He filmed *Greed* as he'd wanted to and then came surprisingly close to having it distributed.

His rebellion may perhaps be read as another reminder of the heady spirit of 1919 – not in the United States but in Germany. In March of that year, a general strike shut down all production; in April, leftists pushed to socialize the entire film industry; in August (as film historian Klaus Kreimeier notes) the legislature of Baden passed a resolution calling for the industry to be nationalized. The Reichstag continued to debate bills for socialization until May 1920. Today, people look back on *Greed* and complacently wonder how anyone could have expected to make a profit on the thing. They forget that the system of profit-making was itself under attack.

But the activism of 1919 gave way very soon to compromises and coalition-building. Although Germany's leading party, the Social Democrats, continued to call for the withdrawing of economic resources from 'the system of capitalist exploitation,' their only tool for doing so was parliamentary pleading. They used force against workers' uprisings, negotiation against the chairmen of the boards. By 1925, they saw Hindenburg, the figurehead of the Reich bloc, take his place as president of the Republic.

In a way, this was Stroheim's story, too, after *Greed*. He was a revolutionary turned Social Democrat. The making of *Greed*, though hardly an act of self-conscious class warfare, was a transpersonal revolt; its implications extended far beyond the status of the filmmaker himself. But later, when Stroheim recast his struggle in terms of the artist's freedom to create, he all but capitulated to the system he had tried to break, and for which he would next direct *The Merry Widow*. Because he was an author, the system should have made room for him.

The Mechanical Bride

Six years after Thomas Edison invented the electric light bulb – and four years before he built his first film apparatus – a character bearing his name and appearance began to haunt the pages of a suitably titled French magazine, *La Vie moderne*. This *doppelgänger* of the world's most famous inventor presided over the serialized novel *L'Eve future* (or *Tomorrow's Eve*), written by Villiers de l'Isle-Adam.

Villiers supplied his fictional Edison with a pleasant evening at Menlo Park and a cigar to enjoy with it, then set the inventor to fantasizing upon missed opportunities. Why had he been born so late? Think of the boon to humanity, had he been present with his phonograph to record the momentous 'Let there be light,' or if, 'lurking behind some secret thicket in Eden,' he had preserved God's words to Adam and Eve. From these meditations on electrical re-creation, Edison passed to thoughts of new creation: the effort to animate mechanical forms of human life.

Many of his fellow inventors had made the attempt; but, 'Poor fools, for lack of the proper technical skills, they produced nothing but ridiculous monsters. Albertus Magnus, Vaucanson, Maelzel, Horner, and all that crowd were barely competent makers of scarecrows.'

A curious list. Its first figure, Albertus Magnus, was said to have constructed an iron man sometime in the thirteenth century – the same period when Roger Bacon supposedly built a mechanical head that could speak. Had Edison cared much about the heirs to such medieval divines – men who were as much alchemists as scientists – his thoughts might have led him next to Faust and his homunculus, or to that 'new Prometheus,' Dr. Frankenstein. But Edison was a thoroughly practical man – an American – and so he thought instead of the showmen–tinkerers of the Enlightenment.

The clockwork figures they built – such as the flutist, tambourine player, and quacking duck made by Jacques Vaucanson – had shown up regularly at fairs, amusement parks, and music halls since the mid-eighteenth century. At the Fair of Saint-Germain, automata went on display in 1748 in the pavilion known as the Magic Palace. That same year, in the gardens of Hellbrunn near Salzburg, an entire clockwork theater presented its shows.

These 'mannequins,' these 'abominable masquerades,' were 'nothing but an outrageous caricature of our species,' thought the fictional Edison. He proposed to do better. Having mastered the proper technical skills – not by any hocus-pocus, mind you, but simply through diligent labor – he would construct an android that would be indistinguishable from a living human.

But the figure that Edison subsequently brought to life, Hadaly, differed from earlier models in more than its degree of illusionism. More important for the history of film, Hadaly took the form of a beautiful woman. This circumstance links Villier's automaton to the android dreamed up by an earlier, German writer. Hadaly is a literary relative of Olympia, the clockwork woman who first met the public in E.T.A. Hoffmann's story 'The Sandman.'

In the 1920s, the offspring of these two mechanical brides would become central figures of two national cinemas in crisis. The embattled German film industry would pin its hopes on a descendent of Olympia: the high-kicking robot Maria in *Metropolis*, directed by Fritz Lang. Around the same time, another director, Marcel L'Herbier, would propose (entirely on his own initiative) to rescue French film by bringing back Hadaly. A version of her, transformed into the heartless singer Claire Lescot, appeared in *L'Inhumaine* (1924).

Convention hides from us the implications of these films. We often speak of *Metropolis* as if it were wholly the product of Lang's authorship, and *L'Inhumaine* as if it were L'Herbier's. We compound the error by discussing Claire and the robot Maria as if they were the fantasies of those men, and of men alone. Yet the robot Maria was created not only by Lang but also by his wife, Thea von Harbou, who wrote both the novel, *Metropolis*, and the screenplay. The role of Claire was dictated, in large measure, by Georgette Leblanc, the real-life diva who portrayed her.

In speaking of these things, we also tend to muddle two related but distinct lines of development. One, the medieval-organic, leads from the works of Albertus Magnus to Paul Wegener's *The Golem* (1920), James Whale's *Frankenstein* (1931), and a host of zombie movies, such as *Night of the Living Dead* (1968) and *Re-Animator* (1988). The characteristic effect in this line is that of horror, accompanied by the chime of adding machines totting up profits. By contrast, the Enlightenment–mechanical tradition leads in film toward grotesquerie and satire: to Claire Lescot, the robot Maria, and bankruptcy. One of the few filmmakers to realize any money on the second tradition was Whale, with *The Bride of Frankenstein* (1935); but that was a sequel, which took advantage of the muddle.

The better to prepare ourselves for the satirical import of the French and German follies of the 1920s – the better to assess the role of women, both real and imaginary, in those productions – let's briskly review the sources.

'The Sandman,' first published in 1816, is one of those undecidable cases in which the German Romantics excelled. It's either the story of a breakdown or else a breakdown on its way toward becoming a story.

The protagonist, Nathanael, is a morose university student who sometimes narrates the tale (in epistolary fashion) and sometimes becomes the object of its narrator. So he's an unstable character in every way; yet he enjoys the love of the faithful and clear-headed Klara, who repeatedly advises him to give up his gloomy moods. If the world seems threatening, she says, it's only because he projects his fears onto it. From time to time, Nathanael responds to this good advice. But then, under the influence of an optical instrument sold to him by the mysterious peddler Coppola, he forgets Klara and becomes infatuated with a neighbor's 'daughter,' Olympia. Coppola's spyglass alters Nathanael's vision; unlike everyone else in town, he cannot see that Olympia is stiff and stupid – in fact, a wind-up toy.

Although readers assign meanings to 'The Sandman' at their peril, I might echo the words of a professor of poetry and rhetoric whom Hoffmann playfully dropped into the tale: 'Most honorable ladies and gentlemen, do you not see the point of it all? It is all an allegory, an extended metaphor.' Beauty – and the love that beauty inspires – is in the spyglass of the beholder. Yet 'The Sandman' disregards symmetry in its extension of this metaphor, which seems applicable only to life's happier sentiments. Klara turns out to be wrong; the evil that pursued Nathanael was more than a projection of his fears.

In 'The Sandman,' a malign force really does stalk the world. But I see no reason to assign the android any part in this evil. As a mere collection of gears, the doll is morally inert; for all it knows or cares, Nathanael could gaze lovingly through his spyglass at a bottle of ketchup. This trait distinguishes Olympia from Hadaly in *L'Eve future*. Although Villier's android at first appears to be just another clever piece of metalwork and wiring, it eventually proves to be a moral agent. What's more, it's benevolent.

First published in 1885–86, *L'Eve future* is the story of a truly noble young Englishman, Lord Celian Ewald, who has fallen miserably in love with a would-be singer and actress, Miss Alicia Clary. Physically, Alicia is a living Venus de Milo; but to Lord Ewald's horror, she regards everything as mere matter, good only for its value in commercial exchange. Her performances are note-perfect but emotionless. Her opinions, which are calculated to please, are hollow. Even her beauty is just a thing to be used, as if it were 'foreign to her *self*.'

Fortunately, Lord Ewald enjoys the friendship of the Wizard of Menlo Park, who volunteers his assistance. Edison will bring to life his automaton Hadaly, having first made it look, sound, and even smell exactly like Alicia Clary. Little does he realize that Hadaly is animated not by electricity but by a condensation of 'the Infinite.' Internally, she is a living ideal, called up long ago by Lord Ewald's dreams and longings. As spirits often do, Hadaly tried to make herself known in the material world, so she might love and comfort the creature who needs her. For all his genius, Edison has done nothing more than provide her with an especially suitable vehicle for reaching Lord Ewald.

Placed face to face with 'The Sandman,' Villiers's novel resolves into a mirror image of the earlier story. Coppola is evil and all-knowing; Edison is good, though ignorant of the central fact about his own 'creation.' Nathanael destroys himself by indulging his fantasies; Lord Ewald, through his imagination, calls down the grace of God. And of course, the flesh-and-blood woman of one story mirrors the android of the other. Alicia Clary takes the place of Olympia – she's the pretty figure without a soul, whom it's embarrassing to desire – whereas Hadaly is like Klara, the pure and noble lover.

Even the objects of satire are reversed. In the broadest terms, 'The Sandman' may be said to poke fun at polite society, in which manners are so conventionalized that everyone might as well be a doll. But to put it more precisely, the story makes fun of men. *L'Eve future* also suggests that society in general might be ridiculous; as Edison dryly observes, Alicia Clary would be 'the absolute feminine ideal for three-quarters of modern humanity.' But for Villiers, Alicia Clary *is* 'modern humanity,' which at its most insipid is made up of women.

But there is one proposition about which both stories agree: machines have no soul. Edison's technology in *L'Eve future* may excite and astonish, but it cannot touch our truest selves. God loves us, so the gizmos are much ado about nothing. In 'The Sandman,' the nightmare figure of Coppola inspires dread precisely because he seizes on such a laughable tool. Think of Olympia's identifying noise: a 'sneeze,' which is the sound of her gears winding up.

Machinery in these stories remains lifeless; and so we may judge its distance from technology as it is presented in *L'Inhumaine* and *Metropolis*. Lang and von Harbou reimagined Olympia as a malevolent android with an active will; L'Herbier and Leblanc proposed that technology might be good enough on its own to transform Alicia Clary into a pure, loving soul. By the time these films were made, machines no longer existed beyond good and evil.

Villiers's novel hints at one reason for this change in attitude. When the author looked around for a credible modern wizard, his obvious choice was an American.

Within a few years of the publication of *L'Eve future*, the World's Columbian Exposition confirmed in European minds the notion that America and modernity were synonymous. Jean-Louis Cohen has written the history of this 'Americanism,' which took root in an 'insidious sense of backwardness *vis-à-vis* the New World.'

The architects, engineers, writers, and politicians visiting the shores of Lake Michigan in 1893 discovered not only the 'white city' of the exhibition site and buildings, but also, behind them, a truly surprising 'black city' of abattoirs, iron- and steel-frame buildings, and advanced mechanical and technical plants. . . . [Commentators] remarked not only on the technical prowess of buildings where 'electricity reigned supreme,' but also on the potential of 'a feeling for beauty' with the entry of women into the architectural profession. French architects who made the trip included Maurice Yvon, Adolphe Bocage, and Jacques Hermant. Writing in the review *L'Architecture*, Bocage underlined the 'advantage' that could be had 'by following the meritorious efforts' and 'the very real results achieved by this new, vigorous people, emancipated from servitude and prejudice alike,' a people that could afford to indulge in fertile 'experiments.' (Cohen, p. 21)

The architectural fantasies that flourished in Europe after the fair, in both professional journals and popular publications, played upon themes of gigantism, power, efficiency, mobility, and speed. The new city, conceived on American models, would not only rise up to the heavens but also plummet deep beneath the ground. The experience was to be nonstop and all-encompassing. Electricity would make the city blaze with light around the clock; airplanes, railroads, and automobiles would zoom through it on all sides. Cohen cites the 'cities of the future' drawn up in France by Eugène Hénard and Louis Bonnier (c. 1910–13); the postcard views of the 'Moscow of the future' published in 1913; the enthusiastically Americanist city-planning studies put forth in Germany by Werner Hegemann, beginning in 1911; and, of course, the 1914 Futurist manifesto of Antonio Sant'Elia.

As soon as World War I had ended, the Europeans got what they had wished for and feared. Americans, and those architects and urban planners who had studied American buildings, were directly involved in the reconstruction of large areas of France and Germany. The organizational methods of Frederick Winslow Taylor (an engineer of human motion) were imitated in some places and discussed everywhere; Henry Ford's methods of industrial organization were not only discussed but applied by Ford himself, who in 1924 opened an automobile factory in Cologne. Modern, American know-how became a topic of daily life in Europe; so did American movies, American music, and American capital. Ann Douglas sums up the situation in her cultural history of the United States in the 1920s:

All historical circumstances in the 1918–28 decade . . . seemed effortlessly to conspire to assure the country's global preeminence. America at the close of the Great War was a Cinderella magically clothed in the most stunning dress at the ball, a ball to which Cinderella had not even been invited; immense gains with no visible price tag seemed to be the American destiny. (Douglas, p. 4)

Not everyone was amused. In a scathingly funny piece titled 'Worshipping Elevators,' written for *Die literarische Welt* in 1926, Friedrich Sieburg parodied the latest America-obsessed novels: 'This is how we begin now: "McCormick reached for the telephone and, with an iron expression on his face, ordered the twelve train cars with wheat for Ohio off onto dead-end tracks."' Sieburg derided such Americanism as 'engineer romanticism, which does not understand the workings of a carburetor and therefore hears the breath of our time in the pounding of six cylinders. . . . The machine can be understood and, to the mechanic, is not a mystical object' (cited in Kaes *et al.*, p. 404).

But Sieburg and his like were in the minority – especially in the film business. At all levels of cinema, in both France and Germany, people were obsessed with America, if only because Americans were eating them alive.

Writing in the 1920s, the critic Léon Moussinac cited the statistic that has since been used to judge French cinema's decline against American competition. Before World War I, '90 percent of the films exhibited throughout the world were French films.' As Richard Abel has since noted in his history of French film in the 1920s, this figure is shaky. Even before the war, he finds, the French share of the world market was shrinking, with more and more foreign films – American, Danish, Swedish, and Italian – being shown in Paris's theaters.

Nevertheless, by 1914 the two dominant French companies – Pathé Frères and Etablissements Gaumont – had become large-scale, vertically integrated businesses, which enjoyed commanding positions internationally. Then came the declaration of war. 'All branches of the industry immediately closed down,' Abel writes. 'The general mobilization emptied the studios of directors, actors, and technicians. . . . The deserted spaces of the studios were requisitioned for military stores and horse barns, and Pathé's film-stock factory at Vincennes was transformed into a war plant' (p. 9).

The French industry never fully recovered. Beginning in 1915, the void in Parisian movie houses began to be filled with Keystone and Chaplin comedies and Pearl White serials. Soon American companies set up offices in Paris, the better to market their films, and were joined by a host of European importers. When French production resumed at last, it did so only fitfully, in part because foreign competitors had so thoroughly crowded French films off the screens and in part because of a financial disincentive. A disparity in customs duties (assessed on every meter of film shipped into or out of the country) made it a safer bet for companies to import films than to produce and export them.

In November 1918, Charles Pathé reorganized his company into Pathé-Cinéma, concentrating on distribution and exhibition. He ordered production to be curtailed and decreed that any new film he financed would have to demonstrate 'a sure commercial appeal beyond France itself.' Léon Gaumont pursued the same policy. He continued to finance Louis Feuillade's serials; but having made 145 films in 1914, he produced only 11 in 1919. He, too, would concentrate on distributing and exhibiting American products. Abel quotes Gaumont's post-war formula for success: 'American technique and French subtitles' (p. 13).

While Pathé and Gaumont cut back, many smaller companies began springing up. Often they were organized by a star, a drop-out from the theater, or a cinephilic journalist, who produced perhaps a film or two. Joining these upstarts were companies composed mainly of Russian émigrés, as well as two or three ambitious, independent firms that attempted to compete against the Americans by making super-productions. Sometimes Charles Pathé or Léon Gaumont put up some money toward one of these efforts; sometimes a chunk of the financing came from the Americans themselves.

In 1922, the French industry produced 130 features, against 474 by the Germans and 706 by the Americans. By 1924, the number of French productions had dropped to 68 – a somewhat misleading figure, as Abel notes, because those 68 tended to be longer and more expensive to make than the earlier pictures. Still, the overall story was one of chronic crisis – of helplessness before American power, and of 'fragmentation, decentralization, and lack of coordination in policy and practice' (Abel, p. 14).

The German industry, by contrast, was characterized by an extraordinarily high degree of centralization and coordination. Its story – until the German industry, too, fell to the Americans – was one of rapid expansion, best summarized by the growth of its most important company, Universum-Film Aktiengesellschaft (Ufa).

Ufa was the creation of the German Supreme Command, which resolved in 1917 'that film be put to work with the highest priority' to ensure 'a successful conclusion to the war.' (So wrote Erich Ludendorff, First Quartermaster General to the Chief of the General Staff of the Field Army, cited by Kreimeier, p. 23.) While battles were still raging, the Ministry of War and the Treasury Office put together a board of directors; the German Bank assembled the financing; and in December 1917 Ufa was incorporated, with the majority interest held secretly by the government.

The new corporation immediately began to buy and consolidate production studios, distributors, and exhibitors; but to the disgust of Ufa's military overseers, the people who actually made the movies kept making movies. Instead of producing tributes to the Kaiser and new installments of *Anna Makes Artillery Shells*, Ernst Lubitsch directed Pola Negri in *Carmen (Gypsy Blood)*, which by chance enjoyed its press preview on November 8, 1918, the night when revolution at last broke out against the Kaiser.

As Klaus Kreimeier argues, the wartime Ufa already behaved as if it were autonomous, a trait that enabled it to go on successfully after the war ended. In 1921, the Ministry of Finance sold its shares, and Ufa became a private company: colossal in size (and often in the taste of its filmmakers), rich in talent, advanced in all phases of technology, integrated both vertically and horizontally.

But Ufa's policy of nonstop expansion required money; and in the early years of the Weimar Republic, when the government deliberately encouraged inflation in order to pay its war reparations with near-worthless currency, the official way to finance anything was to run up debts. For Germany as a whole, the United States offered temporary relief through the Dawes Plan, instituted in 1924, which provided loans to offset the reparations payments. Ufa, too, had to be tided over – not by the American government but by Paramount and MGM. By early 1925, the company had run up about 50 million marks in debts, against liquid assets of half a million marks. In December of that year, in exchange for a loan of $4 million (17 million marks), Ufa contracted to turn over three-quarters of the screen time in its theaters to films imported from Paramount and MGM. In return for this American money, Kreimeier writes, Ufa even 'pawned its own office building.'

Metropolis was made to counter this daunting American power. Having invested almost from the start in superproductions to compete against the Americans, Ufa decided (in the year of the Dawes Plan) to send its head of production, Erich Pommer, to America, so he might study Hollywood's methods. Fritz Lang went with him, perhaps because he had already been designated to direct Ufa's nightmare vision of an Americanized Germany. According to Lang's biographer Patrick McGilligan, Pommer began speaking of *Metropolis* in early 1924. A preliminary script was circulating by February or March, and in July a newspaper reported that Lang and von Harbou were about to put the final touches to the script. This chronology would disallow Lang's repeated claim to have conceived *Metropolis* in October 1924, upon first glimpsing New York's skyscrapers. In no way does it diminish the likely effect of that sight.

In a passage that many people have quoted (including Lang himself), he witnessed a spectacle 'completely new and nearly fairy-tale like for a European. . . . The buildings seemed to be a vertical veil, shimmering, almost weightless, a luxurious cloth hung from the dark sky to dazzle, distract, and hypnotize. At night the city did not give the impression of being alive; it lived as illusions lived' (McGilligan, p. 104). No doubt the scene was as impressive as Lang said, and as influential on *Metropolis*. So, too, was Hollywood. After a long train trip across landscapes that delighted him (he shared with von Harbou a love for Karl May's Western novels), Lang settled down with Pommer to a series of meetings. Ufa's delegates were received by executives and stars; they visited production facilities, toured the sets for *The Thief of Baghdad* and *The Phantom of the Opera*, and saw how miniatures were used to make dinosaurs roam prehistoric forests for *The Lost World*. When Lang and Pommer returned to Berlin in December to begin work on *Metropolis*, they unquestionably hoped to emulate and outdo what they'd seen.

L'Inhumaine was made in much the same spirit. As L'Herbier explained years later in an interview in *Cahiers du Cinéma* (cited in Burch), he thought of the film as 'a sort of summary, a provisional summary, of all that was artistically advanced in France two years before the famous Exposition des Arts Décoratifs' – the international fair, held in Paris in 1925, that established the style and the name of Art Deco. To design the costumes, props, and sets of *L'Inhumaine* and compose its score, he brought together the leading artists in France – or at least the most fashionable of the better artists among his friends. Adolphe Osso, who ran Paramount's Paris office, contracted to distribute the film, encouraging L'Herbier to envision a breakthrough not only in France but in the American market. And for the lead, he had Georgette Leblanc, who had been spending much of her time in the United States. In L'Herbier's mind, this made her an American star – a strange misapprehension, though by no means the strangest feature of the production.

Many people have belittled the story of *L'Inhumaine*, which L'Herbier himself called 'not very distinguished.' To me, the objection seems pointless. L'Herbier never claimed to have cared about the script as such. He spoke of it in purely formal terms, as if it were the figured bass of a musical composition. Upon it, he explained to *Cahiers*, 'I constructed chords, plastic chords, and what was important for me was not the horizontal parade of events but vertical plastic harmonies.' Besides, even the tone-deaf ought to pause before taking the plot seriously. The film is subtitled 'A Fairy Tale, As Seen by Marcel L'Herbier.'

On the outskirts of the City, in an ultramodern home (facade by Robert Mallet-Stevens), lives Claire Lescot – that famous singer, that strange woman, known to her supine public as *L'Inhumaine*. As the story begins, this icy, fabulously wealthy, sexually irresistible woman has convened a dinner party of the world's most powerful men, who have no idea why they've been summoned but nevertheless have shown up in swallowtail suits, which look decidedly out of place in her dining room.

Designed by Alberto Cavalcanti, the space is perhaps less a dining room than a neo-Aztec nightclub. Against the back wall, semimetallic draperies hang like a theater curtain, flanked on either side by staircases leading to nowhere, each stepped back like a wedge cut from a pyramid.

In the middle of the room is a large rectangular pool, stocked with swans. Protruding into the midst of the pool is a platform, decorated in a bold black-and-white pattern of interlocking, multijointed Y-shapes; and on this stands the U-shaped dining table. The servants (all of them deaf-mute, according to the intertitles, to ensure discretion) wear waistcoats in a *faux*-Kandinsky design with checkerboard piping. Circulating through the room, they bow continually, their faces hidden behind grinning, chubby-cheeked masks of somewhat Asiatic aspect.

The powerful men in black swallowtail suits wait for Claire Lescot.

Then, emerging from the midst of the servants, comes a white, off-the-shoulder satin wrap designed by Paul Poiret, with wraparound black feathers on the bias and a feathered turban to match. Within this get-up is the much-anticipated *femme fatale*: tall, fleshy, fiftyish Georgette Leblanc. Holding aloft a chin of uncertain firmness and smiling as if waiting for her photograph to be taken, she maneuvers the dress into a diamond-backed chair designed by Pierre Chareau. A jazz band plays (those wild, modern Americans). The powerful men come to the table. One guest has yet to arrive; but Claire plunges ahead and makes an announcement. She intends to leave – yes, leave – unless Something holds her. What might that Something be?

As in any fairy tale, three suitors immediately vie to answer the riddle. The first is Frank Mahler (Fred Kellerman), a jowly, cigar-smoking American millionaire. Although he owns the twelve top theaters in the United States, Claire laughs sadly at his attentions. She has already conquered every theater worth mentioning. Next comes the Apostle of Humanity (L.V. Terval), a fiery-eyed, lank-haired fellow, who wants to remove Claire to Mongolia. (The scene abruptly shifts to a dingy interior, where the walls are painted with slogans in Cyrillic letters. The Apostle and Claire, dressed as commissars, oppress a teeming mass of Mongolians.) Claire lifts her chin even higher. She cares nothing for Humanity – only for exceptional beings. Finally, as the floor show begins – jugglers use their feet to toss around a barrel decorated in a nice geometric pattern – Claire hears from the tall, stiff, pop-eyed Maharajah of Djorah (Philippe Hériat with his face slathered in tan make-up). He will offer her the crown of Djorah. Perhaps the Maharajah is not yet sufficiently familiar with French to know that the word for 'crown' also denotes a funeral wreath. 'I'm not dead yet,' Claire snaps. 'Kill me first!' As in any fairy tale, the suggestion will be taken seriously.

But first, the late-arriving guest produces himself. He is the brilliant, wealthy engineer Einar Norsen (Jaque Catelain), by far the youngest and dewiest of the men at the party. Einar joins Claire in the winter garden (a Rousseau-like forest of cardboard cutouts, designed by Claude Autant-Lara) and confesses his love, even as the floor-show continues. (Two seminude Africans are now doing a fire-eating routine.) Driven to desperation by Claire's coldness, Einar threatens to kill himself. In reply, the heartless Claire has one of her servants hand him a tiny dagger, the delivery of which is intercut with scenes of the African performers staging a sword fight.

From here on, things become less plausible. The events include an apparent suicide, committed by racing car; a scandalous concert, filmed on location at the Théâtre des Champs-Elysées (where an audience of 2000 was actually incited to near-riot by the piano-hammering of George Antheil); an apparent resurrection, accompanied by an early demonstration of television; a murder by snakebite; and finally a real resurrection, carried out with much bustle in a laboratory designed by Fernand Léger.

In this climactic setting, this bi-level jumble of geometric cutouts – a triangle juts up from the floor, a pair of arcs sticks to the wall, a perforated rectangle hangs down like a pendulum – disks whir, four assistants in black vinyl jumpsuits swing up and down on ropes, and Einar (in a white jumpsuit and elongated welder's mask) produces sparks and smoke from a switchboard. To keep pace with this frantic but meaningless activity, the screen fragments into swish pans and superimpositions, rapid cuts from long overhead shots to close-ups, bursts of light that are (or were, in the original print) jolts of pure red or blue or white. The original score, by Darius Milhaud, apparently calls for nothing but percussion, until the dangerous experiment is concluded and Claire rises from the dead. Thanks to Einar and his machines, she has become a new Claire. To replace the brutally cold diva of before, who was as much a stranger to emotion as Miss Alicia Clary, Einar has manufactured a creature as loving as Hadaly.

In later years, L'Herbier was unkind enough to say that he, too, had wished for a new Claire Lescot; she should have been played by Brigitte Helm or Marlene Dietrich. To soften this criticism, he sometimes remarked that no one at the opera cares when a woman in her fifties impersonates a young beauty. Still, when you read the interviews, you can all but hear him shrug. L'Inhumaine was a complete failure, critically and commercially, and someone had to be blamed.

It's true – as Claire, Leblanc is laughable in the wrong way. She's all the more laughable for having been cast opposite L'Herbier's close friend, trim little Jaque Catelain. Leblanc was twenty-five years older and could have used him for a toothpick. And yet, when L'Herbier began shooting at the Joinville studio in September 1923, his choices for Claire were limited. Helm was then unknown; Dietrich was a semi-anonymous bit player. Perhaps L'Herbier could have gone back to Eve Francis, who had taken the lead in his successful 1921 feature *El Dorado*. But Leblanc provided certain advantages that Francis could not. First, she brought with her a commitment of 130,000 francs from Otto Kahn, the American financier and Paramount insider. This was half the projected budget.* Second, Leblanc really had been famous, before the war. Third, she embodied for L'Herbier the world of aestheticism in which he'd wrapped himself in his youth, and which he now seemed to want to destroy and reproduce in a single gesture.

Leblanc had become a star in the 1890s at the Opéra-Comique, where one of her roles was Carmen. (Like Miss Alicia Clary, she came to the stage by way of a brief marriage, which had usefully removed her from her home town in the north.) In the mid-1890s she met Maurice Maeterlinck, whom she married in 1901. Although denied the chance to appear in the premiere of her husband's *Pelléas et Mélisande*, she nevertheless exerted a strong influence on his work, receiving credit in the press for having moved him away from 'morbid, puzzling' plays to pieces that were more 'hopeful.'

Leblanc did not live near Paris in a Purist construction by Mallet-Stevens. She made her home near Rouen, in the semiruined Norman abbey of St. Wandrille. There, in her heyday, Leblanc played Lady Macbeth, Charlotte Corday, and (at last) Mélisande for small, invited audiences, including L'Herbier. When not entertaining in this fashion or gardening, she devoted herself to philosophy, which meant crystal-gazing, Buddhism, Vedanta, and Theosophy. In 1911, rumors circulated that she had written a much-discussed, unsigned magazine article declaring women to be the future rulers of the world. Leblanc denied authorship. 'Woman doesn't need politics,' she explained to an interviewer that year while on her first American tour. 'She has enough, enough that she can do far better, and without sacrificing her greatest charm – femininity.'

In his autobiography, L'Herbier recalled meeting Leblanc in 1912, when he was 24 years old and suitably impressionable. On the day they met, she was 'helmeted like a Valkyrie' and seemed like a 'Viking' to the young would-be poet.

The son of a consular magistrate – 'a great humanist,' as he told one interviewer, 'who spoke Latin and brought me up to know and love the great composers and authors' – L'Herbier studied for both a diplomatic career and the law. Around 1910, he put his father's humanism to the test and abandoned all professional pursuits, devoting himself instead

---

* It was not, however, an enormous sum. In the early 1920s, Richard Abel notes, most French productions cost between 100,000 and 200,000 francs, the equivalent of $20,000–$40,000. This was about 10 to 20 percent of the usual budget for American pictures. L'Herbier himself had spent 248,000 francs on *El Dorado* and about 850,000 francs on *Don Juan et Faust* (1923).

to musical composition and literature. In music, his idol was Maeterlinck's collaborator, Claude Debussy. In literature, he was under the sway of Villiers, Maurice Barrès, and Oscar Wilde.

This, too, is a curious list. In Villiers, L'Herbier had a hero whose politics had been royalist and whose religion was ultramontane. Barrès, author of *Le Culte du moi*, was the leading literary figure of the anti-Dreyfus faction and an enemy of everything cosmopolitan and democratic. Instead of being drawn toward a world-reforming aestheticism, of the kind that had led Wilde to get dirt under his fingernails building a road near Oxford, young L'Herbier seems to have favored the aestheticism of exclusivity and self-conscious superiority – of 'exceptional beings,' as Claire Lescot would have said. Given these tendencies, L'Herbier could have learned only two things from Wilde: how to wear his homosexuality well (he was open about his preferences), and how to play his refinement of taste as a trump card, to his own amusement and the discomfiture of others.

It must have meant a lot to this young man to become a protégé of Madame Maeterlinck – to be received by her at the abbey at St. Wandrille, and to have her recommend one of his writings to the *Mercure de France*. What was the tone of his writing? Here is a stage direction for his play *L'Enchantement du mort*, written in 1917:

The curtain parts, disclosing a sumptuous room of immediately disconcerting effect; – a large room where, by a bold transgression of all 'historical verisimilitude,' one finds, chaotically juxtaposed, objects and decor belonging to all the styles that characterize the various epochs of decadence, romanticism, and effeminacy through which humanity has passed until now. Here one sees, side by side in a vast synthesis deliberately full of anachronisms, whatever has been called up by epochs as dissimilar as the Byzantine, the Alexandrian, the Moorish, and our own. (Cited in Burch)

Note the author's early taste for the Higher Eclecticism. As for the action: A man and a woman, Faustus and Eva, engage in a dumbshow that culminates in the pulling back of a curtain to reveal a vast landscape of 'PURPLE . . . brutal, sudden, magnificent, torrential.'

You might think that World War I would have put an end to this kind of thing. For L'Herbier, it did and it didn't. In 1917, after having been shunted from one wartime assignment to another, he was posted to the Army Cinematographic Service. 'My life was turned upside-down,' he later testified.

I was face to face with the awful reality. Everything that was filmed at the front passed through our hands: we cut, we spliced, we chose what could be shown. I watched scenes of horror; I saw soldiers who had been eviscerated, cut in two, decapitated. People who weren't at the front couldn't have taken the sight. In doing that work, I discovered that the camera's eye saw what human eyes hadn't been able to see. There are images that will never fade from my memory. That shock revealed to me that I had to become a filmmaker, perhaps to be able to show what normally could not be seen. (di Giannoli)

As he later put it, art is the age-old process of humanity reflecting upon the world. But film is something new: a mechanical, objective process that at last allows the world to reflect upon human life.

Perhaps the shock of his wartime work really did reveal to him this potential of film; and yet his first feature, *Rose-France* (1919), showed little evidence of change from his prewar mindset. It was dreamy, nationalistic, symbolic, aestheticized, and (without meaning to be) thoroughly silly. Moreover, L'Herbier still felt great pride in his three-act 'miracle in purple, black, and gold,' *L'Enchantement du mort*, and was delighted when it was presented in 1919 by the experimental theater group Art et Action.

The group was led by the parents of Claude Autant-Lara: architect Edouard Autant and actress Louise Lara. They deserve a moment's attention as admirers of yet another member of the antidemocratic avant-garde, the Futurist manifesto-writer F.T. Marinetti, who is known to have attended at least one of their shows. Giovanni Lista has traced these connections and points out that the Futurist influence persisted even after 1919, when Gaumont offered L'Herbier a three-year contract to direct films for his new line of low-budget productions, Série Pax. In 1921, the same year that L'Herbier made *El Dorado* for Gaumont, he participated in his first collaboration with Claude Autant-Lara and Darius Milhaud, and his first experience of filming before a live audience. The work was not *L'Inhumaine* but a Futurist-derived 'instantaneous drama,' *Prométhée mal enchaînée*, performed at the Théâtre Colisée in January 1921.

The Futurists, too, crowded the decade's roster of 'progressives'; and like some others who claimed that title, they enjoyed a cozy relationship with wealth and power. Their ideology, like Claire Lescot's, was made for self-styled 'exceptional beings' and flowed all too smoothly into that other forward-looking movement of the 1920s, Fascism. *L'Inhumaine* strikes the characteristic note by deriding Bolshevism on the one hand and American (perhaps Jewish) capitalism on the other. (L'Herbier made a similar gesture in *Prométhée mal enchaîné*, in which the protagonist was a modern banker, chained to his desk by telephones for the sin of having stolen gold, tormented by his speculation on a stock issue known as the Caucasian Eagle.) Politically, Futurism represented continuity for L'Herbier. It allowed him to extend his prewar enthusiasm for Barrès into a congenial period for the right-wing avant-garde, a period when the Bloc National reigned triumphant in France.

But in another sense, Futurism represented something new for L'Herbier – as was only appropriate, since novelty was the movement's subject matter and rallying cry. Futurism did not just welcome modernity but demanded it. Its passion for machinery (such as Einar Norsen's racing car) fitted in perfectly with L'Herbier's recent fascination with motion pictures. Its cheerfully destructive attitude toward the past allowed L'Herbier to define a new identity for himself – active and entrepreneurial – against those decadent, nontechnological prewar moods of which Georgette Leblanc had been a part. Hence the emotional conflict that is one of the most engrossing traits of *L'Inhumaine*: the filmmaker's apparent indecision about whether to worship Leblanc or mock her.

His star and principal funder was a woman in a position at once painful to herself and potentially ludicrous to others, of having to restart her career in middle age, having been brutally dumped by her husband in December 1918. With *L'Inhumaine*, L'Herbier may be said to have rallied to her side. In her guise as Claire Lescot, Leblanc remains above the ignorant herd, as we see when the ugly, common people (goaded by a vengeful Apostle of Humanity) gossip and conspire against her. After she's been murdered, Einar lays her out like a Valkyrie on an immense stone bier, and we understand that nothing less is owed to the former Madame Maeterlinck. But then, she did need to be killed off. As the Futurists insisted, the old world must be wiped away before the new world can be built; and there's no question which of the two Leblanc belongs to. Surely L'Herbier knew: she looks like Einar's mother.

Whether Leblanc knew remains undecided. Unlike L'Herbier, she was no filmmaker and could not easily have foreseen the figure she'd cut. We know she fussed continually over her make-up and hair, as might be expected of an aging diva; she also demanded many changes in the script that L'Herbier had cooked up with Pierre Mac Orlan. But she assented to the overall contour of the story (including Claire's techno-resurrection) and by L'Herbier's own account accepted direction easily. I would guess that Leblanc, too, saw *L'Inhumaine* as an opportunity for self-modernization.

For this purpose, the crucial sequence might take place during Claire's first visit to Einar's house, when she enters his laboratory and helps to launch his new invention: television. She will 'travel by telephone wire,' Einar tells her, and in return the 'whole world' will be brought into the lab. Claire can't wait to try it. Only recently, she had been all but hooted off the stage of the Théâtre des Champs-Elysées. Now (although the intertitles gallantly refrain from making the point) she will no longer need to face an audience. Her voice will go out to listeners around the world, and their images will be sent back to her; but she will not be seen.

The demonstration begins. Claire sings, and the television screen comes alive with an image of three Arabs swaying happily before the horn of a gramophone. The next image: Claire sees an African woman in the bush, sitting on the ground in a grass skirt and listening with open-mouthed delight. Somewhere in Europe, a painter and his half-naked model pause in their work to hear Claire's voice. Then comes the final picture, which shows Claire someone she has seen before: a peasant woman, who on the night of the big party had incongruously shown up driving a donkey cart.

In sum: television transports Claire by allowing her to look at people who are not modern, offering her a spectacle of colonial subjects, rural folk, and figures from *La Bohème*. The contrast intensifies the thrill of her own newly electrified status; the one-way method of transmission ensures that her modernity will not be questioned, now that it's been achieved. Her listeners (unlike the movie audience) may go on dreaming of Claire Lescot, instead of being disappointed at the sight of Georgette Leblanc.

It's as if Leblanc had dreamed of updating herself by substituting television for her prewar crystal ball. Too bad for her that L'Herbier, too, had need of updating. By allowing Leblanc to appear as she was – a matronly star of 1911 who had strayed into a setting of 1923 – he implicitly highlighted his own advanced status, much as he highlighted Claire's by setting it against a backdrop of burnoosed Arabs.

And yet, in his aspiration toward modernity, L'Herbier turned out to be only too much like Leblanc: admirable, but touchingly risible. Unlike his immediate rivals in Exposition-building – civic leaders, government officials, the directors of business empires – L'Herbier could not pour a unifying coat of money over his creation. Nor could he command the large forces of talent and capital that had been available for *Intolerance*, despite Griffith's status as an independent filmmaker. L'Herbier had only his friends to rely on. As a result, his fairground of the latest French art looks flimsy. More to the point, it flaunts its flimsiness, as if to boast of its origins in a coterie. As deliberately discontinuous and cheerfully absurd as a series of skits, *L'Inhumaine* looks like an early example of the 'playing dress-up' mode of underground cinema (to borrow a concept from Parker Tyler), only much, much bigger – another of the self-contradictions that have become, with time, the film's greatest charm. In this respect, *L'Inhumaine* was an aggravated case of the more general disorder of 1920s French film production.

After his contract with Gaumont had lapsed in 1922, L'Herbier followed the usual French model by setting up his own production company, Cinégraphic, for which he drew on financing from two wealthy acquaintances. The pictures he proposed to make may be described, accurately if a bit too harshly, as showcases for himself and his clique, a goal that clearly marked the production of *L'Inhumaine*. Milhaud signed on as the composer partly because he was the cousin of one of L'Herbier's backers. Léger (the second choice to design Einar's laboratory, after Francis Picabia had declined the invitation) showed up at the Joinville studio one morning and simply began building the set, sawing and hammering away on his own. Picabia was curious enough to drop by to see the work in progress, as did Erik Satie and many others.

Shooting started at the end of September 1923 but came to a premature halt on October 24, when Leblanc left for a round of engagements in the United States. In her absence, L'Herbier sent some members of his circle on location for another production and took a Cinégraphic ski vacation in Gstaad (where he offered to produce a new film by Catelain and considered a project proposed by René Clair). Leblanc didn't come back until spring 1924, at which time L'Herbier quickly wrapped up the shoot. But the long hiatus may have been one cause of the absence of *L'Inhumaine* from the preview screenings held each summer for exhibitors. As Richard Abel notes, the film opened cold at the Madeleine-Cinéma in November 1924, competing against superproductions such as *Le Miracle des loups* and *The Ten Commandments*. At some screenings, L'Herbier later recalled, people tried to rip out the seats.

They had already seen the world of the future, thanks to American movies; and they knew it did not resemble the melange of 'pastiche, parody, and quotation' (as Alan Williams calls it) of *L'Inhumaine*. And so, despite the jolt of electricity, Georgette Leblanc did not change into a new Hadaly, fully modern but spiritual; nor did French cinema in L'Herbier's hands become a 'carnival of Futurism,' superior to America's crass products. The Exposition he'd put together with his little group actually succeeded in avoiding Americanism. (It's a place of modern architecture but not of skyscrapers, of industrial products but not of factories.) But the result – greeted with amusement by some, contempt by others – was blatantly a small, private production that happened to be caught up in delusions of grandeur.

Metropolis, by contrast, came from a studio that was the world's largest and arguably its most advanced. The film really is big; and in its form, it is far more coherent than *L'Inhumaine*, despite the production's scale and complexity.

Whereas the sets (and set pieces) of *L'Inhumaine* are as discontinuous as scattered playing cards, the urban spaces of *Metropolis* could conceivably hold together in the physical world. All the necessary, Americanist infrastructure is here: factories, utilities, workers' housing, a transportation network, and (for the managerial class) a cluster of skyscrapers grouped around the 'New Tower of Babel.' Nor is this all. 'Somewhere in this city,' Dietrich Neumann writes (p. 34), 'are a Gothic cathedral, a sports stadium, a nightclub, and pleasure gardens for the *jeunesse dorée.*' As in a European architect's fantasy of New York or Chicago, the elements of this City of the Future plunge far into the depths of the earth and rise high overhead. Lang and his production designers, Otto Hunte and Erich Kettelhut, paid as much attention as would a practicing architect to the vertical connections among these strata. 'Staircases, steeply inclined tunnels, and especially elevators play a central role in the film,' as Neumann notes. The ensemble is 'a complex, three-dimensional entity.'* And yet *Metropolis* has this in common with *L'Inhumaine*: its central female figure is not just a robot but a robotized mother.

Because Ufa withdrew the original version of *Metropolis* from distribution in spring 1927, only a few months after its premiere, and then re-released the film in a chopped-up American version prepared by Paramount, the maternal theme fell into obscurity for decades, until the archivist and film historian Enno Patalas brought it to light through a painstaking restoration project. Thanks to him, the story dreamed up by Thea von Harbou can again be known, if not understood:

A young man named Freder (Gustav Fröhlich) romps thoughtlessly through the sunnier precincts of the twenty-first-century Metropolis, until the day he glimpses a beautiful but somber young woman buttoned up in a chaste, plain dress. She shelters under her arms a crowd of

---

* One reason for this specificity may be found in Lang's background. His father was a successful, high-bourgeois *Baumeister* in Vienna: not an architect (as Lang later claimed) **87** but something more like a general contractor and structural engineer. Lang prepared half-heartedly to enter this profession, until in late adolescence he switched to studying women, cafés, and the latest paintings by Egon Schiele.

children. Immediately, Freder drops the pampered, half-naked flirt with whom he's been cavorting and runs after the mysterious figure. So he sees, for the first time, the underground city to which the workers are confined.

Horrified, Freder returns to the surface and angrily confronts his father, Joh Frederson, who oversees the affairs of Metropolis from high in the New Tower of Babel. The father (Alfred Abel) is lean, tall, and solemn; he thoroughly dominates a son who still wears breeches, and who seems all the more juvenile for his manner of tossing himself about with each fit of emotion. Yet somehow the overwrought lad finds strength to defy the Master. He descends once more into the workers' city, where he tracks down his pure-hearted, child-protecting ideal deep within the womblike space of the catacombs. He now learns she is Maria (Brigitte Helm), a preacher of peace and reconciliation. But while Freder is busy gazing into her eyes and gently stroking her fingertips, the audience is getting another part of the story.

Rather like *Snow White*'s queen, who also can appear as an ugly old witch, Joh Frederson has a counterpart. The Master works in uneasy alliance with a wild-haired, wild-eyed scientist, Rotwang (Rudolf Klein-Rogge). Years ago, these two competed for the love of a woman, who died giving birth to Freder. Now, in an attempt to make her live again, Rotwang has created a robot. On Joh Frederson's orders, this same robot becomes a diabolical double of Maria – which means Freder spends the rest of the film chasing after the image of his own mother and being frightened at the change that's come over her. She now spends half her time in nightclubs, driving men into a sexual frenzy, and the other half in the catacombs, rousing the workers to self-destructive violence.

When a case cries out so loudly for Dr. Freud, we may perhaps dispense with his help. Let us assume von Harbou and Lang knew what they were up to. (A bit of internal evidence that they did: they took care to kill off both the bad mother and the bad father. The robot Maria is burned at the stake, to cries of 'Witch!', while Rotwang falls to his death from the roof of a cathedral. This leaves the family romance neatly resolved. Joh Frederson having been rendered harmless, the lad steps forward with a new manliness, so that possession of Maria may be transferred from father to son.) Yet questions remain. Why should the Oedipal struggle be mechanized, or the industrial class struggle Oedipalized? Apart from the rhetoric of the intertitles, does anything link the robot Maria's two acts of malice: arousing the upper class and misleading the workers?

The first point to be made is the obvious one: by presenting the robot Maria as a nightclub-frequenting hussy, von Harbou and Lang were satirizing the Weimar Republic's much-publicized New Woman. I stipulate 'much-publicized' because slender, short-haired, athletic, sexually active but childless career women were not nearly so common in Germany as they seemed to be at the time.

That they suddenly seemed so prominent may be explained in part by the recent extension of suffrage to women, and by the modest increase in the number of single women working in the cities. Writing in 1931, the journalist Hilde Walter added another layer of explanation:

all the consumer-goods industries geared to female customers were very quick to recognize the attractiveness of ... catchwords [such as 'accomplishment' and 'women's abilities'] and make full use of them in their advertisements. Even the most poorly paid saleswoman or typist is an effective billboard; in a provocative get-up she becomes the very emblem of endless weekend amusements and the eternal freshness of youth. (cited in Kaes et al., p. 210)

The New Woman had an image much like that of the robot Maria: fashionable and sexy but 'unfeminine,' incapable of abandoning herself to love. Such heartlessness and consumerism were among the marks of her affinity with America.

As an article in the satirical magazine *Uhu* pointed out, America had contributed to German speech a number of new terms – five o'clock, flirt, dancing, cocktail – among which the most recent and important was 'sex appeal.' The term banished any mystery; it seemed to come from a realm beyond human will, like 'atom' and 'radio wave.' And this pointed to another Americanized aspect of the New Woman: she seemed to many observers to be an industrial commodity.

Of the chorus girls (those sisters of the robot Maria) who proliferated in the postwar years, Siegfried Kracauer wrote, 'in that era the girls were mass-produced in the USA and exported in waves to Europe. They were not merely American products but a demonstration at the same time of the vastness of American production' (Kaes et al., p. 565). Friedrich Sieburg also made the connection; in his essay 'Worshipping Elevators,' he described a California beauty pageant as an example of the Taylor system at work. Among the judges, 'One concerns himself only with the legs, the other with the line of the back, the third takes the face into account, a fourth measures bottoms, so that the result is achieved rather quickly.' The process was all very efficient; and being efficient, it prevented anyone from enjoying the goods on display.

So it is with the robot Maria, who inspires such lust in men that they fall to fighting over her, never realizing that she is literally a mechanical product. In 'The Sandman,' only one highly imaginative student fell for Olympia; but in *Metropolis*, every able-bodied man of the upper class seems vulnerable to her allure. As if to drive home the notion that the nightclubbing New Woman is a kind of collective hallucination, *Metropolis* has her appear in a fever dream to Freder, who (like Nathanael) habitually suffers from poetic visions. But unlike Olympia, the robot Maria initiates the seductions, using an hypnotic power of her own. In his role as *Metropolis*'s Coppola-figure, Rotwang can only look on, confessing, 'I have lost control of the robot.'

The first object of this satire, clearly, is anyone who has been so foolish as to become fascinated with the New Woman. The second is the New Woman herself. Had von Harbou and Lang wanted to challenge the myth surrounding her, they could easily have put the New Woman into context. In 1920s Germany, nearly as many women worked in industry as in all other job sectors combined, except for agriculture. This wasn't a secret; and yet you don't see any women slaving away in the underground factories of *Metropolis*. The laborers who gather to hear Maria preach are all men. Women show up very late in the underground city, and then not to work but to riot.

They do so under the influence of the robot, who has hurried underground to serve as an *agent provocateur*. But even though an evil machine can pass into the workers' city, the New Woman apparently cannot. The impassioned, violent figure who now comes before us evokes no associations of smart, athletic career women or libidinous chorus girls. She might be likened instead to a blonde, fine-featured Rosa Luxemburg – except she doesn't seem even that modern. Her simple dress and oratorical gestures would pass without remark in a film set in the late nineteenth century. Something similar might be said for the working-class women she calls up out of nowhere: dressed in all-purpose sacks and shawls, they look as if they could be rural peasants instead of the urban poor. Somehow, as the satire passed from above ground to below, its timeliness dropped away. So, too, has the film lost the architectural specificity that was earlier so impressive.

Once the working-class women make their long-delayed appearance, they resemble nothing so much as a flood, rushing violently to the surface – an image that is suggested by more than mere coincidence. Just when the infuriated women break through to the world above, the film shows a real flood pouring upward into the workers' city, threatening to drown all the children. By this point, the illusion of architectural coherence has been so well established that the viewer may ignore the improbability. Perhaps the lower levels of Metropolis are like a mineshaft, which must be kept clear with pumps. But the film neither offers this explanation nor rules out a competing range of fantasies. The city may have been built on water; its power plant may exist chiefly to hold back the primordial flood. The image does not quite make sense on a literal level – or at least, the literal level is not the overriding one.

In search of a fuller explanation, the viewer may ask if there have been other conjunctions of women and fluids. One comes to mind: a clear liquid bubbles around the encased form of Maria when Rotwang transfers her likeness to the robot. It begins to seem as if an unseen hydraulic system must be operating in the city. Flowing from a single good woman of the working class, its waters run upward to the New Woman and then back underground, in the process becoming a raging torrent of bad women.

No viewer can ignore this component of the city's infrastructure; and yet, compared with the roads and elevators, it goes undescribed, as magical systems must. An element of the uncanny runs through *Metropolis* from the beginning: the fable of the Tower of Babel, the visions of Moloch and the Whore of Babylon, the creation of the robot beneath an inverted pentagram. But by the time we reach the climax, with its witch-burning mob and Gothic cathedral, nothing modern is in sight to counterbalance the spookiness. Social satire and Americanist fantasy have broken off, tacitly but sharply, as if the goal of *Metropolis* had been to replace them with psychology and German folklore.

Lang used to speak slightingly of the conclusion of *Metropolis*: a brief political allegory, in which society's head (capital) and hands (labor) are reconciled by the heart (that newly empowered Social Democrat, Freder). As political slogans go, this one is certainly bland – yet it sums up hopes actually held at the time by Germany's centrist political groups. At the least, the finale ought to be strong enough to set off saddened head-shaking. That even such a slight force should be lacking suggests that something has been interrupted, cutting off whatever energy might have gone into the scene.

The connection between the two levels has been cut: between the upper and lower cities, between modern satire and Grimm Brothers fantasy. The interruption happens at the very moment when the women of the workers' city are about to burst into a political space. The robot Maria was allowed to occupy that space, in her role as the New Woman; but the modern arena dissolves at the approach of the proletarian women, who are left in a space of psychology and myth.

And yet the landscape of the finale does incorporate one looming political presence. It is the Gothic cathedral, which stands out among the futuristic sets as the one work of architecture that is unambiguously German. *L'Inhumaine* countered the American challenge with novelty: the European modernism of Mallet-Stevens, Cavalcanti, and Léger. *Metropolis* counters it with something very old.

Metropolis, a product of the most modern developments in technology and business, is a film in full flight from modernity – especially where women are concerned. If we ask whether this internal conflict matches any feature of the contemporary scene, we won't have to look far for an example.

Thea von Harbou *was* the New Woman. After first embarking on a career as an actress, she became a popular novelist and then one of the most prominent screenwriters on the Ufa payroll. When she met Lang in 1919, she was not only two years older than the director but far better known. She was also married, to Rudolf Klein-Rogge, the actor who would eventually play Rotwang – an inconvenience that did not prevent her from diving into an affair with Lang (who also was married, and was half Jewish into the bargain). Since von Harbou was by this time a public figure, her subsequent divorce and remarriage were as scandalous as anything done in a cabaret by the robot Maria.*

Von Harbou also maintained the image of the New Woman in her avocations, her tastes, her style. She was an avid horsewoman and claimed to have climbed Mount Kilimanjaro. In Lang's company, she frequented the most fashionable restaurants, bars, and sporting events. In the couple's apartment, featured in the magazine *Innendekoration*, von Harbou had an office of her own, decorated with artworks and exotica from around the world. Her dress was generally simple and elegant; but when production began on *Metropolis*, she changed into a costume of unmistakable significance: high-heeled shoes, a suit with a knee-length hem, a short, bobbed haircut.

And yet the New Woman was more than a short skirt, lipstick, and a salary. She was also someone who refused to 'be a woman'; who in the name of 'objectivity' (another catchword of the time) denied there was any essential difference between herself and a man. In that sense, von Harbou was anything but New.

Although Patrick McGilligan writes respectfully of her ladylike upbringing – the music lessons, the language lessons, the passages memorized from Goethe and Schiller – Kreimeier knows better and situates her with brutal accuracy. Born into 'an impoverished family of

* Another major element of the scandal is discussed in some detail by Patrick McGilligan: the violent death of Lang's first wife, Lisa Rosenthal, which was ruled a suicide.

The folly comes to town and becomes an amusement park: view of the Jardin de Monceau in Paris, etched by Jacques Couché after a design by Carmontelle (1717–1806). Published 1779 in *Jardin de Monceau, près de Paris, appartenant à Son Altesse Sérénissime Monseigneur le duc de Chartres.* (Collection Centre Canadien d'Architecture/Canadian Centre for Architecture, Montréal)

The amusement park becomes a World's Fair: the Tower of Jewels at the Panama-Pacific International Exposition of 1915. (San Francisco Public Library)

The World's Fair becomes a film: construction begins on the Babylon set of D.W. Griffith's *Intolerance*. (The Museum of Modern Art Film Stills Archive)

In the skull of the world-historical artist: the Wagnerian grotto where King Ludwig II lives out his *Lohengrin* fantasies, in Luchino Visconti's *Ludwig*. (Photofest)

Expensive fantasy: Erich von Stroheim's reproduction of Monte Carlo, constructed on the Universal lot for *Foolish Wives*. (The Museum of Modern Art Film Stills Archive)

Expensive naturalism: Erich von Stroheim, on Polk Street in San Francisco, directs the funeral cortège for *Greed*. (The Museum of Modern Art Film Stills Archive)

Modern America as tower and grotto: view of 'The City of the Future: A Bold Solution to the Traffic Problem.' Relief halftone after a drawing by Harvey Wiley Corbett (1873–1954), reprinted from *Scientific American* in *L'Illustration*, 9 August 1913. (Collection Centre Canadien d'Architecture/Canadian Centre for Architecture, Montréal)

The German future becomes American: the Erich Kettelhut–Otto Hunte design for Fritz Lang's *Metropolis*. (The Museum of Modern Art Film Stills Archive)

A French reply to the American challenge: Fernand Léger's geometric-abstract laboratory set for *L'Inhumaine*, by Marcel L'Herbier. (The Museum of Modern Art Film Stills Archive)

A German reply to the American challenge: the quasi-Gothic laboratory in *Metropolis*. (The Museum of Modern Art Film Stills Archive)

Tanning up in Texas: Austrian-born Tilly Losch, made up as an Indian, dances on the bar of a typical Southwestern cantina, in David O. Selznick's *Duel in the Sun*. (Photofest)

Follies girls come to Rome: Nubian dancers prepare the way for Elizabeth Taylor, in Joseph Mankiewicz's *Cleopatra*. (The Museum of Modern Art Film Stills Archive)

Ceremonies of guilt and absolution: celebration of the Mass amid a helicopter attack, in Francis Ford Coppola's *Apocalypse Now*. (Photofest)

Going too far in the jungle: Klaus Kinski, as Brian Sweeney Fitzgerald, shapes up his Indian forces in Werner Herzog's *Fitzcarraldo*. (Photofest)

Confronting the folly of a rational economy: Jacques Tati, as M. Hulot, looks out over the corporate maze of *Playtime*. (Photofest)

the landed aristocracy,' von Harbou was educated by governesses and 'absorbed a governess's limited view of the world and of human nature.' Her writings (especially the patriotic stories and novels she turned out during World War I) bear witness to the pan-Germanic milieu of her youth, offering a 'special blend of maudlin sentimentality and bloodthirsty inhumanity' (Kreimeier, p. 140).

However provocative the circumstances of her marriage to Lang, she subsequently acted out the role of the good wife, ignoring his flagrant adulteries while for a long time engaging in none of her own. She enjoyed entertaining at home and often was happiest going to bed early with a book. When Lang held production meetings in their apartment, as he often did, she cooked dinner for everyone. When hundreds of malnourished children from the slums of Berlin were brought onto the set of *Metropolis*, essentially to play themselves – they were to be the workers' children, abandoned by their rebellious mothers – von Harbou was the one to offer them food, warmth, and toys, though she (like the New Woman) happened to be childless.

No such contradictions plagued Georgette Leblanc, and for a simple reason: France did not have a New Woman. According to James McMillan's history of women in the Third Republic, French feminists were 'an isolated and ineffectual lobby' after World War I. The radicals amounted to a sect, tiny and obscure, while the mainstream movement (such as it was) belonged to 'a handful of upper-class women,' led by a Catholic elite. Although the Chamber of Deputies passed a resolution in 1919 to extend the vote to women, the Senate delayed debate until November 1922 and then rejected the measure, on the grounds that women would vote for clerical candidates and so undermine the Republic. The proper role for a French woman – according to an opinion that went almost unanswered in public debate – was to serve as a baby machine, replenishing a war-depleted populace. To further the cause of obstetric patriotism, the Ministry of Health established a Conseil Supérieur de la Natalité in 1919, and new laws were passed in 1920 and 1923 against contraception and abortion.

These norms spilled into films, as Richard Abel notes. During the war, the most popular women on the French screen were vamps such as Musidora and daring adventurers such as Pearl White. After the war, these risk-taking, convention-breaking figures faded away, their places taken by mothers and wives in domestic dramas. One notable, and therefore scandalous, exception was *L'Inhumaine*. Leblanc may have looked like Jaque Catelain's mother, but as Claire Lescot she flaunted her indifference to the maternal project, ignoring every Frenchwoman's duty for a chance to wear Poiret designs and appear on television. This attitude proved to be disastrous at the box office but was good in a different way for Leblanc and L'Herbier, whose laughter in *L'Inhumaine* was unencumbered by the burdens of propriety.

For von Harbou, matters were different. In her society, women had broken into the public arena as never before. She was one of them. But how shabby, to be one of many! As her writings reveal, von Harbou was a habitual self-dramatizer, always narrating to herself the events of her life as they happened, always finding the right adjective to describe that special von Harbou quality. She, too, claimed to be an exceptional being; but unlike Claire Lescot, she was surrounded by tens of thousands of other modern women, which somewhat strained her exceptionalism. Besides, she didn't know if she even wanted to be modern.

Such attitudes are easy to deplore, especially when you know where her muddleheadedness would lead. (As Lang drily observed, speaking of the demise of his marriage: 'The only thing that divided us was National Socialism.') But since *Metropolis* is far too confused to be taken as prescriptive – what policy, exactly, would *you* carry out on its advice? – I prefer to think of von Harbou's screenplay not as a foretelling of 1933 but as a representation of her own chaos in 1926, and of the chaos experienced by a multitude like her. Sometimes von Harbou appears before us in her old-fashioned, pan-German mood, in the guise of the saintly Maria. (We know she's projected herself into the character because Maria is singular; no other women in the workers' city compete with her for attention.) Sometimes, in her modern mood, von Harbou turns into a robot (the transformation is effected on screen by her former husband and behind the camera by the present one), and then she lives out excesses of New Womanhood beyond anything she actually would have dared. And sometimes she has to be burned as a witch. Laughing and unrepentant, she atones for those masses of women who foolishly tried to be like her, to break into the new world of easy sex and big, exciting machines.

One figure is missing from this account: the director. Fritz Lang had willingly assumed the task of satisfying everybody: connecting von Harbou's mysterious hydraulic system to the more intelligible infrastructure of Metropolis, dissolving the Americanist city of the future into a German Gothic city of the past, resolving the Oedipal struggle, ending the class struggle, giving Erich Pommer the unprecedentedly big movie he demanded, and saving the German film industry from bankruptcy. All this, while fulfilling his own need for infinitely precise craftsmanship. It's a wonder anything got onto the screen at all.

The script was evidently complete by December 1924, when Lang returned from the United States and launched into production meetings. Through the winter and spring, sets were designed and constructed (including the miniatures that would be shot with Eugen Schüfftan's trick photography), the cast was assembled (including 19-year-old Brigitte Helm in her first screen role), rehearsals were held. On May 22, 1925, shooting began at the immense Ufa studio at Neubabelsberg.

It would continue through October 30, 1926, for a total of 310 days and 60 nights, during which time Ufa went to considerable lengths to publicize its extravagance, much as Universal had done with *Foolish Wives*. Among the unverifiable numbers given out to the newspapers: the production had employed 36,000 extras, including 11,000 women, 750 children, 100 Africans and 25 Chinese. The budget, originally estimated at 1.5 million marks, eventually rose to 5.3 million (more than a million dollars) – though here, too, the figures are unreliable, since Ufa's executives wrote off expenses of all kinds against *Metropolis*.

The production, though already in its seventh month, had not yet reached midpoint when Ufa entered into its desperate loan agreement with Paramount and MGM in December 1925. The following month, alarmed at the rising cost of *Metropolis*, the board of Ufa threatened to cut its losses by aborting the film. But too much was already invested; the board contented itself with firing Erich Pommer, thereby eliminating the one person who was exerting any control over Lang. Pommer remained in touch with the *Metropolis* set until April 1926, when he left for the United States. His replacement as Ufa's head of production was Major Alexander Grau, a veteran of the Ministry of War's press office – a likable, cultivated man (in Kreimeier's judgment) who for the next six months could do nothing for *Metropolis* except let the shooting take its course.

The film was given its premiere at the Ufa-Palast am Zoo in Berlin on January 10, 1927. Many of the reviews were admiring; but given the scale of the investment in *Metropolis*, 'many' was not good enough. Ufa would have needed to persuade everyone in Germany to see the picture; and even then, it would have lost money. The fortunes of *Metropolis* depended upon the international market, meaning the United States, into which it was released in March 1927, beginning with New York City.

Unfortunately, this premiere was entirely in the control of Paramount. The company prepared for it by hiring the dramatist Channing

Pollock to cut *Metropolis* from sixteen reels to nine. Along the way, McGilligan notes, he not only junked entire episodes but also rearranged the sequence of events and rewrote the intertitles, in the service of a story of his own invention. I think it likely that this was the version seen by H.G. Wells, who in a widely circulated review awarded it the title of 'the silliest film.' *Metropolis* did not conquer America.

In late March 1927, faced with the need to sell its offices on Potsdamer Platz and possibly its theater chain, the Ufa board accepted a buyout offer from Alfred Hugenberg – publishing magnate, former chief executive of the Krupp steelworks, and 'conservative revolutionary,' who would eventually become a minister of the Third Reich. For a total of 16.5 million marks, Kreimeier records, Hugenberg acquired a controlling interest in Ufa. He did not wait to make himself felt. On April 7, Ufa's management asked its American-controlled distributor, Parufamet, to allow *Metropolis* to continue playing in a handful of provincial German cities, 'in the American version and if possible with the Communistically tinged subtitles removed.' Instead, Parufamet withdrew the film entirely, the better to prepare for a re-release in August 1927. The version they distributed, in Germany and around the world, was the American cut. The original was lost.

In this way, *Metropolis* joined *Greed* on the list of famous but unseeable films. It was not, however, as unseeable as some.

Unlike *L'Inhumaine*, which all but vanished between 1924 and its revival in a 1968 retrospective, *Metropolis* continued to be a presence and an influence, even in its mutilated form. Perhaps it was even more of a presence than if it had been intact. What its images lost in coherence they gained in portentousness and inexplicable power, once they had been cut loose from their narrative underpinning. People often assert that movies are like dreams, thereby passing over their resemblance to certain other things: archival documents, abstract compositions, and arguments (usually unfair). *Metropolis*, more than most films, really did become a kind of dream, living in people's memories as a confused series of very sharp images: overpowering buildings, ghostly bodies in a fog, a surging riot, a metallic woman ringed with light. Fritz Lang was unquestionably the author who had made these images unforgettable; while Thea von Harbou, writer of the disposable script, was forgotten.

It's worth noting that L'Herbier himself borrowed from *Metropolis*, casting both Brigitte Helm and Alfred Abel in his 1929 film *L'Argent*. That film, too, failed gloriously. Still slightly out of step with his times,

L'Herbier managed to release this fancy-dress lampoon about stock traders just when it would seem neither acute nor amusing: in the year of the Wall Street crash.

L'Argent was to be (with one or two exceptions) L'Herbier's last fling with the cinema of excess. During the 1930s, he made himself adapt to the introduction of sound, and to the more regimented production system that accompanied it. French methods were still far more artisanal than those practiced in America; but even though French producers did not attempt to compete against the Thalberg assembly line – even though they went so far as to foster, for marketing purposes, a nonindustrial image – every aspect of their work was becoming standardized, from the length of the films to the running speeds of the projectors. From 1930 until the outbreak of World War II, L'Herbier chastened his exceptionalism and made nineteen features and two short subjects, which in general were both conventional and successful. He continued to make films throughout the Occupation, during which time he gave employment to screenwriter Henri Jeanson (who could not be credited because of his Jewish background), and in 1943 he founded the French national film academy, the Institut des Hautes Etudes Cinématographiques, which he directed until 1969. The memory of Leblanc's role in making *L'Inhumaine* died out in moviegoers' minds, as did von Harbou's role in *Metropolis*. But for an entire generation of French filmmakers and critics, the project of a popular yet avant-garde cinema remained alive, embodied in L'Herbier.

In many ways, he enjoyed a happier career than did Lang. On March 23, 1933, the German Parliament passed the Enabling Laws, making Hitler dictator. On March 28, the Minister of Propaganda, Josef Goebbels, called the leading figures in the German film industry to the Hotel Kaiserhof, just for encouragement. The evidence suggests Lang attended the meeting. A few days later, Goebbels called Lang to his office and proposed that he become head of film production for the Reich. According to the story Lang told many times afterward, he fled Germany that same night, taking a train to Paris with whatever cash and valuables he had on hand.

He didn't, of course. Writing in the spring 1990 issue of *Film Quarterly*, Gösta Werner revealed that Lang's passport told a different story: he took a trip out of Germany in late June and then left definitively at the end of July. McGilligan, who enjoys being hard on Lang, makes the most of this discrepancy, using it as an occasion to repeat unattributed accusations of Lang's 'slowness or indifference' to Nazism. Granted: after it had become clear that the worst had indeed happened,

Lang took all of four months to abandon a highly successful career, uproot himself from his adopted home, and (in passing) complete his divorce from von Harbou. I suppose some people might have been in a greater hurry to choose expatriation; but I can't see what was blameworthy about Lang's manner of leaving Germany, except for its being less exciting than the tale he invented.

As for the reason why Goebbels proposed making Lang the Nazis' chief filmmaker: in some of the accounts he gave of the conversation in the Ministry of Propaganda, Lang reported that Hitler had 'loved' *Metropolis*. This assertion cannot be verified. We do have reliable evidence that at the March 28 meeting in the Hotel Kaiserhof, Josef Goebbels singled out a Fritz Lang–Thea von Harbou film for the highest praise, saying it was already a work of Nazi art. That film was the immediate predecessor to *Metropolis*: *Die Nibelungen*.

An Interlude

As part of its contribution to the 1937 Paris World's Fair, Germany exhibited the architectural model for a work in progress: the Nazi Party's Nuremberg rally site, designed by Albert Speer.

The project was a culmination of work Speer had done at Nuremberg since 1934. Within the public yet private space of the rally site – public because thousands gathered, private because they did so only at the Party's pleasure – Speer created settings for events that were spectacular: made to be seen, by on-site viewers and by the camera's eye. Of these events, the one that had served the party best was staged in large measure so that an antimodern, antifeminist New Woman, Leni Riefenstahl, could create *Triumph of the Will*. With the exhibit at the Paris World's Fair, the Nazis promised their viewers an even greater work of total cinema.

Budgeted at 700–800 million marks, the rally site was to cover 65 square miles. At its south end was a parade ground, the Marchfield, encompassed by grandstands with seating for 160,000 spectators. Guests of honor would sit on a platform dominated by an allegorical sculpture that was to be 197 feet tall. As Speer noted in his memoirs, such a figure would have been 46 feet higher than the Statue of Liberty. The Marchfield itself, he pointed out, would have covered twice as much ground as the palace of Kings Darius I and Xerxes in Persepolis.

Leading north from the Marchfield was a processional avenue. It was to be a mile and a quarter long and 264 feet wide, with a reviewing stand on the right and a colonnade for the display of flags on the left. At the end of this avenue stood the Great Stadium, which was to seat 400,000 spectators. (The Circus Maximus in Rome, Speer wrote, had held at the most 200,000.) Beyond the stadium was a reflecting pool, or more properly lake; and beyond that stood two more buildings: a Kongresshalle and a Kulturhalle, the latter designed especially for Adolf Hitler's speeches on cultural affairs.

The judges in Paris awarded Speer's design a Grand Prize. Despite this success, Germany declined to contribute a pavilion to the World's Fair held in New York in 1939. When that exposition opened, on April 30, its most popular attraction proved to be the Futurama, a ride-through exhibit in the General Motors pavilion, designed by the scenic artist Norman Bel Geddes. Visitors moved past the model of a clean and happy Metropolis of 1960; upon exiting, each received a pin that read 'I have seen the future.' As for Hitler's work of art of the future: he invaded Poland on September 1.

The war, too, was staged for the cameras; it was a continuation of the Nuremberg rallies by other means. The German nation got to see itself in a starring role, with a great many tributary peoples, prisoners, and stiffs cast as extras. Produced for Hitler by a group that prominently included his Minister of Propaganda, Josef Goebbels, the war played successfully on screens in Germany and its occupied lands for month after month, augmented by radio broadcasts, concerts, newspaper and magazine articles, and still more rallies.

Of course, this all-encompassing production also had its commercial aspects. Goebbels noted one of these in a diary entry for October 21, 1939: 'The financial success of our films is altogether amazing. We are becoming real war profiteers.'

The movies to which he referred seldom forced an explicit political message upon the audience. As writers such as Eric Rentschler have shown, Goebbels wanted the regime's films to serve as come-ons; most of them were musicals, melodramas, light comedies, adventure yarns, biographical dramas about great men of the past. So long as they accorded with the tone the Nazis wanted to set, these genre pictures were allowed to leave the preaching to other films: the newsreels, documentaries, and short subjects that were shown on the same bill. Only a handful of each year's features were propaganda vehicles. Their messages varied with the needs of the moment.

In 1940, for example, the Nazis wanted to step up their promotion of anti-Semitism. The Jewish population of Germany had shrunk from 503,000 in 1933 to 234,000 at the onset of the war. Then, through conquest, the regime quickly added some 8 million Jews to its European subjects. Goebbels, having planned ahead, was ready with two films to meet the challenge: Fritz Hippler's pseudo-documentary *Der ewige Jude* (*The Eternal Jew*) and Veit Harlan's costume drama *Jud Süss*, about the wiles of a Jewish moneylender who perverts and debauches the court of Württemberg. As Erwin Leiser notes, *Jud Süss* 'was shown to the non-Jewish population when the Jews were about to be deported. Concentration camp guards saw it. And at the Auschwitz trial in Frankfurt former SS Rottenführer Stefan Baretzki admitted that the effect of showing the film was to instigate maltreatment of prisoners' (pp. 84–5). *Jud Süss* was Germany's biggest box-office hit of 1940, attracting more than 20 million admissions.

Beginning in summer 1941, Hitler withdrew from public view. Perhaps to compensate for his absence, Goebbels increased production of the genre known as genius films. Although the Führer had become invisible, figures who exemplified his most celebrated qualities showed up in many productions released in 1942–43: *Mozart, Andreas Schlüter, Diesel, Rembrandt, Paracelsus.*

On January 31,1943, Goebbels began to face the need for yet another phase of the propaganda war: Field Marshal Friedrich von Paulus surrendered his 90,000 troops to the Soviets at Stalingrad. Two weeks later, in a speech made at the Sportpalast, Goebbels called for austerity measures and the mobilization of all citizens. For the first time, many Germans began to face the possibility of defeat – a notion that was driven home on May 12, when a quarter of a million Axis troops surrendered to the Allies in North Africa.

On June 1, 1943, Goebbels wrote a memorandum to Veit Harlan, the director who had served him on *Jud Süss*:

I hereby commission you to make the epic film *Kolberg*. The film is to demonstrate, through the example of the town which gives it its title, that a people united at home and at the front will overcome any enemy. I authorize you to request whatever help and support you deem necessary from all Army, Government, and Party agencies, and you may refer to this film which I have hereby commissioned as being made in the service of our intellectual war effort. (Leiser, p. 122)

According to Harlan's memoirs, Goebbels had spoken of making a film about the town of Kolberg as early as 1940. Now, wanting to ready the home front for a period of sacrifice and suffering, Goebbels committed unlimited resources to a film about a citizens' army of the early nineteenth century, defying the forces of Napoleon despite impossible odds. In his diary, he wrote that *Kolberg* 'fits exactly the political and military landscape we shall probably have to reckon with by the time the film can be shown.'

Within one month after Goebbels commissioned the film, a four-night air raid on Hamburg destroyed 80 percent of the city and killed 30,000. The Allies invaded Sicily, Mussolini was deposed, and the German army failed in its all-out attack against the Russians at Kursk. Meanwhile, at the Ufa studio, Veit Harlan worked on completing *Opfergang (The Great Sacrifice)*, an Agfacolor melodrama with a sub-Nietzschean theme. Its hero was torn between his duty toward one woman (representing a wan, indoor realm of books and music) and his passion for another (representing a vibrant, outdoor world of horseback riding and skinny-dipping). Girl number two (played by Harlan's wife, Kristina Söderbaum) was clearly to be preferred, though a lingering death was somehow the consequence of her living as a blonde beast who thinks with the blood.

Around this time, Auschwitz II (Birkenau) went into full operation, its four new gas chambers/crematoria having been inaugurated between March and June 1943. Farther east, forces under the command of SS Colonel Paul Blobel were destroying evidence of an earlier, less efficient phase of genocide. In June, one of the Blobel units was in Lvov, digging up mass graves and burning the corpses; in August, another such unit began work near Kiev, at Babi Yar. During these months, the Nazis also devoted significant resources to rounding up the few Jews who remained alive in the ghettoes. As Goebbels's ally in the home front mobilization, Albert Speer, began to centralize military production in September 1943, Germany was deporting some 2000 Jews from Minsk to Sobibor. By September 25, the Nazis had wiped out the Vilna ghetto.

In early October 1943, Veit Harlan and Alfred Braun finished the screenplay for *Kolberg*. (Klaus Kreimeier writes that Thea von Harbou was said to have been an uncredited collaborator.) Filming began on October 28, with interiors shot in Neubabelsberg and exteriors in Königsberg and on the Baltic coast near Kolberg itself. In order to have a town he could blow apart and burn, Harlan also began constructing a Kolberg-folly in Gross-Glienicke, a suburb of Berlin near Potsdam and Wannsee. In November, as production started to move forward, the Allies began their bombing campaign against Berlin. That same month, some thirty Jews in the Janowska camp staged a revolt; off the set, too, there were acts of defiance, despite impossible odds.

The filming of *Kolberg* continued through August 1944. According to Harlan's account, the production cost 8.5 million marks – more than twice the usual budget for a first-class feature – and eventually employed 187,000 people, including entire army units. For one sequence, in which Napoleon's soldiers attempt to advance across flooded fields, Harlan drafted 4000 sailors to serve as extras. (Soldiers could not be trusted to fall into the water properly.) When the Admiralty refused the request, Goebbels overruled the Admiralty. Harlan also managed to requisition a hundred boxcars of salt (to sprinkle over the fields as fake snow) and 6000 horses. Factories were put on overtime to manufacture blank bullets for the production. Some 10,000 period uniforms were sewn; when those ran out, the soldier-extras who were to march in the rear ranks were told to dye their own uniforms and decorate them with sashes made of toilet paper. The Western Allies landed at Normandy, the Soviets began their offensive against Army Group Center, Colonel Claus von Stauffenberg attempted to kill Hitler, Goebbels was named Reich Plenipotentiary for Total War, and still the shooting continued on *Kolberg.*

Harlan wrapped the production in August, around the time the Allies entered Paris and the Nazis began the final deportations from the Lodz ghetto: another 67,000 Jews sent to Birkenau. The following month, Goebbels began organizing a Volkssturm, or People's Army, made up for the most part of very young and very old men. Children aged 10 to 15 were conscripted to work on farms and at antiaircraft installations. Women, too, were conscripted in large numbers for the first time; exemptions were discontinued, and the age limit for women for compulsory labor was raised from 40 to 50.

In November 1944, Harlan attempted to hand over *Kolberg;* but Goebbels declared the picture a complete disappointment. He demanded extensive cuts, especially in sequences that showed too vividly the sufferings of war. Harlan later estimated that the excised footage had cost 2 million marks to shoot. Around this same time, the Nazis began to dismantle the gas chambers and crematoria at Birkenau and to destroy the camp's documents. On Christmas Day 1944, Goebbels held his final discussion with Harlan about the editing of *Kolberg.* The following day, an Allied air strike all but finished Germany's counter-offensive in the Ardennes.

The film was ready for its scheduled premiere on January 30, 1945, the twelfth anniversary of Hitler's appointment as Chancellor of Germany. Goebbels was determined to hold the premiere on the Atlantic coast of the Reich. By this time, Germany held only one position on the Atlantic, La Rochelle. Since it was behind Allied lines, Goebbels had the print of *Kolberg* dropped in by parachute. The commander of La Rochelle sent back his thanks:

Profoundly moved by the heroic stand of the fortress at Kolberg and by this artistically unsurpassable rendering of it, I convey to you . . . a renewed vow to emulate the heroic struggle of those on the home front and not to lag behind them in endurance and commitment.

On January 31, *Kolberg* was given its premiere in Berlin, at the Ufa-Theater on Alexanderplatz and at the Tauentzien-Palast. (Ufa's greatest theater, the Palast am Zoo, had by this time been destroyed by Allied bombing.) According to Kreimeier, the guests at the Tauentzien-Palast were given only a cold buffet, 'consumed in haste by a worried public eager to get home before the next air raid.'

On March 19, 1945, in the face of the Red Army's advance, German forces evacuated Kolberg (today known as Kolobrzeg). That had pretty much been the result in 1807, too, despite what Harlan and Goebbels showed in the film.

Kolberg is narrated in flashback. The frame story, set in 1813, begins with thousands of citizens marching through the streets of Breslau. Although they sing most stirringly of their desire to fight Napoleon, King Friedrich Wilhelm III holes up in his palace, refusing to hear. Into his inner chamber strides General Wilhelm von Gneisenau (Horst Caspar), who reminds the out-of-touch leader of the events of seven years earlier, in Kolberg:

With Napoleon victorious at Jena and Austerlitz, the military commander of Kolberg, Colonel Loucadou (Paul Wegener), seemed prepared only for token resistance. So the burgermeister, old Nettelbeck (Heinrich George), took matters into his own hands: organizing a militia, bringing in his own artillery, and otherwise showing up the furious Loucadou. Nettelbeck was assisted by a dashing cavalry officer, Ferdinand von Schill (Gustav Diessl) and later by Gneisenau himself, once he took over the military command of Kolberg.

Put in a love story, Goebbels had said. Harlan, never slow to give his wife a job, cast Kristina Söderbaum as Maria, a farmer's daughter, who falls in love with von Schill. She also crosses enemy lines to convey a message to Queen Luise, consents to have her home burned to the ground to prevent its use by the French, and provides a useful contrast to her brother Klaus (Kurt Meisel). The latter is one of Harlan's whipping-boy characters: a culture-besotted weakling who swoons over the *Moonlight* sonata when real men should be fighting and making love, who toasts the French on demand, who dies (as he should) trying to rescue his violin from a flood.

For those interested in establishing auteurist credentials for Harlan – an initiative taken up in recent years by a number of writers – this figure of the degenerate art-lover should be of some consequence. It is unquestionably one of Harlan's thematic signatures; his most notable stylistic tic is a tendency in dialogue scenes to push the actors toward either somnambulism or apoplexy. (In *Kolberg*, the exchanges between Heinrich George and Paul Wegener look so much like spitting contests, they might have been directed by an oral surgeon.) Those who feel that Nazi cinema was redeemed by such traits may seek more of them in Harlan's work. I will note only that his authorial credit for *Kolberg* must be shared with Goebbels, who closely supervised not only the editing but also the screenplay (sections of which borrow from his speeches) and who seems to have thought of the film as his answer to *Gone with the Wind*.

Goebbels also seems to have conceived of *Kolberg* as a personal testament. According to Harlan, Goebbels spoke of Nettelbeck as the hero of the film and identified with the character. But I think Goebbels was much closer to Gneisenau, both in physical type (he somewhat resembled the thin, sleek-haired Horst Caspar) and in the role he played: making speeches and providing an interpretive frame for events. If we imagine Gneisenau to be a self-portrait of Goebbels, then we may find in *Kolberg* some instruction on how to be a Minister of Propaganda. When the French send an envoy to request surrender, Gneisenau steps out onto a balcony and addresses the citizens gathered below, informing them that he chooses to fight on. Anyone who disagrees, say so now, Gneisenau orders; and everyone remains silent. Anyone who agrees, go back to what you were doing; and the crowd disperses in all directions. A striking picture of the mechanism of consent: those who would object must find the courage to speak up as individuals, while those who accept their leaders' policies need only go about business as usual.

Not that anything was still usual by 1943. If we ask why Goebbels, as advocate for total war, should have allocated military resources to a mere film, precisely when Germany's situation in the field was crumbling, we also must ask why the Nazi regime simultaneously allocated its shrinking resources toward the completion of genocide. The mystery becomes intelligible only if we realize that the Nazis were carrying out not one war but three; a war of geopolitical conquest, an intellectual war (to use Goebbels's phrase), and a war against the Jews. These three were related, of course; Himmler, for example, made it plain to his chain of command that the presence of a Jew – any Jew at all, anywhere in Europe – should be considered a danger to German forces. Similarly, certain productions of the intellectual war clearly were expected to influence for the better the war in the field. But the hierarchy among these three projects was never stable. Sometimes the Nazis produced films to help their troops make war; but they also made war for the sake of producing films, or killing Jews and other undesirables.

To speak in this way, linking the production of *Kolberg* with the systematic murder of millions, is to compare small things to great, and in the most tasteless way possible. I am tempted to write 'grotesque.' Yet in its original sense, as applied to the wall paintings of Nero's Golden House, that word described something far removed from the Nazis' enormities. 'Grotesque' described a style in which incommensurate things were mixed to create a decorative pattern, for the amusement of sophisticated people at their leisure. (Strictly speaking, this book is grotesque.) As a domestic refinement, the grotesque had no deep connection to its presumed Dionysian origin in the archaic, disorienting rites practiced in caves and caverns. Far from inspiring awe or ecstasy, the grotesque in Nero's time probably functioned as an ironic contrast to the Empire's above-ground, Apollonian system of temples – which (for the upper classes) were themselves sites of disbelief.

It was the conviction of the young Nietzsche that a full-blooded engagement ought to be restored between Dionysus and Apollo, the grotto and the temple. This engagement, he felt, should be sought not in religion but in art, specifically in the music-dramas of Richard Wagner. Nietzsche's later, horrified recantation of this notion does not concern us here; nor is this the place to do justice to Wagner by considering the actual texts of the music-dramas as distinguished from their aura. For our purpose, it is enough to understand that what Nietzsche analyzed and articulated a century ago, many other people were sensing and acting upon. The 'progressive' culture of which Wagnerism was the highest expression brought together people with many different agendas, and so it generated many results. In one of them, the temple became a rally site in Nuremberg; the grotto, a crematorium.

And the connection between the two? Conventionally, we speak of a dialectic, as if one were succeeded by the other in an endless cycle. Perhaps the folly of *Kolberg* may remind us that there is a third term that temporarily resolves the dialectic, a type of building that exists between the extremes. The midpoint between a grotto and a temple is a ruin.

Follies Girls

As for the man who'd made *Gone with the Wind*:

During the early years of World War II, David Selznick busied himself as a talent scout, an agent, a packager of films, but not as a producer. His situation might be compared to that of D.W. Griffith after *The Birth of a Nation*: having created something that was as much a sociological event as a motion picture (and from a literary source as distinguished as *The Clansman*), Selznick did not know what to do next. As he remarked to a colleague during one late-night working session, 'I know when I die, the obituaries will begin, "David O. Selznick, producer of *Gone with the Wind*, died today," and I'm trying like hell to rewrite them' (Thomson, p. 459).

The origins of his suffering lay as far back as 1935, the year he resigned from MGM to form Selznick International Pictures, which he made into the most visible of Hollywood's independent production companies. Writing to his financial backers, Selznick declared, 'There are only two kinds of merchandise that can be made profitably in this business, either the very cheap pictures or the very expensive pictures' (Schatz, p. 178). Like Griffith before him, Selznick saw no reason to settle for the former; and his judgment on this point was sound. In his book *The Genius of the System*, Thomas Schatz notes that in the late 1930s Selznick could make more money 'turning out one or two big hits per year than eight or ten competitive A-class features.' But until *Gone with the Wind* (1939), even Selznick did not anticipate how *much* money could be made, or what the resulting tumult might do to him.

He was an heir to Griffith in another way as well: when he set up on his own, he contracted to release his films through United Artists, the distribution company that Griffith had helped found in 1919.

Throughout the 1920s and 1930s, UA did much to keep alive a remnant of those artist-entrepreneurs who once had dominated filmmaking. Producers such as Selznick and Samuel Goldwyn needed screens on which to show their movies; the studios, which owned chains of theaters, needed a steady flow of pictures. By acting as go-between, United Artists served both parties, while implicitly casting doubt on the notion that 'independence' might entail more than a business strategy. Everyone in Hollywood understood that Goldwyn and his like could not make movies without drawing on resources maintained by the studios – their physical plants and personnel. The studios, in turn, enjoyed having Goldwyn cover some of their overhead.

This symbiosis allowed Selznick to bring out eleven films between 1936 and 1940, with the list reaching a climax in *Gone with the Wind* (released through MGM) and *Rebecca*. Then Selznick rested. In 1940, through a stock transaction, he liquidated his company, so the profits from *Gone with the Wind* would be taxed at a lower rate, as capital gains rather than income. (Another motive – so his biographer David Thomson believes – was simply to enjoy pocketing a huge wad of cash.) Although he immediately reincorporated himself as David O. Selznick Productions, he did not bring out another picture until 1944. Instead, reversing his earlier relationship with the studios, he became a supplier of resources. He loaned Alfred Hitchcock to RKO, Ingrid Bergman to Warner Bros., Gregory Peck (with the rights to *The Keys to the Kingdom*) to Twentieth Century-Fox, Vivien Leigh (with the rights to *Waterloo Bridge*) to MGM.

For the while, Selznick had cocooned himself; but we would be mistaken to think that he alone felt himself growing into a different creature. Metamorphosis was general in the Hollywood of the early 1940s.

The war fed the studios: the domestic box office grew from 80 million admissions a week in 1940 to almost 100 million a week in 1946. The war also starved the studios, carrying away the very contract personnel who were needed to turn out the product. Of the top-level people who stayed behind, many chose to wriggle away from full contracts; a war-related change in the tax code made it profitable for them to limit their activities. Adding to the irregularity of the work force, another group of film-industry figures from Europe had recently fled to the United States. Producers could hire short-term help from among these refugees, or (as in the case of Max Ophuls) could let them languish in the reserve army of the unemployed.

Given this shift in conditions, the studios themselves began to encourage independence. More and more, they turned to outsiders to organize the production of major films, thereby limiting their own involvement to financing and distribution. Even a large-scale independent might take advantage of the situation. Late in 1943, Selznick hired Dore Schary away from MGM and put him in charge of a new company he'd formed, called Vanguard Productions. Each year, Vanguard was to deliver six or seven films for Selznick to release: the sort of 'cheap pictures' he once had disdained.

Duel in the Sun (1946) might have been made as one of these cheap pictures. Instead, it turned into a production to rival *Gone with the Wind*: a monument to a time of change in the film industry, and to the personal chaos of David Selznick.

The woman at the center of that chaos was at first just another performer who might be hired out for profit. Phylis Walker, a stage actress who also had appeared in two low-budget films, came to Selznick's New York office to audition in July 1941. He gave her a contract and at the end of August tried her out in a play that John Houseman was producing for him in Santa Barbara. This was the start of an extensive makeover. Selznick put his acquisition through multiple screen tests; he sent her to acting classes in New York. In February 1942, he gave her a new name: Jennifer Jones.

The date when Selznick and Jones became lovers cannot be specified so precisely. It's possible that the affair had begun by the end of 1942, when he loaned her to Twentieth Century-Fox for her first starring role, in *The Song of Bernadette*. By summer 1943, when he cast her as a supporting player in *Since You Went Away* – the first new production he'd undertaken since *Rebecca* – their relationship was the subject of gossip on the set.

On March 2, 1944, Jennifer Jones won the Academy Award for her performance in *The Song of Bernadette*, the story of a young girl who is granted miraculous visions of the Virgin Mary. Selznick sat next to her at the award ceremony; his wife, Irene Mayer Selznick, did not attend. One day later, Jennifer Jones, though a Catholic, filed for divorce from her husband, Robert Walker.

Selznick had chased many actresses, and more than a few had allowed themselves to be caught. But this relationship was serious; it threatened his marriage and complicated his business affairs. As the man who had discovered Jennifer Jones, he now might be expected to give her a starring role, not in a loan-out but in a picture of such prestige that only David O. Selznick could have produced it. But to do so would run against the cost-cutting strategy he'd adopted – not only his lucrative practice of talent-peddling, but also the more recent decision to make his equivalent of B pictures, using properties such as *Duel in the Sun*, which had just come to his attention. It was a Western – the sort of story most producers would have made on the cheap. What's more, another studio owned the rights, and merely wanted to pay him for one of his stars. But the star in question was Jennifer Jones, and the role she was to play seemed to work on Selznick's imagination.

Niven Busch had written the story as a novel, which he later sold as a package to RKO, with himself as producer and Oliver Garrett as screenwriter. The studio assigned John Wayne to play Lewt McCanles, the tougher, wilder, and therefore sexier of the sons of a powerful Texas rancher. But RKO could not decide whom to cast as Pearl Chavez, the untutored young *mestiza* who is introduced into the McCanles household and inadvertently disrupts everyone's hormones. Then word got around that Selznick wanted to hire out Jennifer Jones.

The role wasn't exactly Bernadette of Lourdes – but might Jones be available? Selznick said he would consider a loan, if RKO improved the project. He doubted John Wayne would be right for Lewt; he felt the script should be rewritten. He also insisted that Jennifer Jones needed a producer more experienced than Busch – though of course Selznick himself would not have dreamed of assuming the job. Then again, he did dream of it. Instead of loaning out Jones to RKO, he bought the property for her in November 1944. And though he made the deal through Vanguard, he began rewriting the script himself and somehow forgot to hand it over to Dore Schary.

To direct *Duel in the Sun*, Selznick hired one of Hollywood's best-known figures, King Vidor (who had made, among many other films, *The Big Parade*). He gave the role of Lewt to Gregory Peck (a far better choice than John Wayne) and cast Joseph Cotten as Jesse, the contrasting McCanles son, who is sufficiently polite and pacific to deserve Pearl's love and therefore can never win it. To complete the cast, Selznick brought in Lillian Gish, Lionel Barrymore, Walter Huston, Herbert Marshall, Harry Carey, and also much cattle. Shooting began on March 1, 1945, at a location near Tucson. The script, though unfinished, was 170 pages long – enough, by rule of thumb, to yield 170 minutes of screen time – and Irene Mayer Selznick had just asked for a divorce.

Somehow, Selznick was still entertaining fantasies of a budget production. As shooting began, he instructed King Vidor on the importance of 'getting speed at the outset' and accomplishing 'extraordinary dispatch' from 'the very first setup.' Warning against losing 'valuable minutes,' he asked Vidor to be a director who completes each morning's first set-up 'so fast that it startles everybody, even if it is not exactly what he wants . . .' (Behlmer, pp. 345–6). Such slam-bangery was not to last. Only two weeks later – to take one example among many – Selznick sent a sharply different memo to his supervising film editor: a sequence of horsemen riding to a showdown was so magnificent, he wrote, that it ought to be shot again, this time with even more horsemen.

'Mr. Selznick would arrive . . . around three or four in the afternoon with new scenes that he had written or rewritten during the night before,' King Vidor wrote in his memoirs. 'I would point out that I had been shooting these scenes since nine o'clock that morning and in another hour would complete the episode. "But don't you think these versions are better?" Mr. Selznick would ask.' So they were redone, for a 'slight improvement,' while the script kept growing longer and the producer kept searching for the cause of the delays. In April, he explained in a memo that the problem was the lack of a production designer, which caused 'indecision on the set.' Simultaneously, he second-guessed King Vidor by hiring another of Hollywood's best directors, Josef von Sternberg, as 'special visual consultant.' What Sternberg had done for Marlene Dietrich, he must do for Jennifer Jones.

It wasn't unusual for Selznick to involve himself in the writing of a film, or to go into production with an incomplete script. Directors who agreed to work with him also knew he would demand retakes; that he would seize control of the editing; that he would test the picture on preview audiences and then (like Thalberg) make still more changes. But beginning with *Since You Went Away*, Selznick also had come onto the set, to watch run-throughs of scenes before they were shot. In a letter to King Vidor's attorney, Selznick proudly testified to the extent of his interference on *Duel in the Sun*: 'It was on the love scenes especially that . . . I was on the set morning, noon, and night, redirecting the actors, the camera, and even the lighting' (Behlmer, p. 345). He claimed that 'Not even a single angle of a single scene' was shot until he had reviewed it; and by his own account, 99 times out of 100 he changed what he saw.

King Vidor controlled himself until August 10, 1945, when (according to one account) he was busy trying to direct the climax of the picture, a love–death shoot-out between Pearl and Lewt. Selznick, judging the latest of many takes to be insufficiently dramatic, took the liberty of dashing stage blood over the actors. 'You can take this picture and shove it,' Vidor told him, then got into his car and drove away. This was five days before Irene Mayer Selznick moved out of the Selznick house.

August 16 found the producer coping with his impending divorce by sending Vidor yet another memo. Selznick seemed to believe this one was conciliatory: 'I was much more mad at you in subsequent days than I was out on the Mesa when I realized what there was left to shoot in the way of annoying bits and pieces. At least you might have left me one decent scene!' (Behlmer, p. 349). Somehow, this line of argument failed to bring Vidor back. Selznick installed William Dieterle as director, and *Duel in the Sun* ground on.

The picture was before the cameras for a total of 167 days, from March through November 1945, with retakes continuing into April 1946. During this time Jennifer Jones had to be sent home from the set because of exhaustion. News of her liaison with Selznick finally broke into the gossip columns, to the distress of both, and one night (according to David Thomson's account) she took too many sleeping pills and had to have her stomach pumped. Then came another six months of suspense and irritation during post-production. Arguments erupted between Selznick and the man he'd hired to make *Duel in the Sun* into a true *Gesamtkunstwerk*, composer Dimitri Tiomkin, who provided both a love theme and a desire theme but got into difficulties over the requested orgasm theme. Litigation broke out between Selznick and his distribution partner, United Artists, which was angry at him for having released some pictures through RKO. Selznick, angry in return, broke away from UA and formed his own distribution company, the Selznick Releasing Organization, whose first major picture would be *Duel in the Sun*. This was in November 1946 – a full two years after his B-movie unit had bought the rights. The picture had now cost Selznick $6.48 million – $3.7 million more than the original budget, and $2.9 million more than he'd spent on *Gone with the Wind*.

What kind of film had Selznick got for his money? That was just the problem: whereas movies are expected to conform to a type, *Duel in the Sun* was a Technicolor mishmash.

Ostensibly, it was a Western, one that could claim a certain influence on the postwar revival of the genre. The two most significant Westerns of the period, Howard Hawks's *Red River* and John Ford's *Fort Apache*, came out in 1948, shortly after the release of *Duel in the Sun*. Both were uncommonly monumental for the genre, and both were independent productions (released through United Artists and RKO, respectively). In a few sequences, *Duel in the Sun* seems to foreshadow those pictures: in the gathering of the McCanles horsemen, for example (which Selznick found so magnificent), and the ceremonious procession of the U.S.

Cavalry. But like so much else in the film, these are set pieces, whisked onto the screen and then whisked off again. Unlike a real Western – or *Gone with the Wind,* for that matter – *Duel in the Sun* does not draw upon a sense of national history. Selznick conceived its landscape as mythological, beginning with a frame narration about a spurious Indian legend. In that sense, we might say the film foreshadows a second genre: it anticipates the wild landscapes and bustling crowd scenes of Cecil B. DeMille's *Samson and Delilah* and many subsequent sword-and-sandal epics. Witness the opening scene, which features a 'Southwestern *cantina*' that's as big and crowded as one of DeMille's pagan temples during its high-priestess floor show.

Perhaps *Duel in the Sun* was also groping its way toward a third type of 1940s film, one that was not a true genre but rather a tendency within cinema: *film noir.* In its setting and visual style, *Duel in the Sun* hardly fits the *noir* image; but to qualify for the honor, a picture needs more than an urban crime story plus exaggerated shadows. *Noir* also implies a certain attitude toward the characters' moral sense, or lack of one. The principal male character of *Duel in the Sun* is brutal and lawless, emotionally weak but sexually enticing; in Selznick's own words, 'the worst son of a bitch that's ever been seen on a motion-picture screen.' The principal female character, like Rita Hayworth in *Gilda,* would like to be a good woman but is just too sexy to be left unmolested. At last, she decides she might as well live down to her image.

For viewers today, part of the fascination of *Duel in the Sun* lies in this confusion of genres. If Selznick shredded everyone's nerves, it may have been because the film he envisioned didn't correspond to type; so he kept trying to make several types at once, and was dissatisfied with them all. But for viewers at the time, one aspect of the picture clearly dominated all others: the character of Pearl Chavez, who wanted to live as a good girl but had to die as a bad woman. Selznick had made *Duel in the Sun* so his lover could play such a role. The fortunes of the film, and its reputation, rested on Pearl.

The premiere was held on December 30, 1946, at the Egyptian Theatre in Los Angeles; but Selznick delayed the general release until May 1947, when he opened *Duel in the Sun* in 300 movie houses across the United States. Until then, prestige productions (as Selznick would have called them) had invariably been shown first in a handful of movie palaces and only later put into wide release. *Duel in the Sun* was the first such film to be released almost as if it were a programmer. To Selznick, this multiple-run strategy was a 'tremendous milestone in motion-picture merchandising and exhibition,' marking a 'revolution . . . for handling big pictures.'

It was, in fact, one of *Duel in the Sun*'s chief legacies to the film industry. This variation on the theme of 'take the money and run' is now standard practice with blockbusters, to make them critic-proof during the first week in release. Yet in its initial trial, the strategy may have been less successful than it seemed. In his biography of Selznick, Bob Thomas reports that *Duel in the Sun* brought in $750,000 during its first week in New York City and earned $17 million nationally during its initial run. These figures were impressive enough to win it the reputation of being a great hit. Selznick took away perhaps $10 million of the box-office revenue, with the remainder going to the exhibitors. But as David Thomson notes, Selznick's share had to cover not only the $6.48 million that had been invested in production but also the costs of prints and administration. The latter item could not have been small; by his own reckoning, Selznick had opened his own distribution offices in thirty cities. And then there was the cost of promotion: $2 million.

Selznick later complained to his director of publicity, Paul MacNamara, of the loss of prestige he suffered because of the 'ballyhoo' that had been drummed up. (Among MacNamara's tricks: dropping *Duel in the Sun* weather parachutes over sports events such as the Kentucky Derby, and paying people to talk up the film at bars in Hackensack.) But how much dignity can attend the release of a scandal? Such was the nature of *Duel in the Sun*, on screen and off. By May 1947, through the gossip columns, the public had learned that two broken marriages lay behind the picture, and that the producer and his star were probably living in sin. For anyone who had seen the film, there was worse news still: Selznick had debauched a saint.

As Hedda Hopper wrote in an early, widely syndicated article, 'Jennifer Jones as Pearl Chavez is no *Bernadette*.' She was, in fact, closer to Jane Russell in *The Outlaw*, the peep-show Western over which America had professed outrage in 1943. Selznick had turned Bernadette into a dark-skinned dancing girl with a heaving bosom. When summoned to pray – not by the Virgin, but by a rumbustious preacher called The Sin-Killer – she presented herself dressed in nothing but an artfully draped blanket. When sexually assaulted – having just waggled her rump directly into the camera – she removed the onus of rape from her attacker by returning his embrace, at twice the force.

Hollywood's self-censorship office, the Production Code Administration, objected to some of these doings; but that was only the beginning of the uproar. Archbishop John J. Cantwell of Los Angeles announced publicly that Catholics could not watch *Duel in the Sun* 'with a free conscience.' The Church's Legion of Decency, whose influence extended far beyond Catholic circles, threatened to condemn the picture. (Selznick eventually secured a mere B rating, for 'objectionable in parts.') A more dangerous response came from Washington, where John Rankin railed against the picture from the House of Representatives. In June 1947, he read into the *Congressional Record* a letter calling *Duel in the Sun* 'a barbaric symphony of passion and hatred, spilling from a blood-tinted screen.'

A critic today could hardly compose a more apt description. Unfortunately, the Congressman and his correspondent did not intend theirs as flattery. Rankin was one of the film industry's principal enemies in government, and also one of the leading anti-Semites in Washington. As a member of the House Committee on Un-American Activities, he eagerly promoted the notion of a conspiratorial Hollywood, as it was described by the self-proclaimed Christian Nationalist Gerald L. K. Smith. 'There is a general belief that Russian Jews control too much of Hollywood propaganda,' Smith told the committee at Rankin's invitation, 'and that they are trying to popularize Russian Communism in America.' In May 1947, just as the Russian Jew Selznick was disseminating his multi-million-dollar insult to Christian morality, the committee came to Los Angeles for two days of hearings – an episode that marked the beginning of the blacklist period.

I am describing confluence, not cause and effect; I'm also writing of a producer who was unharmed by the blacklist and protested only faintly against it. Yet I'm sure the notoriety of *Duel in the Sun* made it easier for Congress to begin treating filmmakers as if they were Soviet spies. The film was inescapable in the summer of 1947 and intolerable to conservatives, not only because of its atmosphere of sexual frenzy but also because of its suggestion that miscegenation might be condoned. The film's moral arbiter, Jesse McCanles, would not have hesitated to marry Pearl; and yet she simply was not white. The film emphasized this inconvenient fact by giving Pearl a kind of double, or shadow: an even darker woman, played by Butterfly McQueen, who was made to flutter behind Jones in the endlessly irritating role of a witless servant.

Inadvertently, Selznick had contributed to an atmosphere in which anyone who seemed troublesome might be driven out of Hollywood. Hundreds of experienced filmmakers were about to be thrown out of work, expatriated, or forced into an underground economy. This was, of course, only the best-publicized part of a national campaign that affected millions, the repercussions of which lie far beyond the scope of this book. But I might mention one result that has often been overlooked: the blacklist caused a further diffusion of Hollywood's labor pool, attended by an acceleration of the trend toward quasi-independent production. Although the victims would have taken small comfort from the thought, their suffering hastened the demise of the studio system. Perhaps this, too, may be counted among the legacies of *Duel in the Sun*.

One of those who left Hollywood in the wake of the blacklist was Joseph L. Mankiewicz: a man who (like Selznick) had won Academy Awards two years in a row. In 1949, Mankiewicz received Oscars as best writer and best director for *A Letter to Three Wives*. In 1950, he repeated the feat with *All About Eve*, which also won the award for best picture.

No one should have felt more at home in Hollywood. Mankiewicz had worked in the film business since 1929, when his brother Herman got him a job as a junior writer at Paramount. A young producer at the studio, David Selznick, soon assigned him to write his first lines of dialogue, for *Fast Company*. A few years later, after both men had gone to MGM, Selznick brought Fritz Lang to America, and the task of collaborating with the studio's new employee went to Mankiewicz, who was fluent in German and had once been the Berlin correspondent for the *Chicago Tribune*. He undertook the hazardous duty of being Lang's producer on *Fury*.

Mankiewicz subsequently enjoyed a fine career as a producer; and in 1946, he began to direct, starting as a replacement for no less a figure than Ernst Lubitsch. In 1950, as *All About Eve* was nearing release, he gained official status, accepting the presidency of the Screen Directors Guild. And yet, soon after his triumph, Mankiewicz announced he was leaving Hollywood, declaring on his way out that he was departing a 'cultural desert' and 'intellectual fog belt.'

Why did he leave? Perhaps his awareness of superiority no longer amused him. Mankiewicz had actually read the books David Selznick talked about. He now intended to move back to the city he saw as his true home, New York, where he could devote himself to the stage, including the opera. He would make, at the most, one film a year. But there was also a second reason for his defection: the willingness of his colleagues to label people as traitors. As his biographer Kenneth Geist records, a faction of the Screen Directors Guild wanted to help enforce the blacklist. Mankiewicz fought hard to block their efforts. After he succeeded, he walked away in disgust.

The background to the episode was the passage in 1947 of the Taft–Hartley law, a Congressional response to labor unrest. From 1944 through 1946, America underwent a wave of major strikes, with unionists demanding a share of corporations' wartime profits and a degree of workplace control. At first glance, this agitation might be compared to the near-uprising that followed World War I; though in this case, the unrest was contained without mass arrests and deportations, let alone the hangings that an outraged President Truman proposed at one point. Most workers were beginning to enjoy unprecedented comfort, thanks in part to the nation's new anti-Soviet policy, which kept industrial production at a wartime level. For workers who would consent to business as usual, the Cold War provided immediate benefits. For those who would not consent, the same Cold War provided an occasion for discipline.

The Taft–Hartley law was part of that discipline. It not only imposed new impediments on unions but also sought to decapitate them. The law required union officers to sign an affidavit affirming they were not Communists. As those who drafted it could easily have foreseen, the measure was unacceptable to the more militant leadership of the labor movement – not only active Communists, but also civil libertarians and those who in the past had made common cause with the Party. They protested without success and were cut out of power.

As an officer of the Screen Directors Guild, Mankiewicz was required to sign the loyalty oath, and he complied. But while he was on vacation in the summer of 1950, the Guild's board of directors, led by Cecil B. DeMille, pushed through a new bylaw, making the Guild the first craft union to demand a loyalty oath from all its members. The full list of those who had signed – and of those who had not – could easily be given to producers.

Infuriated, Mankiewicz declared that even though he had signed the oath as a union officer, he would refuse to do so as a member. *Variety* reported his decision on October 11, 1950. On October 12, DeMille and his faction on the board circulated a ballot calling for Mankiewicz to be recalled from the Guild's presidency. *All About Eve* had its New York premiere on October 13, the same day the trade papers carried an advertisement taken out by the DeMille group, announcing the 'tabulation' of the Guild ballot requiring 'the non-Communist oath.' The figures were as unimpeachable as poll results from Moscow, or Chicago for that matter.

Mankiewicz forced the issue at an emergency meeting of the Guild, held at the Beverly Hills Hotel on October 22, with about five hundred members attending. DeMille and his allies grew ashen-faced as the meeting turned against them. First Rouben Mamoulian spoke movingly in defense of Mankiewicz. Then John Ford rose, introducing himself with heroic understatement as a man who made Westerns, and proceeded to force the resignation of the entire board of directors. Mankiewicz had prevailed. Three weeks later, he declared he was leaving for New York.

He would, of course, operate as an independent. In April 1953, he announced the formation of his own company, Figaro, Inc., which had reached an agreement to make one film a year for release through MGM. Financing for the first two Figaro productions would come from United Artists.

This circumstance is significant in itself; it demonstrates that by 1953, UA and the studios had become much more alike. The latter had been stripped of their theaters by a federal antitrust action, the so-called Paramount consent decree of 1948, and were beginning to rid themselves of production facilities and contract personnel. UA, recently reorganized under the leadership of Arthur Krim and Robert Benjamin, was stepping up its activities as a financier, while facing sharper competition from the studios for the right to distribute independent productions.

The first of the UA-backed Figaro productions was *The Barefoot Contessa* (1954), a film that proved independence was still not easy to attain. Mankiewicz had to pay MGM a high price for the loan of Ava Gardner, with the result that he soon had to loan out Figaro's only star – himself – to direct *Guys and Dolls* (1955). Mankiewicz was also learning that independent production did not necessarily yield personal filmmaking. In October 1955, he amended his financial arrangement with United Artists, contracting over a four-year period to make nine films, of which he was to write and direct only five. He was splitting his time between working for himself and taking on assignments for others, between acting as a hands-on filmmaker and being a relatively hands-off producer. He even had to split the ownership of his company; in June 1956, he sold NBC a 50 percent stake in Figaro.

Someone had to supervise the four extra productions Figaro had contracted to make; so around the time Mankiewicz sold a stake to NBC, he brought in another independent producer, the experienced and self-consciously high-toned Walter Wanger. Among his many other accomplishments, he, too, had worked with Fritz Lang, having formed a short-lived company with him in the 1940s. (Lang memorably directed Wanger's wife, Joan Bennett, in *Scarlet Street* (1945).) But by the early

1950s, Wanger was having a hard time staying independent – especially after he was sent to prison for putting a bullet into the groin of his wife's overly attentive agent. Although the time spent inside inspired Wanger to adopt a more common touch in his filmmaking, he did not regain the confidence of Hollywood decision-makers. Nor did his brief period with Figaro provide the refuge he needed, since Mankiewicz, too, turned down most of his projects. In October 1958, Wanger accepted a job offer from Twentieth Century-Fox. On paper, he was still his own man, since he had loaned himself out from his own company. In practical terms, he had reverted to being a contract producer.

Perhaps these dealings seem arcane. But they are crucial for understanding how Joseph Mankiewicz wound up directing *Cleopatra* (1963): the most expensive film that had ever been produced; the sort of movie that might sooner have been expected of DeMille; 'the hardest three pictures I ever made,' as Mankiewicz called it; a disaster for its studio, and a cataclysm for the man who attempted to be its author.

Almost as soon as Fox had hired him, Wanger proposed making a film about Cleopatra. The studio agreed, envisioning a picture that would cost anywhere from $1 to $3 million. The higher figure quickly became more likely, as Wanger first drummed up enthusiasm for an elaborate set by John De Cuir and then succeeded in his campaign to sign Elizabeth Taylor as the lead. Fox would have preferred a cheaper star; but Taylor's recent part in the Debbie Reynolds–Eddie Fisher divorce made her advantageously notorious, while her role in *Suddenly, Last Summer* (1959), directed by Mankiewicz, added to her reputation as both a sex symbol and an actress. Her salary was to be $1 million, plus added payments for schedule overruns and living expenses.

Despite the colossal sum he was willing to pay his star, Wanger did not want *Cleopatra* to be primarily a spectacle film, like so many others: *Alexander the Great*, *The Ten Commandments*, *Solomon and Sheba*, *Ben-Hur*. 'The entire picture,' he wrote in a memo, 'is one of intrigue, conspiracy, suspense and adventure. It will not be presented – as historical films usually are – in a pompous manner, with endless pageantry, but rather in the speed and tempo and cliff-hanger excitement of an underworld picture.' He asked Hitchcock to direct; but when he got an immediate refusal, he allowed Fox to give the assignment to Rouben Mamoulian, a director known for his light touch and visual flair. Peter Finch would play Caesar, and Stephen Boyd would be Antony.

Everything proceeded normally through midsummer 1959, when De Cuir began building Alexandria on the Fox lot. Then, in September, came the order to stop. The president of Fox, Spyros Skouras, had estimated he could save $1 million by transferring principal photography to England, making *Cleopatra* another of the American industry's growing number of runaway productions.

It had taken about ten years for such overseas relocations to become common. In the late 1940s, at the same time as the studios were stripped of their theater chains, they tightened their grip on the international market by making a number of trade agreements. These allowed the studios access to foreign screens so long as a set percentage of the box-office revenue was spent within the country. The need to make use of these blocked funds, the availability of cheaper labor and tax breaks, the desire to cut overhead – all these factors spurred American studios to go abroad for production. As they did so, unemployment rose in Hollywood, while the pace of production fell off. In the years 1944 through 1951, Hollywood turned out 350 to 400 films a year. The figures dropped to 258 in 1958, 181 in 1959.

Received wisdom tells us these were symptoms of a Hollywood in crisis, and that television was to blame. Perhaps so; but the existence of television cannot in itself account for the decline, since the drop-off in theater attendance began before ownership of TV sets became widespread. Nor is it sufficient to point to another well-known factor, the studios' loss of their theater chains. I think we need to take a step back, to the beginning of World War II, and see that the film industry had been scaling down for several years before the 'crisis' hit. Perhaps we should think of the postwar events as having been not just setbacks but also stimuli, which encouraged the studios to continue a managerial trend – a pioneering one at that. In the 1950s, studio executives were among the first to move toward multinationalism (as it became known in the 1960s) or globalization (as we now call it).

Some of the traits of globalization have become familiar since then: firings, a greater reliance on freelance labor, a drop in productive capacity. But there was also a symptom peculiar to the film industry: gigantism. As everybody noted at the time, movies were swelling up. The most obvious explanation, again, was television: in order to distinguish itself from the small screen, the big screen got bigger. But even though the domestic box office was shrinking – from 90 million admissions a week in 1948 to 40 million in 1958 – there was still plenty of money to be made, especially with foreign revenues thrown in. A studio could produce fewer pictures while turning a greater profit on each. One obvious strategy for doing so was to make the films look big and important. Overseas production put the means at hand.

So De Cuir started building Alexandria again, this time at Pinewood Studios in London. No one foresaw that the studio would be too small to handle De Cuir's sets easily, or that the English laborers, only too aware that they were cheap help for the rich Americans, would take their sweet time doing anything. Somehow, shooting started on September 28, 1960, only about a month later than planned. But the temperature at Pinewood was 40 degrees Fahrenheit – so cold that the 'Alexandrians' emitted puffs of steam every time they spoke – and as yet *Cleopatra* had no script.

Nigel Balchin and Dale Wasserman had both failed to produce satisfactory drafts. Wanger asked Lawrence Durrell to try, but Mamoulian refused to read his version past page 25, declaring it to be 'sensationalism.' Shooting of a sort proceeded, but it was interrupted on November 18 when Taylor fell ill from the cold and damp. Wanger took advantage of the break to call in veteran screenwriter Nunnally Johnson. But even after shooting resumed, the production had no momentum, and Taylor was openly unhappy. In January 1961, Mamoulian sent Fox a letter of resignation, his fourth, as a stratagem for gaining control of the project. He assumed Spyros Skouras would refuse to let him go. Instead, Skouras assented to Taylor's wishes. She wanted a new director: Mankiewicz, who had helped her win an Oscar nomination for *Suddenly, Last Summer*.

By a curious coincidence, Mankiewicz was already preparing a film set in Egypt. It was to be *Justine*, based on the first novel of Lawrence Durrell's *The Alexandria Quartet*. This, too, was a Walter Wanger project, which he had persuaded Fox to initiate with the help of his friend David Selznick (who wanted Jennifer Jones to play the lead).

In June 1960, Fox asked Mankiewicz to write the script. He had severed his ties to that studio in the early 1950s, after its founder, Darryl Zanuck, had taken control of the editing of *Five Fingers* (1952). But Zanuck was no longer at Fox, having decided that he, too, wanted to be an independent producer; while in the intervening years, Mankiewicz had been chastened, not only by his troubles with Figaro but also by the suicide of his wife, Rosa, in 1958. He took the assignment and threw himself into work.

Following standard procedure, he began by writing a summary of the action: a document known as a treatment, which in most cases can be scanned by a producer in five minutes. Mankiewicz's treatment, according to Geist, ran on for 151 pages. For many reasons – his past success with dialogue-laden scripts, his personal and professional troubles, his habit of medicating himself to wake up in the morning and go to sleep at night – Mankiewicz had lost touch with his early training in the studios, back when he'd watched the senior writers walk into a meeting with a producer and spin out their 'script' using the cigar trick: each man improvising a story until he ran out of ideas, at which point he'd put his cigar into his mouth as the signal for the next writer to start talking. When Mankiewicz broke off writing the first draft of *Justine*, he was on page 674.

He told Fox he wanted to continue with that project, rather than take over *Cleopatra*. So Skouras offered to make him truly independent. In addition to paying a salary and expenses, Fox would buy Figaro for $3 million, with half the money going to NBC and the other half to Mankiewicz. He would get more money than Elizabeth Taylor; the great majority of his payment, taking the form of capital gains, would be shielded from taxes; and he would be rid of a company that had never worked out.

On February 1, 1961, Mankiewicz arrived in London to begin work on *Cleopatra*. With production overhead costing $45,000 a day, Fox demanded that he resume shooting on April 4. Mankiewicz plunged into rewriting the script with Lawrence Durrell and Sidney Buchman (who had lost his job at Columbia because of the blacklist). Then, in early March, Taylor came down with a serious case of lung congestion. In the wake of a much-publicized near-fatal illness, she won the Academy Award for *Butterfield 8* (1960) (bringing still more attention to herself and *Cleopatra*), and Skouras at last decided that Pinewood Studios would be unworkable. The film had now been in production for six months and had cost $7 million, with only ten and a half minutes of film having been shot.

After some dithering, Skouras ordered photography to resume in Los Angeles in summer 1961. Two boatloads of sets and costumes left for California, traveling through the Panama Canal, while De Cuir prepared to set up his third Alexandria. Mankiewicz got to Los Angeles on June 12, one week before Skouras decided that *Cleopatra* should be shot instead in Rome, at Cinecittà. The taxes would be less onerous, and Fox needed every available inch of its lot for another costume epic, *The Greatest Story Ever Told*.

Meanwhile, Lawrence Durrell had been replaced on the screenwriting team by Ranald MacDougall, who was known for his speed. Living up to his reputation, MacDougall roughed out a screenplay based on Sidney Buchman's outline; but Mankiewicz simultaneously wrote his own script, expanding on the same Buchman draft. He intended to make the film in two parts, dramatizing the events of twenty years, from Cleopatra's first meeting with Julius Caesar until her death. As Geist points out, this was a spacious conception, covering approximately the same territory as Shaw's *Caesar and Cleopatra* and Shakespeare's *Antony and Cleopatra*, with *Julius Caesar* thrown in. Mankiewicz also added a new element to Wanger's concept of an Egypto-Roman *film noir*: he built in an Oedipal theme. Antony, tortured by feelings of inadequacy toward his father-figure, Caesar, would compensate by attempting to claim the lover–mother. When the Mankiewicz phase of *Cleopatra* at last went before the cameras, on September 25, 1961, the author was only halfway through the script for 'Caesar and Cleopatra', the first part of the film. For the duration, he would need to write by night and direct by day.

By this time, Mankiewicz had replaced the original Caesar with Rex Harrison and the original Antony with Richard Burton (who had to be bought out of his contract in the Broadway musical *Camelot*). 'I've got to don my breastplate once more to play opposite Miss Tits,' Burton informed his friends. While the actor braced himself for the ordeal, Mankiewicz was failing to shoot a couple of big sequences. There was a delay in filming Cleopatra's entrance into the Forum, for which Taylor was to ride atop a sphinx drawn by 300 slaves. The animals brought in were foul beyond expectation, and heavy rains drenched the set. The sequence was postponed until spring. Caesar's landing at Alexandria also proved to be troublesome. The production designers had secured the use of Prince Borghese's private beach near Anzio as the site of Egypt's royal compound but had scouted the location only from sea, using a speedboat. They later discovered the harbor was blocked by a hidden sandbar and was still dotted with mines from the war, and was within earshot of a NATO firing range.

The delays so alarmed Skouras that he ordered the budget to be capped at $10 million. Mankiewicz informed him that a more realistic cost would be $15 million. As Matthew Bernstein points out in his biography of Walter Wanger, these figures were purely notional, since there was still no screenplay on which to base a budget. It wasn't until October 20, almost four weeks into principal photography, that Mankiewicz finished the script for 'Caesar and Cleopatra.' It was 197 pages long. By Christmas, he had got as far as writing the first 50 pages of Part Two, 'Antony and Cleopatra.' Wanger was now estimating a total cost of $25 million, and Liz Taylor was again experiencing medical problems, this time with her leg.

Burton played his first scenes with Taylor at the beginning of 1962. By the final week of January, the affair had started, amid rumors that

Wanger and Mankiewicz were making hurried visits to the Fisher–Taylor household. In February, Burton decided he'd had his fun and attempted to return to his wife Sybil, at which point (in the words of Jack Brodsky and Nathan Weiss, who were publicists for Fox) Taylor went 'coconuts' and checked into the hospital. The publicists informed reporters that the problem was food poisoning – an explanation that fell apart when Burton's press agent made the mistake of denying the existence of any affair. Since none had been reported, the story exploded.

'I've had affairs before,' Burton muttered. 'How was I to know she was so fucking famous?' The scandal immediately dwarfed *Cleopatra* itself – a considerable feat, since at the end of March 1962, as Taylor and Burton went public with their romance, Skouras was forced to announce that the picture would not be ready for another year. In early May, with some of the most expensive and complicated sequences yet to be shot – such as Cleopatra's entrance into Rome – Mankiewicz assembled a rough cut of what he'd done so far. Nathan Weiss, who saw this interim version, praised the work to Jack Brodsky, though without the oomph a studio might hope for from its publicist: 'The film is both scholarly and showmanly, no mean achievement.' It also ran for four and a half hours.

At this point, early in June 1962, Fox's current chief of production, Peter Levathes, dismissed Wanger from the picture. At the end of June came Skouras's resignation as studio president. He was no longer able to defend himself to his board of directors. Mankiewicz threatened to resign as well, since he was outraged over Fox's demand that he do without the battles of Pharsalia and Philippi. But he stayed on, and location shooting began in the Egyptian desert on July 18, sparking riots between the extras and students who wanted to be hired as extras. Around this time, the nurse whose injections helped Mankiewicz cope with his round-the-clock schedule happened to hit the sciatic nerve. Mankiewicz had to be carried about on a stretcher. John De Cuir encountered him in this condition as he was being conveyed through Alexandria, all the while scribbling on a pad. 'How's it going?' De Cuir asked. Mankiewicz replied, 'I'm writing the last page.'

More pain was to come. On July 25, Darryl Zanuck returned to Twentieth Century-Fox as its president. Not only was he a past antagonist of Mankiewicz, but he was finishing an epic of his own, *The Longest Day* (1962), which had cost $10 million and was scheduled for a Paris premiere in September. A famously decisive man, Zanuck had neither the time nor the patience to play around. Among his first moves upon assuming the Fox presidency was to close the studio rather than let it lose any more money. On July 28, 1962, with the director incapacitated and the studio shuttered, second unit director 'Bundy' Marton completed the ten months of principal photography on the Mankiewicz phase of *Cleopatra*.

Or so it seemed. In mid-October, Zanuck summoned Mankiewicz to Paris to screen a rough cut. The running time is in dispute: it was either four and a half hours or seven and a half. We do know that Zanuck demanded a film of no longer than three and a quarter hours, that Mankiewicz responded by removing only thirteen minutes, and that Zanuck immediately took the editing out of his hands. But Mankiewicz still was not through with the film. When Zanuck realized he'd been left with a patchwork, he recalled the director, who agreed to go to Spain in February 1963 to reshoot the opening sequence, set in the aftermath of the battle of Pharsalia. He also shot for another eight days with Burton at Pinewood Studios, finishing his work on March 5, 1963.

Cleopatra – screenplay by Joseph L. Mankiewicz, Ranald MacDougall, and Sidney Buchman, from Plutarch, Suetonius, Appian, other ancient sources, and *The Life and Times of Cleopatra* by Charles Marie Franzero – received its world premiere on June 12, 1963, at the Rivoli Theatre in New York, in a version that ran four hours and three minutes. For the first run, this was cut to three hours and forty-one minutes, with subsequent prints running three hours flat. It was easily the most talked-about film since *Gone with the Wind* and the most expensive ever made. Fox eventually settled on $31 million as the negative cost – the equivalent, in current terms, of $155 million. (This budget was not topped until 1995, with the release of *Waterworld*.)

During the four and a half years when Fox was making *Cleopatra*, William Wyler released *Ben-Hur*, Stanley Kubrick directed *Spartacus* (which along with *Exodus* gave screenwriting credit to Dalton Trumbo and so ended the blacklist), and David Lean brought out *Lawrence of Arabia*. The Bay of Pigs invasion and the Cuban missile crisis came and went; the August 1963 March on Washington was at hand. If any movie caught the spirit of the times, it was Kubrick's new picture, *Dr. Strangelove*. Mankiewicz's emerged looking like the relic of a bygone era. In a famously devastating review, Judith Crist in the *New York Herald-Tribune* called the picture a 'monumental mouse.' Few revisionists since then have tried to tickle into life a film that resolutely lies inert beneath the fingers.

Yet in its physical trappings, *Cleopatra* is much as Wanger wanted it to be: light and animated. Although De Cuir's sets overload the eye with decorative 'archaeological' detail, they also organize space into something like the free flow of a Mies van der Rohe interior. Inspired assemblages of gauze draperies and gilt flats, the sets soar to the top of the frame, giving the impression that they must continue upward forever. Leon Shamroy, who irritated Mankiewicz with his old-timer's sagacity, won *Cleopatra* an Oscar for cinematography. The focus is crystalline; the colors, soft and mixed, spring to life from the 'ancient frescoes' that introduce each major episode. Irene Sharaff took on the challenge of making gowns for Elizabeth Taylor – 58 in all, so that Taylor might wear a different outfit in each scene she played, except where the editors were left with a gap in continuity and had to show her in two. For each scene, Sharaff found a fresh way to drape fabric around the starring cleavage.

All this may be credited to Wanger – including the cleavage, which was among his chief reasons for hiring Taylor. Who knows what effect she might have had as the underworld moll that Wanger envisioned: a royal Egyptian equivalent, perhaps, of Joan Bennett in *Scarlet Street*? Some evidence of this Cleopatra peeks out whenever Mankiewicz allows the character to enjoy a private exchange in the midst of public ceremony. She whispers a lover's half-mocking endearment when Caesar joins in her coronation; she concludes her triumphal entry into Rome by giving Caesar a wink. Taylor could be convincing with such flirtations. With the rest of the role, she had far less success. But could anyone have played Cleopatra as Mankiewicz conceived her? The character is part sorceress (who insists she is the incarnation of Isis), part scholar (who rails at Caesar for burning the Alexandrian library), part Wendell Wilkie Republican (who dreams of establishing a pacific, one-world government), and all Macedonian (as the screenplay is at pains to point out, amid its hundreds of lines of expository dialogue). Often within a single scene, Taylor has to hold forth on statecraft and geopolitics, engage in private reminiscence, toss off a few remarks about ancient religion, and then act unsurprised and unresisting when her interlocutor leaps upon her.

Never before had Mankiewicz written a script so cumbersome or directed so heavily. (Caesar is dead and Cleopatra sailing back to Egypt before the camera provides any illusion of movement – just in time for intermission.) His disgust at DeMille may explain the failure, up to a point. Politically and artistically, DeMille pandered to the worst in people; as Mankiewicz put it, he 'had his finger up the pulse of the public' (Geist, p. 173). In *Cleopatra*, Mankiewicz intended to demonstrate the right way to make an epic; he would create a serious, literate drama that just happened to have lots of sets, costumes, and cleavage.

This had been tried before, notably by another DeMille antagonist, Philip Dunne, who had written the screenplay for Fox's *David and Bathsheba* (1951). But Dunne knew himself to be a contract writer; his script existed to serve director Henry King and the chief of production of a still functioning American studio, which used California chaparral as a stand-in for Judean grazing land. By contrast, Mankiewicz was an author – not in the full French sense (which had only begun to penetrate American film culture) but in traditional theatrical terms. 'I am essentially a writer who directs,' he said. Given his record of success, and the industry's move toward independent production, we may understand how he could imagine himself as the Shakespeare and Shaw of *Cleopatra*. The production existed to serve his words – not an easy trick, since the huge apparatus was already up and running while those words were being written.

To some, Mankiewicz's attitude might seem like one more instance of hubris. I prefer to see it as a valiant attempt to claim responsibility when no one else would. The same managerial decisions that had allowed him to glimpse the possibility of independence had also inspired Fox to invest in a project it could not supervise. While the production with its international crew and train of reporters roamed from England to Italy to Egypt to Spain, behaving like nothing so much as a traveling fair, Fox was running through four heads of production (Buddy Adler, Bob Goldstein, Peter Levathes, and Darryl Zanuck), leasing its facilities to other companies, firing 1000 contract employees, and selling 260 acres of its lot to real-estate developers. Thanks to the logic of globalization and downsizing, the only person other than Mankiewicz who could claim to be in charge of *Cleopatra* was Wanger; and he, too, was supposedly independent.

So we come back to Truffaut and the *politique des auteurs*.

'I am essentially a writer who directs.' Had Truffaut known how Mankiewicz would describe himself, he might have reversed the formulation, thereby providing *Une Certaine Tendence* with its missing definition: an auteur is a director who writes. And given the emphasis on visual style that has since become conventional in film criticism, especially as it has flowed from *Cahiers du Cinéma*, we might indeed think of Mankiewicz as the opposite of an auteur. Nevertheless, his works appeared consistently on the *Cahiers* lists of the year's best films. Over the years, the magazine's composite list cited *All About Eve*, *The Barefoot Contessa*, and *The Quiet American*.

To see why, we must understand in what sense the auteurs seemed politically virtuous. A good place to begin might be a wonderfully overheated article by Jacques Rivette, published in the December 1955 issue of *Cahiers*. In it, Rivette placed Mankiewicz among those American filmmakers who were 'refusing the dictatorship of the producers and trying to create a work that is personal. They are all *liberal* filmmakers, some openly left-wing.' I cannot say precisely what Rivette meant by this (especially since he called these people 'revolutionaries' for good measure). Perhaps he was imagining each honest filmmaker as Chaplin's Tramp caught in the gears of *Modern Times*, or Stroheim throwing his monkey wrench into Thalberg's assembly line. But if we look again at those Americans who qualified for authorial status, we will see that something more was at stake than the struggle of the individual spirit against a world of grinding mass production.

Rivette and other *Cahiers* writers tended to favor Americans who had become expatriates (Welles, Chaplin, Jules Dassin, Joseph Losey) or who had set themselves apart from the blacklist and other Cold War enthusiasms (Mankiewicz, Nicholas Ray, Herbert Biberman). By doing so, these Americans in effect refused to participate in the colonization, cultural and otherwise, in which the United States was then engaged. And that gave them something in common with other filmmakers championed by *Cahiers*.

The Italian neorealists, too, might have been loosely described as liberal or left-wing, starting with Visconti, who was an out-and-out Communist. But, more to the point, the neorealists represented an alternative to Italy's revived tradition of superproductions, such as Mario Camerini's *Ulysses* (1954): films that were financed internationally and shot with polyglot crews on that new Hollywood by the Tiber, Cinecittà. France, too, was seeing more of these gaudy international co-productions, made with an eye toward the export market: Christian-Jaque's *Fanfan la Tulipe* and *Nana*, Autant-Lara's *Le Rouge et le noir*, Jacques Becker's *Ali Baba et les quarantes voleurs*. The filmmakers who excited Truffaut's scorn, Aurenche and Bost, were those who presented a false alternative to this big-budget frippery. Like front men, they put a respectable face on a cynical industry. They even appealed to the guardians of French pride, though all the while they, too, were doing their bit to turn the world's cinemas into so many versions of 'Hollywood.'

So the auteur critics were responding not only to long-established notions of industrial slavery but also to very recent shifts in imperial power. For the most part, though, they did not respond as leftists. I see them more as cinematic Gaullists: deeply indebted to Americans and fascinated by them, but determined to stand against the dominance of America – meanwhile staying away from the Soviet camp.

In this sense, auteurism was an attempt to promote a cinema that would be true to local realities, without the advocate's falling into the ready trap of nationalism. It also was an attempt to find anti-imperialist (or at least nonimperialist) models among the Americans themselves. The urgency of the need should be apparent. Truffaut published 'Une Certaine Tendance' in the same year that France withdrew from Indochina and began its long, losing struggle for Algeria. The liberation of Tunisia and Morocco would soon follow, in 1956; so, too, would the costly Franco-British-Israeli co-production, *The Suez Invasion.*

Faced with these grand movements of capital and armies, the auteurists generally did not recommend the Wagnerite strategy. Recent events had given a bad name to artists with world-encompassing ambitions. Better to follow the neorealist method of working cheaply, with street locations and nonprofessional performers; to sneak one's ideas into low-budget genre pictures (as did Nicholas Ray or Robert Aldrich); to move to New York and become independent, like Mankiewicz. Then one might open up some precious, free space.

But as Mankiewicz was to discover, the economic logic that spread American influence around the globe could sometimes put a super-production into the hands of an auteur. When that happened, it was even possible for the auteur to challenge the imperialists on their own ground.

Max Ophuls did just that when he made the most famously ruinous of European co-productions, and perhaps the most dazzling: *Lola Montès.*

He was among the auteurs pictured in 'Une Certaine Tendance', even though his status as a French filmmaker was purely elective.

Born in the border town of Saarbrücken in 1902, Max Ophuls started life as a German, became French after 1918, and later gave everyone the impression that he was Viennese. He did live in Vienna, but only for ten months in 1926, when he served as director of the Burgtheater. (His dismissal was in part the result of anti-Semitism; before adopting the stage name of Ophüls, he had been Oppenheimer.) His career in film began at Ufa in 1930, continued in other countries (principally France) after 1933, and then went through an American phase. He spent the years from 1940 through 1946 looking for work in Hollywood, then made four pictures from 1947 through 1949, including a Walter Wanger production, *The Reckless Moment.* In 1950, he returned to France (where he had obtained citizenship in 1938) and made *La Ronde* – a big, lush, but infinitely graceful adaptation of Arthur Schnitzler's play *Der Reigen*.

As Alan Williams remarks in his history of French cinema, *La Ronde* and Ophuls's subsequent films – *Le Plaisir* (1951) and *Madame de . . .* (1953) – bear the external markings of the 'tradition of quality' that Truffaut so despised. Yet in 1955, we discover Truffaut corresponding with Ophul's production manager, Ralph Baum, in an unsuccessful attempt to get hired as an assistant for his work-in-progress, *Lola Montès*.

This, too, was an international co-production, and (on the face of it) was to be of the flimsiest kind. The literary source was a none-too-elevated novel by Cécil Saint-Laurent, author of *Caroline chérie*, the film of which had helped launch the career of Martine Carol, who was to star in the new film. The executive producer was Albert Caraco of Gamma-Films (in co-production with Florida Films, Paris and Unionfilms, Munich), who intended to have the picture shot back-to-back with a film called *Frou-Frou* (which lived up to its name). As Edgardo Cozarinsky remarks, this detail alone indicates the level of entertaiment *Lola Montès* was expected to reach.

How did Ophuls, of all people, become involved with such a project? 'Since *Madame de . . .*, I had begun and abandoned three films without being able to impose my conception on the script,' he later said. 'I'd reached the point of thinking, I have to make a film' (Annenkov, p. 85). Ralph Baum recalled sitting with him in Fouquet's one night until two or three, all the while insisting to Ophuls, 'We absolutely have to make a commercial film, not very expensive, something we can shoot in six, seven weeks.' To which, Baum testified, Ophuls had said, 'Agreed. So long as we find a good subject' (Beylie, p. 141).

The next day, Albert Caraco of Gamma-Films called Baum. He needed someone to replace Jacques Tourneur, the initial director of Caraco's proposed *Lola Montès*. Baum suggested Ophuls, then left at once for Germany to work on another project.

Since Caraco not only entertained Baum's suggestion but later approved Ophuls's extraordinary scheme for *Lola Montès*, he was perhaps not so sleazy an operator as later events made him seem. Following a brief career in journalism, Caraco had become a producer in 1932, when he was in his mid-twenties. Among the directors with whom he worked was Marcel L'Herbier, for whom he produced *Forfaiture* (1937). During the war, he lived in England, where he worked for the cinematographic service of the Royal Air Force. From what I can tell, he wasn't the sort to put art before profit – but with Ophuls, he wouldn't need to. He'd have a remarkably stylish director whose *La Ronde* had been a commercial success.

In fact, Ophuls seems to have been the one who hesitated. 'The subject was absolutely foreign to me,' he later recalled. 'I don't like life stories where a lot happens.' Just thinking about the proposal made him feel 'dizzy and full of pity: pity for this poor Lola, pity for the filmmaker who took the assignment!' (Annenkov, p. 85).

And yet, thinking about the life of Lola Montez, Ophuls also thought about the latest scandals in the newspapers: 'Judy Garland's nervous depression, the romantic entanglements of Zsa Zsa Gabor . . . And then, once more I reread Pirandello' (Guérin, p. 184). When Baum got back to Paris, he learned that Ophuls had given Caraco a proposal for a film that would cost the considerable sum of 400 million old francs. If we ask for that much money, Baum said, 'we might as well shoot it in CinemaScope.' He knew Ophuls's opinions on that subject; the very mention of 'Scope was likely to make Ophuls scale down his proposal. But instead of backing off, Ophuls accepted the challenge of working in wide screen, so long as the budget were enlarged to 500 million – a figure that soon rose to 600 million, when Ophuls figured out a system to mask the lens and so change the shape of the 'Scope frame.

The film was shot in Paris, Nice, Munich and their environs from February through July 1955. Gradually, the budget rose to 650 million francs – about $1.5 million, which at the time was considered to be extravagant. But as the set designer, Jean d'Eaubonne, pointed out, *Lola Montès* wasn't all that expensive compared to an average Hollywood film. True, in his intoxication at shooting in color for the first time, Ophuls put in an order for a cistern of colored water, so a certain road could be repainted each morning. True as well that Ophuls did something unusual to an old inn, which had been chosen as the setting for Lola's good-bye to Franz Liszt. Since the stone walls weren't the right autumnal color, Ophuls had gauze flown in from Brussels – kilometer after kilometer of tulle – and draped it over the building. Was this an indulgence? Just the opposite, d'Eaubonne wrote: 'We worked cheaply to make expensive sets' (Beylie, p. 149).

The high cost of *Lola Montès* may be imputed in part to the producers' decision to shoot the film in three versions at once: French, German, and English. (Such were the rigors of international co-production.) But then, even in one language, the film as Ophuls conceived it would have been complex to shoot; and his methods were painstaking. Peter Ustinov, who played the role of the Ringmaster, recalled with admiration that 'He would cut a scene because he found the flicker of an eyelid excessive, as tactless as a fanfare at a funeral.' We also have a reminiscence from Walter Kiaulehn, himself a director, who played a cameo role as manager of Bavaria's royal theater. For a scene in which various attendants wait for the king to appear, Ophuls took care to have each character act out his boredom in a different way. Yet when he studied the effect, he felt a detail was still missing. Perhaps, he thought, the theater had an old dog, which had lost the habit of barking, and which would be lying asleep amid the general ennui. Only after a dog was produced and had been properly settled did filming begin. 'We shot the scene twenty times', Kiaulehn remembered. 'We were bored in German, in French, and in English' – a total of seven hours of 'photogenic boredom.'

Ophuls was not bored; by his own account, he had become entirely caught up in the picture. That was also the recollection of his costume designer, Georges Annenkov, who testified that Ophuls at last accepted even CinemaScope. While shooting Lola's flight from Bavaria, he suddenly shouted, 'CinemaScope! CinemaScope! Don't tell me any more lies about it! It isn't big *enough*! I need a screen twice as big! A square CinemaScope!'

The product of his enthusiasm had its debut at the Marignan Theater in Paris on December 23, 1955. Evidently, the public expected the usual Martine Carol vehicle in Eastmancolor and 'Scope. In an article written two weeks later, Truffaut described the response: '*Lola Montès* divides the Parisian public to such a degree that the police have had to intervene several times at the Marignan Theater, and the film is now preceded by an announcement: the public is advised that it is about to see a film that is "out of the ordinary", and there is still time to ask for one's money back before it begins.' The uproar was so great that a group of filmmakers and critics – including Roberto Rossellini and Jean Cocteau – wrote an open letter to *Le Figaro*, defending *Lola Montès* as 'a new, daring, and necessary enterprise.'

Such praise can be enough in itself to induce panic in a producer. While Ophuls was away in Germany, Caraco pulled all the prints out of circulation and reedited the film, cutting it to 90 minutes, putting the events into chronological order (instead of having them play as a fantasia or hallucination) and adding a voiceover narration. This version was given its premiere in February 1957, and it, too, was a flop. Ophuls died of a heart attack a month later, having just directed a production of Beaumarchais's *The Marriage of Figaro* in Hamburg. As for Caraco, his Gamma-Films went bankrupt, having earned 100 million francs on

Lola Montès, according to the estimate of film historian Claude Beylie. Only after the company sold its remaining prints was *Lola Montès* reconstructed. It received a United States premiere in something close to the original form at the 1963 New York Film Festival.

The irony was, Ophuls had given the audience everything it might have wanted in a film about Donna Maria Dolores de Porris y Montez, the scandalous Spanish dancer, who began her life in Cork, Ireland, under the name of Eliza Gilbert. Self-invented on the London stage in 1843, Montez soon took her skirt-shaking routine to the Continent, where she augmented the fame won in theaters with an even greater notoriety, achieved through social performance. She wore exotic costumes, smoked cigars, cultivated a reputation as a crack shot with a pistol, and acquired as lovers only men who could be recognized in public. These ranged from Franz Liszt through King Ludwig I of Bavaria, the father of Wagner's patron. Ludwig's subjects did not share the royal opinion of Montez; they came close to revolution in 1848 and chased her out of Munich. A period of wandering brought her to America, where in 1852 she played the title role in a successful stage production, *Lola Montez in Bavaria*. She died in New York City in 1861, a recent convert to evangelical Christianity – the only part of the above account that Ophuls omitted.

Surely anyone paying to see this tale enacted must want romance! adventure! scandal! and so on – all of which commodities are faithfully supplied by the film, as promised at the start by the Ringmaster. For Ophuls chose to set the film in an American circus, where Lola Montez appears nightly in a pantomime of her life story. Chandeliers descend, a bandleader in an Uncle Sam suit whips up the music, tumblers and trapeze artists whirl through the ring, and the camera whirls, too, as a fairy-tale carriage bearing a veiled Lola Montez circles past the prowling Ringmaster, who cries out (to the echo of juggling showgirls) that what we are about to see is authentic. 'Authentique!' Ask your questions of her, even the most indelicate, the Ringmaster commands, dispatching red-clad pages into the tiers of seats, which are occupied by papier-mâché figures and photo cutouts. The camera spins past Lola: dark, subdued, obedient. Does she remember? calls someone from the audience. Yes, she remembers. The image of her face dissolves into a landscape, and a second layer of story-telling is added to the circus pantomime: Lola's memories, or fantasies, or fever dreams.

Critics such as Susan M. White and Alan Williams have pointed out that one of the explicit themes of Lola's reveries is motion; she recalls herself as someone for whom movement was life itself. As the film's audience gradually learns, she now moves no more. Having become an attraction of the Mammoth Circus, this 'wild animal' (as the Ringmaster describes her) finishes each show in a kind of menagerie, where she passively accepts men's kisses at a dollar a smack. And what of the circus act, which replays the events of her life in a shriller key? The performance bursts so giddily from the screen that its exuberance passes at first for spontaneity. Before long, though, Ophuls has revealed what a practiced, routinized extravagance we're watching; Lola goes through it every night, no doubt with matinees thrown in on the weekends. The outward tumults and memories churning within come together in stasis: in the figure of an exhausted, ailing woman.

So Ophuls goes one better than the Ringmaster. He delivers not only romance! adventure! scandal! but also a quiet sadness, without which *Lola Montès* would feel overbearing. There is a heart inside this teeming, co-produced international star vehicle, a heart that gives the film its lightness and delicacy. Such, perhaps, was the true scandal of *Lola Montès*: that Ophuls had sneaked something no bigger than a garden folly into a production of World's Fair proportions.

But, of course, there was the other scandal, too: Ophuls's mockery of the big-time movie business and of the public around the world that let itself be suckered by 'Hollywood' fare. The multinational circus of *Lola Montès* doesn't just spin you through the sufferings and scandals of its heroine; nor does it close the ring when it's whirled you past Lola into the life of the star. (Martine Carol, born in 1920 as Marie-Louise de Mourer, first acted in films in 1944 but did not make a name for herself until 1947, when she dived into the Seine. Since a photographer just happened to be standing nearby, the suicide attempt was fully covered, though her suddenly famous body was not.) *Lola Montès* seems to encompass all instances of female notoriety as it has been industrially manufactured in our century – especially after World War II, particularly under American influence. What if Jennifer Jones had appeared in a film in which she remembered her life as Pearl Chavez? What if Elizabeth Taylor had been allowed to cast a knowing on-screen look at Richard Burton, much as her Cleopatra winked at Caesar?

I'm not surprised that Ophuls, like the Ringmaster, should have fallen in love with a character who can suggest such possibilities. But I am astonished at the coincidence of her being a dancer from a purportedly exotic background. To become Lola Montez, Ireland's Eliza Gilbert took on a semi-Moorish, semi-gypsy disguise. Jennifer Jones, in complicity with Selznick, also made herself darker, changing into a dancer who was part Spanish and part Indian. And even though Mankiewicz kept reminding the audience that Cleopatra was European in ancestry, he shadowed her with Nubians throughout the film and brought her into Rome amid a troupe of African dancers.

'Tanning up,' they used to call it in show business, according to Ann Douglas. On the musical stage, white Americans sometimes wore a light-toned blackface, rather than the coal-black look associated with Al Jolson. Douglas suggests that in the 1920s, when sunlamps and trips to the Riviera came into vogue, the craze for darker skin was an extratheatrical form of tanning up. A certain group of cosmopolitan whites, fascinated by the 'vitality, rhythm, and "virility"' of Harlem life, thought it fashionable to be 'like the chorines at the Cotton Club ... "tall, tan, and terrific."'

But that was in the 1920s, when many Europeans and white Americans worried that modernity was robbing them of raw, authentic life. To take on a slight tinge of negritude in those years was one way to reject the embrace of the Mechanical Bride. The tanning up that was practiced in *Duel in the Sun* and *Cleopatra* (and parodied in *Lola Montès*) seems to me to have had a different meaning, consistent with the late 1940s and the 1950s. Those were years of European decolonization and American expansion, when the contested issue of 'Americanism' was no longer strictly one of mass production. Rather, it was an issue of mass democracy, often in places where the people were not white.

Of course it's facile to retroject such political concerns into the portrayal of characters in films, especially characters who are sexually charged. But then, our political lives are to a great extent conducted on just that level. Americans, who are unwilling to use the word 'empire,' spoke instead in those years of winning the hearts of the people they dominated; they were genuinely shocked each time their love was not returned. Meanwhile the French, struggling with the loss of something they admitted was an empire, looked across the ocean at the Yankees and saw a bit of themselves in the rejected lover. If we want to find an allegorical figure to represent the anxieties of filmgoers in both nations, as they thought of the dangerous allure of the world's darker places, perhaps we might look to the sexy 'little bobcat,' Pearl; to the freedom-loving Lola, made into a commodity by the Americans; to Cleopatra, irresistible mistress of the Southern Hemisphere's raw materials. The Mechanical Bride had faded from the screen. She'd been replaced by the Follies Girls.

In the Jungle of Cinema

In 1969, when he was a 24-year-old art student, Anselm Kiefer took a tour through Western Europe, pausing here and there to claim territories. Or so it seemed; Kiefer went about staging photographs, in which he showed himself performing the Nazi salute in otherwise deserted settings. As he later explained, he wanted to understand the 'madness' of Adolf Hitler by reenacting the Nazi conquests 'a little bit.' In 1975, these photographs were exhibited in Germany, where Kiefer stirred up considerable controversy with his *Occupations*: images of the solitary artist, dominating with his gesture the unpopulated Coliseum in Rome, an empty plaza in Montpellier, or (in the tradition not only of Hitler but of Caspar David Friedrich) a featureless sea.

Had Kiefer's reenactments been sarcasms pure and simple, I doubt they would have made people so upset, or served so well to advance his career. The pictures hit hard because they were outrageous and yet ambiguous in meaning. The eye found nothing to rule out the possibility that the artist might have been saluting in earnest; nor was Kiefer's explanation reassuring. Had his mimicry achieved its stated goal, the Nazi spirit would indeed have been revived 'a little bit,' both in himself and in viewers.

Of course, Kiefer was not a Nazi. Born in 1945 into Germany Year Zero, he was of a generation that presumably had experienced a complete break with the past (even though, when he was growing up, the institutions of both Germanies were filled with former Party members and veterans of Hitler's army). So he carried his innocence with him on his round of *Occupations*, which in effect were conquests not of space but of time, of a history that had been placed out of bounds. But how secure is anyone's innocence? As Kiefer moved on to painting grandiose works on subjects of German history and legend, including the stories used in Wagner's *Ring*; as he began literally to occupy as much space as possible, covering huge canvases with a pompous and incoherent iconography, a few of the cannier art critics (such as Arthur C. Danto) began to wonder at what point imitation stops being blameless.

A similar question came up with two notable cinematic follies of the 1970s and 1980s, *Fitzcarraldo* and *Apocalypse Now*. In broad terms, we might say they addressed colonialism as Kiefer dealt with the Nazi past. Both films were concerned with good intentions gone bad in the jungle; in both cases, the filmmakers were accused of having lived out their theme.

Fitzcarraldo, set in the early twentieth century, tells of an Irishman who hopes to bring the glories of opera to a boom town on the Amazon; this enlightenment is to be paid for with money from the rubber trade, earned off the backs of Indians. In the course of making the film, the director, Werner Herzog, underwent an investigation by Amnesty International, which sought to determine whether he had exploited the Indians in and around his production. (Amnesty cleared him; but some of the Indians had a different opinion. A tribal council of the Aguarunas burned Herzog's first jungle location to the ground.) *Apocalypse Now*, set in the midst of the Vietnam War, tells of a mission to find and murder a renegade officer, Colonel Kurtz. Although he was once a gentleman soldier, Kurtz has abandoned America's ostensible project of 'winning hearts and minds' and turned himself into a warlord, ruling through terror. In this case, it was the director himself, Francis Ford Coppola, who ruefully made the analogy between the processes of his production and those of the Vietnam War. 'There were too many of us,' he told Charles Michener of *Newsweek*, 'too much money and equipment, and little by little we went insane.'

These two filmmakers also risked imitation in their relationships to the industry. Herzog was one of the handful of star directors to come out of the New German Cinema. That is to say, he was a proud individualist, who offered his audience 'freedom from the dull round of commercial cinema' (in the words of Timothy Corrigan), purveying 'images of outsiders, iconoclasts, and strange other worlds' (p. 3). Yet at the same time Herzog was a manipulator of the social apparatus of commercial cinema, 'mimicking an industry's tactics for self-promotion and representation.' Coppola, too, was a star director, who in search of independence had relocated from Los Angeles to San Francisco in the late 1960s and formed his own company. 'I wanted to do little Antonioni films, little Fellini films, and get my own theatre company and do experimental writing,' he later told David Breskin in an interview. Yet in May 1979, just when he was presenting the long-delayed premiere of *Apocalypse Now* at the Cannes festival, Coppola let *Variety* know he was about to buy a production facility in Los Angeles, where he hoped to revive the studio system – in a spirit of benevolence and artistic freedom, of course.

What are we to make of this impulse to inhabit the guilt of other people, reliving their failures, reproducing their corruptions? Whatever its meaning, the gesture cannot be explained simply as auteurism run mad – although that argument was advanced at the time and since then has been repeated endlessly, with and without the French accent. In November 1980, for example, with the premiere of the expensive and deadly boring *Heaven's Gate* (which was, as we shall see, yet another Vietnam War movie, in this case disguised as a Western), the press turned the picture's failure into a moralized tale about a self-infatuated director and the executives who had lacked the nerve to rein him in. The characterization contains this much truth: by the late 1970s, a certain number of directors were enjoying unprecedented autonomy. Whether this had anything to do with the popularization of the *politique des auteurs* remains to be seen.

We may trace the figure of the star director back to Berlin, in 1905. That year, Max Reinhardt received an ovation at the premiere of his production of *A Midsummer Night's Dream*, becoming the first person to be called onstage for a bow without having written or performed anything.* No doubt Reinhardt's fame helped set a precedent a few years later for Griffith's celebrity, and for that of a very few others, such as Frank Capra and Alfred Hitchcock. But even though star directors were not unknown in the first half of the century, it's fair to say they were not produced in any numbers until the 1960s, with the spread of the *politique des auteurs*.

To start with West Germany: in 1962, the word auteurs cropped up in the founding document of the New German Cinema, a manifesto issued by 26 young directors at the festival of short films held each year in Oberhausen. Of course, we cannot equate New German Cinema with the French New Wave on the basis of one telltale word. Historians such as John Sandford and Thomas Elsaesser have noted the distinct features of each movement. For example, only one signer of the Oberhausen Manifesto, Alexander Kluge, went on to a notable career making feature films, whereas the *Cahiers* polemicists became the New Wave's best-

---

* At the Moscow Art Theatre, Constantin Stanislavsky played major roles in his most celebrated shows. When critics thought his acting was bad, they panned him by name. When they thought his directing was good, they praised an authorless '*mise-en-scène*.'

known directors. Also, the New German Cinema was made possible by state subsidies, provided principally through West Germany's ZDF television network, whereas many key figures of the New Wave – Truffaut, Louis Malle, Claude Chabrol – scraped together their funding from family sources and became part of France's long-established network of small-scale, independent producers. Yet there were also many points of contact between the two movements, beyond the merely verbal.

When Rainer Werner Fassbinder made his first feature film in 1969, *Love Is Colder than Death*, he included Eric Rohmer – *Cahiers* editor and New Wave director – in the list of dedicatees. Many leading figures of New German Cinema also sought inspiration at the New Wave's temple, the Cinémathèque Française, looking in particular to one of its curators, Lotte Eisner. Jan-Christopher Horak gives a partial list of the directors she befriended and promoted: Herzog, Fassbinder, Werner Schroeter, Wim Wenders, Herbert Achternbusch. At the Cinémathèque, she introduced many of these people to the films of Fritz Lang and F.W. Murnau, establishing a link between West Germany's young directors and the pre-Nazi cinema. From her base in Paris, Herzog said in an interview, Eisner was the person 'who has so to speak blessed and legalized' New German Cinema.

These trends and ideas reached American filmmakers, too, though in a subtly altered translation. When Andrew Sarris imported auteurism to the United States in 1963, in an epoch-making article in the journal *Film Culture*, he dropped the *politique* and wrote of an 'auteur theory.' Its principal virtue, in Sarris's account, was to bring to light the merits of American genre pictures, revealing artistry in a large body of movies that had been snobbishly overlooked.

This version of auteurism was so highly selective that it deserves to be seen as a critical school of its own. Issues such as nationalism, imperialism, blacklisting, and class bias fell away from the discussion, as Sarris and his many followers concentrated instead on identifying the stylistic and thematic traits of American auteurs, and on assigning those directors to higher or lower artistic ranks. Since condescension toward their own movies was at the time habitual among educated Americans, this polemic seems to me to have been much needed. It came at an opportune time, too.

Only a few years earlier, New York City had displaced Paris as the world's capital of painting and sculpture, with the result that Americans were beginning to abandon centuries of apology and transatlantic emulation and take their own artists seriously. They also were starting to look anew at things that hadn't before seemed to qualify as art: comic strips, cheap advertisements, the front page of the day's tabloid newspaper. Hard upon the revelation of Abstract Expressionism had come the scandal of Pop Art, launched at New York's Sidney Janis Gallery only a year before the publication of 'Notes on the *Auteur Theory*.' Here were two phases of a single cultural moment: Andy Warhol's *Dance Diagrams* and Andrew Sarris's appreciation of *Baby Face Nelson*.

This rough sketch has blurred certain features of American auteurism, principally the enthusiasm it generated for a new range of European art films. Still, I think the image is recognizable: we may characterize this strain of auteurism as a style-conscious, Americanist approach to looking at movies, including those that seemed to be nothing more than mass-produced commodities. Helping to popularize the approach were institutions such as film societies, museums, and revival houses, which provided the raw material for auteurist study: old movies. Television, too, must be counted among these institutions. It had turned every living room into a haphazard film library.

I give this account to explain how, for a significant group of filmmakers who came of age in the 1960s, movies became a fit subject for writing and formal study. Coppola attended the film department of the University of California at Los Angeles. Martin Scorsese both studied and taught about film at New York University. After an early career in the theater, Peter Bogdanovich became associated with the film department of The Museum of Modern Art, for which he wrote auteurist monographs.

But here again we discover the peculiar bias of American auteurism. Having first associated themselves with respectable institutions, the young men I've named broke into the industry with the help of Hollywood's proudest producer of low-budget schlock, Roger Corman. Coppola was the first to seek a job with Corman, for whom he directed *Dementia 13* (1963). Bogdanovich got his start in movies by working on Corman's *The Wild Angels* (1966) and *Voyage to the Planet of Prehistoric Women* (1967). Scorsese, having made prize-winning short films and an outstanding first feature while still at NYU, did not scruple to direct his second feature for Corman: the none-too-highminded *Boxcar Bertha* (1972). Clearly, Corman gave these young directors something more than a paycheck and a chance to build up their résumés. He also offered them a chance to feel like auteurs, in the basic American definition of the term: artists who worked a personal touch into genre pictures.

Had artists in America ever before felt so comfortable with commercial moviemaking? The example of Orson Welles may come to mind; but we should remember that he did not go to Hollywood until RKO offered him unprecedented control over whatever film he might choose to make. Coppola, Bogdanovich, and Scorsese behaved more like Jacques Tourneur signing on at RKO to direct *Cat People* and *I Walked with a Zombie*. Such was the revolution in tastes and attitudes of the 1960s that they could do so and at the same time keep Welles before their eyes.

So as not to overdraw the caricature, I will add that the people under discussion were all keenly aware of how the studio system had constrained filmmakers. (Bogdanovich, for example, was close to Welles and knew the details of his joustings with the industry.) But as much as these young directors wanted autonomy, they also seemed to long for a bygone industrial system. 'There is no one like Zanuck around anymore,' Coppola said wistfully in a 1982 *Sight and Sound* interview, 'and there are no studios like there used to be.'

There was the problem – or the opportunity, depending on how you played it. Auteurs, in the American sense, could scarcely exist outside a studio context; but while the American auteurists were coming of age in the 1960s, the American movie companies stopped being studios, one by one.

Universal became a subsidiary of the entertainment conglomerate MCA in 1962, and in 1966 was made into the feature-film division of Universal City Studios, Inc., a producer of television shows. In 1966, Paramount became part of Gulf + Western Industries, whose core business was oil. United Artists was the next to go, in 1967, becoming a subsidiary of Transamerica, an insurance corporation. Warner Bros. was bought in 1969 by Kinney National Service Incorporated, which also owned parking lots, funeral parlors, and a pest-control business; and in 1970, MGM was acquired by Kirk Kerkorian, an investor in airlines and Las Vegas casinos, who sold off at auction the props and costumes of Hollywood's proudest studio. As for RKO, where Welles had all too briefly played with the best train set a boy ever had: the studio had been dissolved in the early 1950s, its production facility sold to the Desilu television company. By the time auteurism had fully established itself in America, toward the end of the 1960s, only Twentieth Century-Fox and Columbia were still free-standing corporations, engaged primarily in producing and distributing motion pictures.

By this point, 'independent' production in the Selznick–Wanger– Mankiewicz tradition had become a norm in Hollywood. A film 'studio' of the 1970s 'did not produce pictures, it caused or allowed them to be produced.' So wrote United Artists executive Stephen Bach in *Final Cut*, his account of the making of *Heaven's Gate*; and though UA was a special case (having never owned a production facility), Bach's statement was more or less true of all the movie companies. They had turned into so many feudal kings, each served by vassal lords: the production groups and talent packagers that did most of the hands-on work of making movies. Like medieval vassals, these smaller companies were (and are) a fractious lot, of uncertain loyalty. Hence the opportunity for would-be auteurs in the 1970s: a director who was sufficiently bloody-minded could fight his way up (almost always *his* way) through the shifting forces.

But Hollywood was medieval only in its internal relationships. Facing the outside world, it merged into the electronic force-field of global capitalism.

With the early 1970s came the demise of the system of regulating international rates of exchange, its death sentence pronounced by President Richard Nixon: 'I don't give a shit about the lira.' Currencies were now floating freely against one another; capital, flowing as never before. In the eyes of up-to-date businesspeople, a movie company looked very much like any other venture capital firm. Its job was to put money into properties on a short-term basis (perhaps two or three years), then hand up the profits to the parent corporation. This was significantly different from the older relationship between movie factories and New York banks. The new movie companies were in a sense financial institutions in themselves; as such, they were expected to produce not just earnings but the highest possible rate of return.

Hence the problem for would-be auteurs: a renewed emphasis on blockbuster production and marketing, which became fundamental to the industry starting in 1975 with *Jaws* (produced for Universal by the Zanuck-Brown company) and in 1977 with *Star Wars* (produced for Twentieth Century-Fox by Lucasfilm). Although the latter picture cost $27 million, by 1980 it generated gross receipts of more than $500 million, making a profit on the order of 1000 percent – a considerably better return on principal than investors could get in the bond or equities markets.

Coppola had made a blockbuster of his own in 1972, *The Godfather*, which paid back Gulf + Western's investment at a highly competitive rate. While he was at it, Coppola also had created something that auteurists could admire: an artful gangster picture. This put him in a position that was promising but ambivalent. On the one hand, he was attractive to venture capitalists. After *The Godfather*, at Paramount's invitation and with its initial financing of $31.5 million, Coppola got together with Bogdanovich and William Friedkin and formed The Directors Company. On the other hand (as Jon Lewis relates in an illuminating study of Coppola's career), an auteur's projects would not always outperform mutual funds. When Coppola used his new freedom to make *The Conversation* (1974), a movie that burrowed into the mind of a Nixon-era political–corporate spy, Paramount cut its ties to The Directors Company.

This was not the first time Coppola had lost the confidence of financiers. In 1969, before *The Godfather* made him a hot property, he had signed a deal with Warner Bros. to develop low-budget pictures for the youth market. Half a year later, Warner Bros. pulled out, leaving Coppola with nothing but an undercapitalized start-up company – American Zoetrope – and the memory of having pitched a handful of projects that were turned down flat. But by March 1975, Coppola had won a second round of Oscars, for *The Godfather, Part II*. He was powerful enough, even without Paramount's financing, to develop on his own one of those early, rejected projects: *Apocalypse Now*.

In 1969, *Apocalypse Now* had amounted to a script by John Milius, which Coppola's friend George Lucas was to direct in a style of rough immediacy, shooting in 16mm and incorporating newsreel footage. The proposed budget was a modest $1.5 million (and, of course, the Vietnam War was still raging). By mid-1975, on the strength of his own involvement as director (and with the war just concluded), Coppola was able to sell in advance the foreign distribution rights to *Apocalypse Now* for $7 million. Later the same year, United Artists bought the rights to domestic distribution for another $7 million, as an advance against profits. The film's projected budget was set at $12 million.

Now, Coppola did not have a finished script – Milius's screenplay, recently rewritten by Coppola, was undergoing further revision – and he did not have a cast (despite the foreign distributor's demand for stars). So what did a $12 million budget mean?

We may gain enlightenment from Bach's *Final Cut*, in which he explains the budget categories instituted at United Artists only a few years later. A blockbuster – of which UA wanted to have two a year – would cost $10 million. An ordinary drama was to cost $6 to $8 million. So, in hindsight, we may understand UA's commitment to *Apocalypse Now* as a leveraged investment. The company would expose itself to as much financial risk as would be involved in bankrolling an average drama, but would potentially enjoy profit participation in a blockbuster. The rest of the risk would be the responsibility of the auteur without a studio, Francis Coppola.

Shooting began in the Philippines on March 20, 1976, in the jungle location of Baler, six hours from Manila by dirt roads and half an hour away by airplane. The script was still unfinished. The cast had been announced only three weeks before. The paint on Dean Tavoularis's set was wet. Since the rest of the story has become familiar – through Eleanor Coppola's published journal, *Notes*, and Fax Bahr and George Hickenlooper's documentary *Hearts of Darkness* – I may perhaps limit my account to a simple itemization:

- One overly flamboyant battle scene, which set fire to the paint shop and properties warehouse.

- One miscast leading actor, Harvey Keitel, who was fired a month into principal photography.

- One halt in production while Coppola flew to Los Angeles, to sign Martin Sheen as Keitel's replacement in the role of Captain Willard.

- One hurricane, which destroyed the second location, at Iba.

- One unprepared star, Marlon Brando, who showed up without having read the novel on which *Apocalypse Now* was modeled, Joseph Conrad's *Heart of Darkness*. Coppola had hoped to develop the climactic scenes through improvisation, once Brando brought a flesh-and-blood Kurtz before the camera. Instead, with the production costing $80,000 a day, Coppola had to hole up alone with Brando to talk about characters and themes and patch together the dialogue.

- One heart attack suffered by Martin Sheen.

- One rambling memo sent to Coppola's staff back in San Francisco, subsequently made public in *Esquire* magazine as a case study in megalomania.

In addition, there were various miscommunications with the Philippine Air Force, which provided helicopters and pilots on an irregular basis, depending on the requirements of a civil war;

miscommunications between the director and his cinematographer, Vittorio Storaro, who seemed to intimidate Coppola; miscommunications between Coppola and his wife, especially once she discovered he was having an affair; all of the above compounded by the woolgathering and indecision that come with smoking marijuana.

Principal photography wrapped in June 1977, after a total of 238 days' shooting spread over 15 months. That summer, Coppola showed a rough cut of *Apocalypse Now* to an invited audience, calling it a 'work in progress.' The response was troubling enough for him to bring in Walter Murch to supervise the editing and hire Michael Herr (author of an acclaimed book of reportage on the Vietnam War, *Dispatches*) to write a voiceover narration. He tinkered with the film for more than a year before finally showing it to United Artists, in September 1978.

There, too, *Apocalypse Now* was greeted with dismay. 'Color it red – not for politics, for violence!' complained Christopher Mankiewicz (son of Joseph), at the time a production executive for UA. By this point, UA had increased its direct investment in the film to $7.5 million and had lent Coppola a little more than $20 million to cover expenses. More would be needed for post-production. The UA executives might have chosen to increase their stake in the film; but judging the potential return on investment to be less than thrilling, they took a defensive position, protecting as best they could the money they had already tied up. They would continue to lend Coppola the funds he needed and hope he would be able to pay them back.

In part, this decision was based on feudal politics. The executives who had contracted for *Apocalypse Now* had left to form their own company, Orion; the new UA managers were therefore stuck with responsibility for a film from which they could win no glory, and to which they felt no personal commitment. They also had to think about the corporate economy. As Bach makes clear in *Final Cut*, executives of the parent company did not hesitate to remind UA's managers of their duty to boost the price of Transamerica stock. To Wall Street analysts, a loan from UA would no doubt look more prudent than a bigger commitment of capital – even though the loan was secured with nothing better than Coppola's private property.

In this way, Hollywood's political economy made Coppola into a test case in the new meaning of independence. In the past, some directors had worked on the grand scale on the instructions of a producer. Such was the case with Lang, Ophuls, and Mankiewicz (who was first bought out of corporate independence by Fox). Others – Griffith, L'Herbier, Selznick – overextended themselves on their own initiative, acting as their own producers. Then there was Stroheim, who worked big in defiance of direct orders. But with *Apocalypse Now*, we come to our first case in which a company wanted a superproduction and at the same time assigned the greater part of the risk (at least on paper) to an independent producer–director.

Of course, that's not how it played in the newspapers. 'Crazy "Artist" Runs Wild in Jungle' might be a fair composite headline. By midsummer 1979, it would change to 'Visionary Artist Gambles Big and Wins.' First, on his own authority (and to UA's discomfort), Coppola entered *Apocalypse Now* in competition at the Cannes festival, where the film shared the Palme d'Or with a work of New German Cinema, Volker Schlöndorff's *The Tin Drum*. In the United States, curiosity about the picture ran so high that when Coppola held a sneak preview in Los Angeles in early May, people began lining up at 9:30 A.M. for tickets that would go on sale at 6:00 P.M., at the steep price of $7.50. The film ultimately cost $32.5 million to make, but it brought in about $100 million internationally on first release, contributing (in Bach's words) to 'the most successful box-office period' in the history of United Artists.

Meanwhile, Coppola was making direct contributions to the 'Crazy "Artist"/Visionary Artist' headlines. In his interviews, *Apocalypse Now* ceased to be a movie about the Vietnam War and became a tale of Francis Coppola. To Michael Dempsey of *Sight and Sound* (quoted in Lewis), he said, 'I, like Captain Willard, was moving up river in a faraway jungle, looking for answers and hoping for some kind of catharsis,' which sounds right, as far as it goes. But for those who seek meanings in the film beyond the psychological, an instructive comparison might be made between *Apocalypse Now* and another costly project financed by United Artists, Michael Cimino's *Heaven's Gate*.

I include the director's name in honor of Cimino's contract, which specified that he be cited on the title card in the same size type as the name of the film. Through such displays of egotism – and there were many – Cimino made himself the prime example of that semimythical figure of the late 1970s, the out-of-control auteur.

This much was true, as we may judge from *Final Cut*: Cimino was a recently famous director (having just won an Academy Award for *The Deer Hunter*), working for a new and inexperienced management team at United Artists. His first proposed budget for *Heaven's Gate*, $7.5 million, was unrealistic, and was flagged as such by the one veteran executive still on staff. But production went ahead anyway, driven by UA's need for a big year-end release, and by wishful thinking about

Cimino's willingness to deliver on a tight schedule. Shooting began on April 16, 1979, for a scheduled wrap on June 22, and actually concluded in April 1980. The total cost came to $35.19 million.

The premiere of Cimino's cut of *Heaven's Gate*, which ran 3 hours 39 minutes, was held in New York on November 18, 1980, to universal derision. A shorter version also died at the box office. As UA's recently installed head of domestic distribution, Jerry Esbin, told a reporter for the *Los Angeles Times*, 'It's as if somebody called every household in the country and said, "There will be a curse on your family if you go see this picture."' The finale came in May 1981, when Transamerica, humiliated by the picture's failure, sold United Artists to Kirk Kerkorian, who turned the company into a distribution service for MGM.

Since this debacle followed so close upon UA's troubles with *Apocalypse Now*, the two films became linked in people's minds. Allow me to uncouple them. *Apocalypse Now* is a true folly: inconsistent, overly ambitious, profligate, and dazzling. Its faults are the spillover of its virtues: a feverish rush of ideas about the war, the characters, the sources and implications of its story, the formal possibilities of filmmaking. The picture begins and ends with the screen bursting into flames, and the events in between play like a rolling conflagration. *Heaven's Gate*, on the other hand, is merely a long, expensive flop, whose most striking characteristic is an air of utter literal-mindedness. The actors look just like actors, dutifully wearing their costumes and saying their lines; the sets are emphatically movie sets; even the landscape of Glacier National Park somehow takes on the look of a backdrop. I might call *Heaven's Gate* a masterpiece of materialist cinema, except that its flatness lays bare nothing for the audience, apart from the director's mental state.

For *Heaven's Gate* was the result not of extravagance but of a plodding discipline. The crew (according to Bach) thought it an exceptionally well-regulated production, which isn't surprising, since Cimino, despite the reputation he acquired, did not fit the profile of an American auteur. He did not study film in school; he did not write reviews or monographs. Trained as a graphic artist and painter (with an M.F.A. from Yale), he began his career making television commercials. He broke into the movies as a writer, working on the script of *Magnum Force* in collaboration with John Milius, who thus provides one of the two meaningful connections between *Heaven's Gate* and *Apocalypse Now*.

The other connection is the Vietnam War. Cimino wrote the script for *Heaven's Gate* in 1971, a year after the United States expanded the war into Cambodia, a year after the National Guard killed student protesters at Kent State University. A shadowy version of these events may be glimpsed in the story Cimino told: a highly exaggerated version of the history of Johnson County, Wyoming, in the 1890s, when cattle barons hired armed men to enforce the law against rustling, and to keep immigrant farmers off the grazing land. In Cimino's account, the skirmishes became a full-scale war, with the cattle barons' hired killers supported by the federal government and the U.S. Cavalry. Caught in the middle of the conflict was the federal marshal of Johnson County (played by Kris Kristofferson), who chose to be a lawman in the West despite a patrician East Coast background and a Harvard degree. The character, as written, is inexplicable – unless we read him as the self-projection of a Yale-educated filmmaker from a moneyed town on Long Island, who was fantasizing in the early 1970s about the experiences he might have had in Vietnam.

Cimino made a film about himself, though he was not an auteur; whereas Coppola, who really was an auteur, avoided the temptation to collapse the war into his own character. In fact, Coppola took care to encapsulate himself within the movie, as if to deny his status as the picture's controlling intelligence. He plays a cameo role as a newsreel director, self-importantly shouting orders to soldiers as they assault a beach.

Perhaps we would see *Apocalypse Now* more clearly if we thought of it as an expression not of its auteur but of the world around him. To do so, we would need to abandon the image of the solitary artist versus an industrial system and begin to think seriously about the figure of Captain Willard: a man with specialized skills who acts under orders but without explicit authorization from the chain of command, so that he appears to operate on his own. I believe he could adequately represent the contemporary director–producer, working within Hollywood's feudal–capitalist system.

We also might think about Willard's mission: amid unremitting slaughter, he is to help his superior officers project a 'sound' image. Nor is Willard the only one who has to look after appearances. Everyone, it seems, is putting on a show in *Apocalypse Now*: the newsreel director, the USO troupe and its dancing Playmates, Colonel Kilgore (Robert Duvall) with his special-effects music and surfing performance. In the eyes of a sailor who is high on LSD, even the battle for Do Long bridge becomes a *son et lumière* spectacle staged by the U.S. Army. In *Apocalypse Now*, as in the world at large, making mayhem and making images are twin aspects of making war.

Of course, these readings of the film break down once we start to wonder who the Vietnamese might represent. (Producers outside the United States? Small shareholders in Transamerica?) But internal incoherence of this sort need not be a fatal flaw. Not every work of art aspires to the condition of allegory, with its one-to-one correspondences; nor do audiences often demand of artworks a set of sequential, paraphrasable arguments. (I speak of average audiences, not of Plato or professors of film theory.) It's more common for people to want to be carried out of themselves, into a confrontation with realities that overshadow the personal. That's what they got from Wagner's *Ring* (in which the allegorizing tendency is more pronounced, and therefore more jarring), and that's what they got from *Apocalypse Now*. Despite headlines to the contrary, the film did not contract upon the figure of its director; it expanded, like a widening fire in the viewer's mind. Most of the flames sent up resembled those of a specific set of events, known as the Vietnam War; but at times they also could look like one man's flares, or erupt into a universal combustion.

Perhaps that outermost edge of the circle meant the most to audiences. What stayed with viewers of *Apocalypse Now*? Not the borrowings from *Heart of Darkness* – that tale of the savagery of imperialism – but the attack of Kilgore's Air Cavalry, executed to the strains of 'The Ride of the Valkyrie.' Let us pick up that hint and follow the film outward, to see how it touched against the concerns of German artists in the 1970s, as exemplified by the films of Werner Herzog.

To students of New German Cinema, the immediate question will be: why not Hans Jürgen Syberberg instead?

If subject matter, scale, and stylistic eclecticism were my only criteria, then Syberberg's work would indeed represent the ultimate German folly. In 1972, he competed against Visconti with his own version of the story of Wagner's patron, *Ludwig – Requiem for a Virgin King*, which runs 2 hours 14 minutes. Following this, among other works, were *The Confessions of Winifred Wagner* (1975) at 5 hours 3 minutes, *Hitler, a Film from Germany* (1977) at 6 hours 47 minutes, and *Parsifal* (1982) at 4 hours 15 minutes. All these films were awash in Wagner's music, and more generally in Wagnerian culture, which Syberberg called up as the heroes of Greek myth used to call up shades from the underworld, with a mixture of dread, disgust, and inquisitiveness. I do not choose the simile at random; in *Hitler, a Film from Germany*, we see a toga-clad Führer rise from the fuming grave of Richard Wagner.

Even so, I prefer to edge past these immense and highly debatable pictures, since I am concerned with filmmakers who became engaged with commercial production and distribution. Syberberg made his pictures quickly and cheaply and distributed them himself, going directly to the owners of small movie theaters. Despite the amount of press attention he received, especially in France, he belongs to the tradition of defiantly uncommercial art cinema, which runs from the Surrealists of the 1920s to today's network of lesbian and gay experimentalists. Granted, Syberberg's films were more grandiose than the usual productions of this alternative cinema; but at times, so were those of Stan Brakhage and Hollis Frampton.

With Herzog, on the other hand, we have a filmmaker who was not shy about seeking international distribution. When he presented *Aguirre, Wrath of God* in the Directors' Fortnight section of the Cannes festival, he showed the picture in a version dubbed in English – though it was such bad English that the strategy almost failed. Richard Roud, head of the New York Film Festival, told Herzog he would like to show *Aguirre*, but only in a German version, which quickly became available.

Aguirre received its U.S. premiere in 1973 at the New York Film Festival but was not released commercially in America until 1977, a year after Coppola began shooting *Apocalypse Now*. Nevertheless, Coppola had an early opportunity to see the film and to meet Herzog, with whom he quickly became friends. Tom Luddy, who at the time was running the Pacific Film Archives, recalls bringing Herzog and a print of *Aguirre* to Coppola's home in San Francisco in 1973. A year later, Luddy dropped by with Herzog's next feature, *The Mystery of Kaspar Hauser*, which at the time did not have a U.S. distributor. Coppola immediately called the head of Cinema 5 and urged him to pick up the rights, saying the picture was a masterpiece. By the time Coppola was preparing *Apocalypse Now*, he felt close enough to Herzog to ask permission to copy three shots from *Aguirre*. Herzog replied that he would feel honored.

Is an *Aguirre* influence evident in *Apocalypse Now* beyond those three shots? Recall that in 1969, *Apocalypse Now* was a war story for George Lucas to direct in fake documentary style; by 1975, it had become Coppola's own project, reconceived as an epic about the cruelty and madness of those who would seize a jungle empire. In between came the release of Herzog's startling film: the story of a rogue conquistador in Peru, who breaks away from Francisco Pizarro's army and plunges into the jungle with a small force of his own.

There is also the matter of Herzog's approach to telling his story. He filled *Aguirre* with long takes of lush jungle scenery, making the rivers, mists, and monkeys seem as important as the human figures, who sweated and strained through the tropics in their sixteenth-century armor. To judge the impression this made on American audiences, we might turn to an article by Richard Eder in *The New York Times*: 'To talk about Herzog is, first of all, to talk about his landscape. . . . [His places] strike us with the kind of charged and magical significance that our primitive forebears may once have felt.'

When *Apocalypse Now* at last came before the public, many viewers again were struck by the way the film dwelled on hallucinatory landscapes, rather than pushing along a story. *The New York Times* sent a relatively inexperienced filmgoer, Susan Heller Anderson, to cover the premiere at Cannes and was rewarded with a report that is today illuminating in its ingenuousness. 'On the surface it has a plot,' Anderson informed her readers; but 'the film, on its most global level, is a mind-shattering trip. . . . It doesn't even begin like a normal film. There are no credits.' In the same report, Anderson quoted Coppola's confirmation that *Apocalypse Now* was not 'normal': 'I tried to make it more of an experience than a movie,' he said. 'At the beginning there's a story. Along the river the story becomes less important and the experience more important.'

Herzog's $320,000 jungle picture clearly had its effect on Coppola's $32.5 million epic. *Apocalypse Now* would in turn influence the making of Herzog's $6 million *Fitzcarraldo*.

'*Apocalypse Now* was only a kindergarten compared to what we went through,' Herzog told his interviewers (more than once) about *Fitzcarraldo*. I doubt the comparison occurred to him only in retrospect. In the first place, according to Tom Luddy, Herzog lived in Coppola's house while he wrote the script for *Fitzcarraldo*. In the second place, the production history suggests that Herzog went looking for hardships comparable to those his American friend had endured.

Herzog's first attempt to make *Fitzcarraldo* began in November 1979, only a few months after the release of *Apocalypse Now*. As documented by Les Blank and Maureen Gosling in the film *Burden of Dreams* (1982), Herzog set up camp in Peru, near the Ecuadorean border, where oil and lumber companies had been moving in, to the accompaniment of armed battles for control of the land. Herzog chose to bring his crew into this area without any sanction from the Peruvian government. (As *Variety* later explained, officials remembered how *Aguirre* had left 'a long trail of unpaid technicians and extras abandoned in the jungle'.) As for the local population: having already lost territory, they regarded Herzog's people as just another set of interlopers.

'The Indians' general claims are entirely justified,' commented one of Herzog's associates, Alan Greenberg, to Seth Cagin of *The Soho Weekly News*. 'They say their culture is being destroyed, and it is. Werner isn't the one who did it to them, but he walked right into a trap by going into their territory with an invasionary force of 180 whites.' Rumors began circulating that his crew was running guns, raping Indian women, imprisoning Indians who would not work for the production, perhaps planning genocide. Coppola had gone on location some 150 miles away from a guerrilla war; Herzog had outdone him by heading right into the midst of conflict, only to encounter more resistance than he'd expected. He told his people to slip away. In December 1979, armed members of the Aguarunas tribe ordered the remaining crew to leave, then burned the camp.

The filming of *Fitzcarraldo* resumed in January 1981, in Iquitos, Peru. Aiming again at the international market, Herzog shot in English, using a cast that was at least as marketable as that of *Apocalypse Now*. Jack Nicholson had turned down the offer of the lead (as he had refused Coppola), but Herzog succeeded in signing Jason Robards, Jr. to play the role of Brian Sweeney Fitzgerald and Mick Jagger to play the sidekick, Wilbur. Making possible the production was financing from a U.S. distributor: New World Pictures, headed by Roger Corman.

Five weeks into principal photography, with perhaps 40 percent of the picture shot, Herzog had to abandon the production again. Jason Robards came down with amebic dysentery and quit, leaving his agent to explain to *The New York Times* that Robards would sue Herzog over the 'hazardous' conditions to which he had been subjected, with neither a refrigerator nor a physician on the set. Mick Jagger quit, too, complaining through a spokesman that he had been stuck in the jungle without a telephone.

Herzog's response was to look for more trouble: he brought in Klaus Kinski to play Fitzgerald/Fitzcarraldo. Herzog had gone into the Peruvian jungle once before with Kinski, for *Aguirre*, an experience that had led to threats of gunplay. The likelihood of a more amiable outcome on *Fitzcarraldo* may be judged from Kinski's memoirs. Although these cannot guide us toward any external reality, they do leave a vivid impression of the actor's feelings toward Herzog, which may be summed up as murderous rage. In April 1981, Herzog started shooting *Fitzcarraldo* again from the beginning, in the face of his star's unrelenting fury.

All this, of course, was merely a preparation for the real impossibility: filming the sequence that would show Indian workers hauling a 320-ton steamship up a hill.

In interviews, Herzog repeatedly said that *Fitzcarraldo* sprang from his desire to realize this one image, of Indians bearing upward the machinery of European civilization against the force of the jungle, in defiance of gravity itself. This effort, however crazy, serves a purpose for the film's main character; by moving his ship overland from one river system to another, Fitzgerald/Fitzcarraldo will be able to open a new territory for rubber production, thereby making a fortune for himself and enabling him to build his opera house. But for Herzog, the heavy lifting was an end in itself; he made *Fitzcarraldo* expressly to see if he could get the steamship over the hill. It was as if Coppola had made *Apocalypse Now* to see if he could survive hurricanes, heart attacks, and the vagaries of the Philippine Air Force.

In fact, two turn-of-the-century steamships appear in *Fitzcarraldo*, both of them reconditioned at significant expense. Because of the delays in production, Herzog lost the first ship for several months; the rainy season had ended, and the ship ran aground in the shallows. The other ship sat unused at another location while a bulldozer struggled to clear a path for it up the hill, and while Herzog argued with his consulting engineer. The system of cables and pulleys for moving the ship had been devised for a slope of 20 degrees, but Herzog insisted on 40, over the engineer's objections. The engineer quit; Herzog went ahead with the sequence; a cable snapped, as the engineer had feared. Miraculously, no one was killed, but neither did the ship go over the hill. In the aftermath of this failure, Herzog took the ship into the rapids to shoot another sequence and ran it aground on a sandbank. Now both ships were out of use. There was nothing to do but wait for the rainy season. Herzog shut down production in July and used the break to call in a new team of engineers from Lima. When he resumed shooting in October, he succeeded in getting the ship over the hill, though not (as he had hoped) using only muscle power.

Fitzcarraldo finished shooting in November 1981 and had its premiere in March 1982 in Munich, followed by a presentation in competition at Cannes, where Herzog won the award for best director. 'Mon film est une œuvre inimitable,' he announced, 'destinée à encourager l'être à la folie et la fantaisie.' For the most part, critics did not oblige by going mad. But on balance, *Fitzcarraldo* got at least as many good reviews as had *Apocalypse Now*, and on a much lower budget. The disasters of the production were not revisited upon Herzog at the box office.

Yet it's unseemly to count up profit and loss, when a picture has cost human lives. (The broken cable didn't kill anyone, but an airplane crash did.) Love it or hate it, *Fitzcarraldo* made people judge it on a basis other than money, which in this case is perhaps the highest compliment I can pay Herzog.

Those who didn't want to give him that much credit were scathing. In *The New Yorker*, Pauline Kael accused Herzog of 'playing Pharaoh' and said he was so morally obtuse as to have risked lives for the sake of providing a diagonal for his frame. In *Cineaste*, Hans Koning dredged up the name of Karl May (that favorite author of Lang, von Harbou, and Hitler) to help categorize *Fitzcarraldo* as a fantasy about blonde, blue-eyed people subduing a darker race by sheer willpower. The film was therefore a German problem. 'I am . . . not saying that Herzog *per se* must be a racist,' Koning wrote.

He may be a marvelously progressive man; his problem is that there is something almost inherently racist in the very language and culture he is working with, when these go beyond the national German borders. The tale does not come out as that of a crazy, obsessed guy doing the impossible, but as of one more white man who had a great many dark people sweating their asses off at his whim. . . . *Fitzcarraldo* is a kind of movie we would have seen in very large numbers had Germany won its wars. (Cineaste 12, 5)

Other viewers, such as Andrew Sarris, fidgeted to see a fictional character being made to point back so insistently toward its maker. Writing in *The Village Voice* of October 26, 1982, Sarris asked:

Is this . . . not what auteurism originally set out to glorify? Not really. What has been generally overlooked is that the various politiques of the '50s and '60s, and mine was merely one of many, began with screenings and not interviews, with pictures in the dark and not filmmakers on the couch.

This argument against self-promotion leaped to mind all the more readily because *Burden of Dreams* was shown in several American cities even before *Fitzcarraldo* opened.

By its omnipresence, the behind-the-screen story emphasized another problem in the film itself: Herzog cut a more complex and compelling figure in Les Blank's documentary than did Kinski in *Fitzcarraldo*. As several critics observed, Kinski's Fitzcarraldo seems more of a contrivance than a character. His devotion to opera is merely posited, like a geometric axiom. His relationship to the film's one significant female character, Molly (Claudia Cardinale), is as flimsy as most comparable cinematic romances slapped together between a leading man and a prostitute. As Kael wrote, 'It's hard to know quite what Kinski's Fitzcarraldo is because he's not like anyone else in the world – except maybe Bette Davis playing Rutger Hauer.' Or, perhaps, like a stand-in for Klaus Kinski in *Aguirre, Wrath of God*.

What can be said of Kinski's performance may be said in general of *Fitzcarraldo*, which in its parts and as a whole is a stand-in movie. The picture refers us back to *Aguirre*, as if to establish itself as 'a Werner Herzog film'; it recalls *Apocalypse Now*, as if to prove that the European art cinema might dare to outdo Coppola. Even the climactic opera performance is a replacement. At the end, though his mad scheme has failed, *Fitzcarraldo* secures a moment of passing happiness by staging Bellini's *I Puritani* in Iquitos, not in an opera house but on the water. Herzog's original draft called for a different opera, the choice of which was perhaps too revealing: *Die Walküre*.

These many substitutions give *Fitzcarraldo* a phantom quality, which tends to undo the effect Herzog claimed to pursue: the restoration of faith in cinema through the avoidance of fakery, by virtue of presenting to the camera a real steamship on a real hill. If we take this stated goal at face value, *Fitzcarraldo* becomes equivalent (in terms of a *politique des auteurs*) to the Thermidorean reaction: Bazin's once liberating doctrine of cinematic realism leads smack into a tyrannical cult of personality.

But what if we accept the film's insubstantiality? Let us admit that *Fitzcarraldo* is equally a record of an arduous exploit and a dreamlike tissue of allusions. What might change in our image of the film and its artist–adventurer, once we understand Herzog set out to confront not only nature, but also the memory of other works of art?

To answer the question, we must first recall that Herzog pursued ordeals beyond those of *Aguirre* and *Fitzcarraldo*, and even beyond filmmaking.

In November 1974, informed that Lotte Eisner was ill and might die, Herzog took it into his head to walk from his home in Munich to her bedside in Paris, outfitted for the road with only a compass, a jacket, and a small bag. He later spoke of this pilgrimage, which he recorded in a book titled *Of Walking in Ice*, as 'a rebellion against the inevitability of her death' (O'Brien, p. 43), since he believed – knew – that Eisner would not die, so long as he slogged through the rain, snow, and slush. A decade later, in the hope of reunifying Germany, Herzog undertook an even tougher hike. As he explained in an interview with Geoffrey

O'Brien, 'I started to travel on foot all around my own country, following the sinuous border demarcations through the mountains of Austria, then along Switzerland, France, Belgium, Luxembourg, Holland, Denmark, Poland, Czechoslovakia, and Austria, then back to the village where I grew up, which was right on the border.' He estimated he walked for more than a thousand miles before he fell ill and had to end the trip. (For a discussion of Herzog's *Of Walking in Ice*, see Horak.)

If we ask whether anyone else gave physical challenge a central place in art, we will not have to look far for the answer. The key German artist of this period was another practitioner of ordeals: Joseph Beuys.

Did Herzog know of Beuys? Without question. In the late 1960s and early 1970s, after Beuys was dismissed from his post at Düsseldorf's art academy and was fighting to be reinstated, he became not just an artist but a cause. Beuys also played an active role in politics, eventually helping to found West Germany's Green Party. By the late 1970s, he had attained the status of a senior public figure, if a dotty one, sitting in on the 1978 meeting between the Chancellor of the Federal Republic of Germany and the President of France. To Beuys, all this came under the heading of artistic activity, or 'social sculpture,' with the ordeal, or shamanistic ritual, serving as a principal tool for re-forming and healing human relationships.

In 1964, for example, Beuys had himself wrapped head to toe in a roll of felt, then lay for nine hours on the floor of a Berlin art gallery; while immobilized, he spoke intermittently through a microphone, addressing his words to a pair of dead hares that had been placed at his head and feet. In 1974, at the René Block Gallery in New York, Beuys carried out an action titled *I Like America and America Likes Me*, in which he cohabited round the clock for three days with a live coyote. The American representative shredded Beuys's clothes pretty well before deciding it liked, or at least could tolerate, the German artist.

Behind these particular trials lay the myth of a great ordeal, which Beuys claimed to have suffered during World War II. While serving as a Luftwaffe pilot, he had been shot down over Asia. A tribe of nomadic Tatars discovered him and saved his life by wrapping him in layers of animal fat and felt. Beuys emerged from this cocoon of primitivism a new man, no longer a cog in Hitler's grim social machine but now an artist and healer, in harmony with the natural processes of growth, death, and decay.

I sketch this background in the belief that when we speak of 'art cinema,' we ought to specify what kind of art the filmmaker might have had in mind. For Herzog, it seems to me, Beuys's art was a likely point of reference. Time after time, Herzog made films as an exercise in physical endurance carried out in 'primitive' settings, in the face of the forces of nature. By subjecting himself to these rigors, Herzog, too, played the role of shaman. He offered his audience a process of healing and liberation, in which they could participate simply by watching the film.

So it is with *Fitzcarraldo*. The Indians, who all along had a purpose of their own, sacrifice the steamship to the rapids, in fulfillment of a dream-vision. And Fitzcarraldo, far from being crushed by this reversal, turns it into triumph of a sort. By thinking up a new way to present opera – not in a great theater with Caruso, but on an ephemeral, open-air stage – he proves that the experience of machine-heavy torture has opened him to a realm of insubstantial spirit.

As with the character, so with the author. In the course of his trials in the jungle, Herzog may be said to have reproduced colonialism in order to atone for it, for himself and his audience. A shaman for modern Euro-American filmgoers, he bore away their sins, which he carried deep into the wilderness.

Whether this resolution was a bit too convenient for modern Euro-Americans, I leave to others to decide. Nor will I debate whether an Indian should be allowed to be just an Indian and a jungle a jungle, rather than being made into instruments of somebody else's transformation. I prefer to say only that Beuys performed his ceremonies of guilt and absolution before a much smaller public than Herzog's. He did not engage an international system of financing at the $6 million level, nor did he play artistic leapfrog with the director of *The Godfather*. Whatever Herzog's faults – and entire volumes have been written about them – we may credit him with popularizing this new strain of art, bringing it into direct contact and confrontation with the institution of the movies.*

So we return to the question raised by a student of Beuys, Anselm Kiefer, in his *Occupations*: how far can an artist go in enacting guilt without becoming guilty?

The loss of life suffered during the making of *Fitzcarraldo* ought to suggest one limit of innocence. But even if the deaths had not occurred, we might question the wisdom of popularizing a shamanistic art, causing it to balloon out of all proportion.

Performances and actions such as those I've described may have lasted longer than Wagnerian music-dramas, but otherwise they were of a far different nature, being an art of the immediate and the

* The need for popularization may be gauged from the August 26, 1976 entry in Eleanor Coppola's *Notes*, in which she recalled the Conceptualist and performance art she had encountered in New York galleries in the 1970s. 'Dumb and boring,' she called it.

makeshift. They used the humblest of materials, the artist's body prominent among them. The space they occupied was intimate; the appropriate technology for recording them would have been video, not 35 mm film. These characteristics account for a contradiction that was inherent in much of this artwork, which aspired to address everybody while in fact reaching a relatively small, insular audience. That Beuys became a public figure in Germany does not mean his work was widely known.

But then came Herzog and (especially) Coppola, who played the scapegoat on a world stage. In so doing, these filmmakers achieved true Wagnerism; in a spirit of high seriousness, they reunited popular and avant-garde art (which had begun to diverge even before *Intolerance*) and brought a sense of public space into the movie houses. They also revived a Wagnerian cult of personality.

Of course the Master of Bayreuth was no fit model for an auteur, as Sarris might have been the first to say. Even so, auteurism had helped persuade people such as Herzog and Coppola that they could be artists and big-time showpeople at the same time. One had only to look at the result to suspect that 'auteur' might be just another name for the domineering artist–hero. The auteur was also a handy figure to blame if one felt moral unease at watching *Apocalypse Now* and *Fitzcarraldo* – though moral unease, of course, was precisely what those films were meant to incite.

Studio heads and producers may have lacked such sensitivity, but for their own reasons they, too, learned to use 'auteur' as a term of abuse. It meant Cimino; it meant movies that had been marketed on the strength of the directors' names, to the disappointment of investors. Journalists agreed, auteurism having become a handy concept for editors looking to peg a trend piece. Such irresponsibility had to stop – and by the early 1980s, it did.

Whether in the United States or West Germany, newly installed conservative governments were reenforcing corporate discipline. Since the screws that were tightened then remain firmly in place as of this writing, I will state only briefly the worldview of President Ronald Reagan: public good flows exclusively from the pursuit of private gain. It was a happy thought for the managers of entertainment conglomerates and owners of newspaper chains.

Joining in this ideology was Chancellor Helmut Kohl – like Reagan, a man who projected an image of casual good cheer about the use of power. While Reagan grinned out of existence any lingering malaise over the slaughter in Vietnam, Kohl was engaged in his own smoothing-over of the past, the better to prepare for Germany's unification. Unlike Herzog, the Chancellor made it seem as if this goal might be reached without pain or personal struggle.

Little wonder that a shaman couldn't find work in the 1980s. By mid-decade, people had begun to speak of Coppola and Herzog as if they were shambling embarrassments. To the delight of the movie executives he had challenged, Coppola's enterprise foundered upon the critical and commercial failure of his expensive 'little' musical, *One from the Heart* (1982), which cost him his dream of a studio. And Herzog finally succeeded in crucifying himself by making an anti-Sandinista documentary, *Ballad of the Little Soldier* (1984), which convinced his core audience that he was indeed a colonialist and demagogue.

These self-inflicted wounds were bad enough; but even more damaging was the political economy in which the filmmakers found themselves. That follies were strictly forbidden should go without saying. They always had been; but now the executives of the new Hollywood had learned what to guard against. Gladly accommodating themselves to an era of *gai pouvoir*, they invested ever larger sums in their blockbusters, but only when they felt sure of the star, the genre, and the marketing tag-line. Would-be auteurs therefore faced two choices: either to raise money on their own, taking on financial risk and making alliances with other vassals (as did Oliver Stone and very few others), or else to drop down to the circuit of small distributors, art houses, and film festivals.

So normality was restored, as it always is – this time in a decade when the audience for the not-normal had splintered. There was no Wagner in the 1980s to bind together the disparate bands of nay-sayers; no hunger for a Wagner. For people who wanted to feel daring but didn't care to risk anything beyond the price of a ticket, David Lynch offered the smug ironies of *Blue Velvet* (1986). Those who felt more deeply estranged from business-as-usual tended to go their own ways, into various enclaves: lesbian, gay, feminist, Africanist, Third World, even formal-experimentalist (the latter group being especially in-grown and prickly). Some remarkable films came out of these cinematic subcultures; none, of course, was wasteful enough to merit discussion in these pages.

The age of follies had ended.

And yet the folly lived.

In August 1985, one of Hollywood's most powerful people, Warren Beatty, announced that he would put a new production before the cameras in the fall. Budgeted at $30 million, the picture would be shot indoors at New York's Kaufman Astoria Studios and outdoors in Morocco, for release through Columbia Pictures (which had the major financial stake). Described as an up-to-date version of the Bob Hope–Bing Crosby 'Road' comedies, the film would star Beatty and Dustin Hoffman as a pair of utterly talentless songwriter–performers, caught up (through sheer ignorance) in a North African political intrigue. The film was titled *Ishtar*. Its writer–director was Elaine May.

Perhaps no one since Stroheim had so consistently spat in the face of fiscal prudence, or contrived a more magnificent disproportion between expenditure and ostentation. Two of May's previous projects, *A New Leaf* and *Mikey and Nicky*, had generated lawsuits in which Paramount Pictures accused her of kidnapping the film. On *Mikey and Nicky*, she also spent about $5 million on a $1.8 million budget, shooting 1.4 million feet of film and then working for two years on the editing, all to realize a picture that looked so unassuming that Molly Haskell could describe it as 'one of those long, lugubrious Actors' Studio exercises.' Nevertheless, she had worked with Warren Beatty on the script of his 1978 *Heaven Can Wait*, which did well at the box office and received eight nominations for Academy Awards. Beatty was pleased to offer her $1.5 million to write and direct *Ishtar*. He also paid himself and Hoffman $5 million apiece to act in it and took another $500,000 as his fee for producing the film, putting a sizable dent into the budget before the first frame had been shot.

Needless to say, the production took longer than planned. Elaine May insisted on shooting as many as fifty takes of a single set-up, with the result that the film opened in May 1987, about a year after the premiere might have been expected. Published tallies of the cost began at $36.5 million and went up giddily, with most reports claiming something in the neighborhood of $50 million. To hear an indignant press tell the tale, you would have thought May wanted to filch the full sum from the pocket of each moviegoer.

She had offended many people in her feudal community, being not only litigious but also as sharp-tongued as Mankiewicz. Beatty, too, had made enemies; and as everyone knew, both producer and director had taken cruel advantage of Columbia Pictures and its parent corporation, the Coca-Cola Company. So the failure of *Ishtar* was decided before the film had even been screened. *Variety*, always attentive to company heads and influential with exhibitors, delivered a poisonous early review. At the industry previews in Los Angeles (so I'm told by a reliable source), anyone who dared to laugh at *Ishtar*'s jokes was stared back into silence.

Today, granted the privacy that comes with a videocassette player, a viewer may freely roar. Although *Ishtar* cost a fortune to make, it is one of the great comedies of insufficiency. The main characters – Lyle (Beatty) and Chuck (Hoffman) – lack skill, status, money, wives, careers, courtesy, fashion sense, and self-knowledge, none of which makes them unworthy of sympathy, or even admiration. As Lyle says early in the film, voicing manly encouragement when Chuck is about to leap off a building ledge, 'It takes a lot of nerve to have nothing at your age.'

In style, the film perfectly matches this theme of bravery, however idiotic, on the brink of the abyss. The long sequence to which May builds up has her two characters wandering lost in the desert. As a site of nature in the absolute, a desert is conceptually identical to a jungle and serves the same purpose, testing the moral fiber of Americans who have temporarily donned native costumes. Visually, a desert is the jungle's negation. For minutes on end, the screen in *Ishtar* is all but void, except for sand, the horizon line, a blind camel, and the occasional vulture. Such is the climax of the hilarity. There is no romantic climax, because Isabelle Adjani (in the Dorothy Lamour role) does not get to wear a sarong, but rather is made to spend the film wrapped head to toe in a burnoose – except when Chuck mistakes her for a boy, and she corrects him by matter-of-factly flashing a tit. To bring the plot to its conclusion, May also supplies the excitement of a battle scene, staged with so little firepower as to be insolent.

But the most glaring effrontery was the one that went almost unremarked at the time: the movie's politics. A handful of reviewers went so far as to describe *Ishtar* as having 'liberal' tendencies; the majority avoided even so mild a characterization, preferring to concentrate on (and damn) Elaine May's sense of humor. But of course the film would have seemed unfunny, had you chosen to ignore its jokes about American meddling in the Third World. The bad guys in *Ishtar* are spies for the Central Intelligence Agency; the good guys, Shi'ite Muslim revolutionaries. And the import, in this context, of showing two American entertainers, bumbling about in an Arab country? May drove home her point at the end of the film simply by decorating a CIA office with the portrait of a third American showman, Ronald Reagan.

This was no way for a filmmaker to ingratiate herself, given the political culture of 1980s America. To quote one of Lyle and Chuck's most piercing lyrics, 'Telling the truth can be dangerous business. "Honest" and "popular" don't go hand in hand.' That understood, we may skip the remaining tra-la-la – something about an accordion – and go straight to the conclusion: *Ishtar* became a folly proudly and willingly, for the sake of mocking a more costly foolishness.

Monumental humor was unlikely to erupt in the cinema of the opposite Cold War bloc – despite the Soviet habit of art-making on a laughably grand scale. But follies were possible even there.

I lack the space, and the expertise, to review these Soviet extravagances, from Yakov Protazanov's 1924 *Aelita, Queen of Mars*, with its Constructivist sets and it-was-all-a-dream plot, to Yulia Solntseva's wide-screen, stereo-sound epics of the 1960s, such as *The Enchanted Desna*. Still, there was one such film – perhaps the most remarkable of them all – that demands attention, because of its jungle sequences, its irresistible flamboyance, its history of dormancy and revival.

I Am Cuba is a work of cinematic delirium and great political ambition, of political delirium and great cinematic ambition – a fabulous beast of a movie, part white elephant and part fire-breathing dragon. Co-produced by Mosfilm and the Cuban Film Institute (ICAIC), it went into pre-production in the latter part of 1961, shortly after the Bay of Pigs invasion, when officials in Moscow and Havana were newly keen on investing in a big feature film in support of the revolution. To that end, they made a dramatic intervention.

ICAIC, which was founded in March 1959, until then had devoted its resources mainly to making newsreels and documentaries and to expanding the exhibition circuit. (Among its initiatives was the 'mobile cinema' – a projector loaded onto the back of a Soviet truck, sent to roam the villages.) Feature film production would not take hold decisively until 1966, with Tomás Gutiérrez Alea's *Death of a Bureaucrat*; so for ICAIC in 1961, the project of making a 140-minute fiction was extraordinary. The subsequent evolution of the project into an art film would be utterly inexplicable, were it not for two factors: the context of Havana, and the personality of Fidel Castro.

Havana had for years been a movie-mad city. Under Batista, Hollywood products had crowded out most other fare; but for the curious, there were opportunities to see all sorts of films, opportunities that expanded in the years immediately after the revolution. This rich film culture had its effect on those Cubans who longed to make films themselves. By mid-1961, when the proposal for *I Am Cuba* would have been floating about, there had been just enough production beyond the aesthetic limits of the newsreel to elicit a landmark speech from Castro, 'Words to the Intellectuals.' This was the occasion when he put forth the formula 'Within the revolution, everything; against the revolution, nothing.' Given its timing – two months after the Bay of Pigs – this doctrine was not so much a threat as a daring promise. Despite the all-too-credible prospect of destruction by a vastly superior force, Castro pledged that nonrevolutionary (as distinguished from antirevolutionary) artists would find in Cuba 'a place to work and create, a place where their creative spirit . . . has the opportunity and freedom to be expressed.'

Into this proposed wonderland of personal expression (newly established on an island where northerners had long been accustomed to letting go) came Mosfilm's production team, headed by director Mikhail Kalatozov. A few years earlier, Kalatozov had scored an international hit with *The Cranes Are Flying*; he also had enjoyed a successful bureaucratic career, having served, at various times, as cultural consul in Los Angeles, Head of the Chief Administration in Charge of Feature Film Production, and Deputy Minister of Cinema-tography. On the face of it, he would not have seemed a man to run wild in the tropics. But Kalatozov's tastes had been formed during the Soviet Union's era of heroic experimentation, under the influence of Dziga Vertov and Esther Shub, and his career since then had been marked by frequent gaps, the result of official disfavor over his occasional 'negativism' and chronic 'formalism.'

Even while he was readying *I Am Cuba* for the camera, in October 1962, Kalatozov came under attack from Mosfilm's Art Council on the grounds that he had irresponsibly subordinated the subject matter and characters of his latest film, *The Letter Never Sent*, to the pleasures of direction and cinematography. By the time of this attack, of course, the screenplay for *I Am Cuba* (written by Yevgeny Yevtushenko and Enrique Pineda Barnet) had been finished and the casting was set; everything was in place to make a rhapsody, rather than a manifesto. Still, we may guess that the Art Council contributed something to *I Am Cuba*, inadvertently digging a spur into Kalatozov just as the starting gate clanged open.

He began shooting in late November 1962 – immediately after the missile crisis – assisted by cinematographer Sergei Urusevsky and camera operator Alexander Calzatti. At once, Kalatozov plunged into the sort of death-, convention-, and gravity-defying camera excursion that distinguishes *I Am Cuba*. To show the corruption of Havana in the bad old days, he made his camera wander among the participants in a bikini contest, staged on the rooftop of a 1950s Moderne hotel; then descend as if by elevator to poolside; then take a side trip onto a terrace overlooking the beach, and then (with all this happening in one continuous take) become fascinated by a woman in a leopard-skin bikini, tracking her as she gets up from her *chaise-longue* and following her into the pool, to dive at last beneath the surface. Seal-like capitalists swim by, accompanied by bubble-breathing pimps and bimbos, while the soundtrack modulates into a glub-glub version of the hotel band's jumpin' jive.

This comes close to being a normal sequence in *I Am Cuba*. The film's different sections may vary somewhat in style, incorporating a gauzy flashback here, a bit of suspense-building cross-cutting there. (As with *Intolerance*, the film presents four main episodes, linked not by character and plot but by theme: the people's misery in the city, their hardships in the country, the students' revolt in Havana, and the peasants' uprising in the mountains.) But whatever the episode, the viewer is continually struck by a sense of hallucinatory rapture, conveyed by the black-and-white cinematography (which transforms palm trees into giant white feathers and the sea into molten lead); a willful dizziness, implied by the framing with its nonstop tilts; and above all a breakneck daring, boasted of by the long, hand-held takes. Again and again, Kalatozov invites the viewer to marvel at a never-before-seen shot; he even provides on-screen cues for enthusiasm, in case you're slow to react. When the camera descends to poolside during the hotel sequence, for example, some of the extras stand and applaud. Ostensibly, they're clapping for the participants in the bikini contest; but they might as well be congratulating Kalatozov. Immediately after, as his camera glides past the poolside tables, you see a Batista-era tourist making his own movie with a little Bolex. Miserable capitalist! Can he hope to achieve a socialist camera movement like *this*?

For viewers today, this relentless thaumaturgy can have the effect of underscoring the film's dramatic clumsiness, while at other times distracting viewers altogether from the subject matter. Surely most audiences will chortle over the film's nightclub sequence, in which a chinless, bow-tied American geek (played none too steadily by French actor Jean Bouise) takes sexual advantage of Downtrodden Cuban Womanhood (Luz Maria Collazo). Less funny, though no less kitschy and stiff, is the episode about an old, illiterate sugarcane farmer (José Gallardo) who loses his land to the United Fruit Company. In these sections of *I Am Cuba*, the too-muchness of Kalatozov's style works against any attempt to exercise one's historical imagination, to think oneself back into the core of lived experience that once might have animated what is now a lump of propaganda. But in a more dramatically vivid section – the episode about a student activist named Enrique (Raúl García) – the style can be equally inimical to meaning.

You often ignore the subject – for example, the outpouring of popular emotion that results from Enrique's self-sacrifice – because you're gasping in astonishment at a crane shot you *know* was impossible.

Given the disillusionment or animosity that is common today toward Castro's revolution, why not yield to the virtuosity, and say that nothing was ever worthwhile about *I Am Cuba* except for its flamboyance? By effecting that divorce between style and subject matter, we would treat Kalatozov more or less as certain critics treat Leni Riefenstahl. Are the two in fact equivalent? Would we have any valid reason – other than a belief in the good intentions of one and the bad of the other – for justifying Kalatozov's propaganda but not Riefenstahl's?

I think there's something to be said for good intentions. Put the worst possible construction on Kalatozov's film. Claim that it promoted a dictatorial regime that betrayed and bankrupted the Cuban people; you will still have to admit that *I Am Cuba* was meant to defend the Cubans' right to govern themselves, in conditions that would allow the poor to become a little less wretched. Judged in that way, Kalatozov's faults are essentially aesthetic misdemeanors: sentimentality, overstatement, tone-deafness. (He did not commit the graver crime of hero worship; Castro is mentioned a couple of times in *I Am Cuba*, and that's it.) Now put the best possible construction on *Triumph of the Will*. Claim that Riefenstahl was improbably naive and failed to foresee the ends of Nazism; you will still have to admit that *Triumph of the Will* was meant to praise the force of arms, the glories of regimentation, and the inherent goodness of the Aryan race, all embodied in the figure of the Great Leader. Unlike Kalatozov, Riefenstahl was so deft that she committed almost no aesthetic missteps; but politically, her masterpiece is one giant felony.

It's all the more telling, then, that *Triumph of the Will* was useful to its producers, in a way that *I Am Cuba* was not. Upon the film's release in Havana in 1964, audiences reportedly had a good laugh, then unofficially changed the title to *I Am Not Cuba*. I would guess they cringed at the 'poetic' voiceover narration, murmured in alternating lines of Russian and Spanish, and at the Soviet crew's tireless interest in floor shows and hot babes. Besides, it must have rankled that the job of telling about the revolution had fallen to a bunch of Soviets. Meanwhile, at the Moscow end, there was even less appetite for the film. Mosfilm struck only a few prints, and the picture seems to have quickly dropped out of sight – helped into oblivion, no doubt, by the contemporaneous disappearance of Khrushchev. It was not a moment for eccentricity.

I Am Cuba had to wait until after the fall of the Berlin Wall to reemerge, when it was rediscovered by the very nation it had been directed against. In the early 1990s, Tom Luddy brought the picture to the United States.

Long an enthusiast for Russian cinema, Luddy had known for years about the film but had been unable to pry it loose from the Soviets. With the Cold War at an end, he learned from his contacts in Moscow that a print might be made available, if he would pay for it. He did so and was able to introduce *I Am Cuba*, without subtitles, at the Telluride festival, where it caused a sensation. Luddy then sought to add the subtitles and have the film released. He approached a small distributor in New York, Milestone Film, and also two people who could lend the picture some glamour and financial support: Martin Scorsese and Francis Coppola. So in 1995, with the help of two American auteurs, *I Am Cuba* was released commercially in the United States.

It went into art houses, not movie palaces. Its political force had evanesced. To most audiences, *I Am Cuba* seemed as wonderfully inexplicable as an abandoned temple, stumbled upon in the jungle; which meant it was now only half itself. Half was enough. If mad, grandiose works of cinema could no longer be made in the United States, they could at least be imported and revived. Here was a curiosity, an extravagance, a string of dizzying production numbers, a gorgeous ruin from another time, a monument to the genius of what's-his-name; a folly.

Finales

Historical overview of the folly

Standing on a hilltop on a day far along in this century's wars, we may look out over the fairground of cinema's past and spy in the distance a bluish smudge, barely legible as the ruin of a Crusader's fort. Or is it a pagoda?

No matter. Despite its appearance of antique exoticism, this structure is indigenous to the British Isles and no more than three hundred years old. A thousand such follies spring up on the horizon line of the eighteenth century, built in the name of charm and sensibility wherever common lands are enclosed and private estates enlarged.

A little closer to us rises the folly's urban counterpart: an amusement park. Although it, too, is privately owned, it is open to the city's new throngs, who gather for spectacles and political discussion. Observe the fireworks; listen to the grinding of the clockwork gears.

Still closer to us are the gigantic descendants of the pavilions at Vauxhall Gardens and Ranelagh: the Crystal Palace and Ferris wheel, marking the era of the World's Fairs. Celebrations of the global reach of European power, manifestations of national and civic pride, advertisements for capitalist enterprise, the World's Fairs attract millions to displays that confound art with commerce, private space with public space.

Also notice the ungainly brick structure set up next to the Crystal Palace. Although it might serve the Fair as a factory or warehouse, this building is in fact Bayreuth. Here, a significant number of the city's throngs find renewal in a spectacle as all-encompassing as an Exposition and similarly committed to the ideal of progress (or, in this case, the 'progressive'). Yet the Wagnerian festival also conveys something of the melancholy and nostalgia of the rural folly, where people put up a building for the inward pleasure of contemplating it in ruins.

In the middle distance rise the walls of Babylon, erected by D.W. Griffith in emulation of the Fairs. But in aspiring toward a progressive art, this showman of happy endings also has copied Bayreuth, perhaps without realizing that it is a place of robust pessimism, profoundly divided against itself. And so, having just established the movies with *The Birth of a Nation*, Griffith inadvertently sets off a series of disruptions within that new institution: the tradition of the film folly.

From inadvertence to deliberate sabotage: just this side of Babylon stand the gracious avenues and wedding-cake architecture of Monte Carlo, side-by-side with the slums of San Francisco. The first attraction is a display of Erich Stroheim's famous but entirely fraudulent identity. The second is a kind of leftover: what you see when that identity is withdrawn. Examine the gap between the two and discover how extravagance (which may be sanctioned for its promotional value) can turn without warning into wastefulness (which dooms a career).

Made as the studio system is being instituted, Stroheim's follies strike the eye so forcibly that the fairground seems to warp around them. Babylon shifts in the background, becoming a great commercial failure after the fact, and a monument to its author's self-defeating ambition. But of course this trick of perspective is not caused solely by Stroheim.

Close by his exhibits stand two national pavilions of the 1920s. The first, confected of geometric cutouts and artfully draped cloths, is a Purist–Deco wonderland, built on the grand scale by an avant-garde clique. Such is the work of art of the future as Marcel L'Herbier conceives it, within a decentralized, improvisatory French film industry. The powerfully integrated German industry – organized by the army, the state, and the central bank – produces with the help of Fritz Lang a correspondingly massive vision of the future, one that tucks a medieval world into the shadows cast by its skyscrapers.

These are *L'Inhumaine* and *Metropolis*. Both have at their center a laboratory, where a woman of the past is electrified into modern life. Both call up this Mechanical Bride – or is she a mother? – in the vain hope of rivaling the newly dominant American film industry, with its seemingly inexhaustible supply of showgirls and technical prowess. So a fresh element enters the history of the folly: a sense that failure, when it hits, has been suffered in a good cause and therefore is glorious.

But before that attitude can take hold, the world pauses for another war.

In the aftermath, a Southwestern cantina as big as a football field grows up before our eyes. It is the site of gambling, adultery, miscegenation, and murderous rage; and that's just the first sequence of *Duel in the Sun*. At a moment when the studios are reorganizing themselves, pioneering the trends that will later be known as globalization and downsizing, David O. Selznick builds this pavilion as a monument to his own independence, both personal and professional. Its chief attraction: the Follies Girl, a tan-colored, high-bosomed dancer who wants to be good but can't help being bad.

And here are two more exhibits housing Follies Girls: the Mammoth Circus, where Lola Montez screws up her strength each night to play herself, and Alexandria, where a garrulous Cleopatra models gowns and talks of geopolitics. The din of half a dozen different languages being spoken, the groans and giggles of Max Ophuls and Joseph Mankiewicz carrying out assignments they thought they didn't want, should not drown out the voice of François Truffaut, who strolls through these buildings reciting instructive sarcasms from the fairground guide he's written.

Even nearer comes an asymmetrical jumble of architectural pieces – part Cambodian temple, part suspension bridge, part open-air nightclub – lit up by fireworks and wreathed in the air by helicopters that perpetually blare 'The Ride of the Valkyries'. This, of course, is *Apocalypse Now*. Here, Griffith's American movie tradition at last converges with an imported French theory, with Wagnerism, and also (at one or two removes) with a new German art movement – in this case not a successful public enterprise like the Bayreuth Festival, but a small, avant-garde clique like L'Herbier's.

So we reach the moment when the past bumps into our hillside. History ends – and we still know little more about the films themselves than we did when we started out.

Morphology of the folly

When fully developed, the folly will resemble Leos Carax's *Les Amants du Pont-Neuf*.

I Modes of storytelling are mixed; fantasy coexists improbably with a pronounced naturalism. In the opening sequence of *Les Amants*, a homeless young man named Alex (Denis Lavant) suffers an injury and is taken to a public shelter on the outskirts of Paris, at Nanterre. This shelter was real; the writer–director, Leos Carax, spent many nights there, filming men who were truly homeless. The same writer–director chose to represent the intoxication of Alex and his homeless love-object Michèle (Juliette Binoche) by showing them sprawled in a huge, studio-built gutter, constructed on such a scale that a cigarette butt dwarfs the giddy couple.

2 The sets, which combine authenticity with other-worldliness, are uncommonly costly. For *Les Amants*, Carax went to the countryside near Montpellier and built his own replica of the Pont-Neuf, with water underneath and false fronts to represent the buildings on either side. Carax's bridge was approximately full scale in the center but tapered down to perhaps two-thirds on either end, providing a forced perspective. A long, twilit vista toward the Samaritaine department store could lead the eye along a penumbral corridor, away from a foreground of dirt and crumbling masonry toward an unattainable Beaux-Arts fairy castle, shining against the purple sky. The expense of constructing Michel Vandenstien's set provided for such basic effects. To restage the fireworks display for the bicentennial of Bastille Day, so his homeless couple might view the celebration from their perch on the bridge, or to give them the benefits of healthful recreation by letting them water-ski along the Seine, Carax pushed the budget further toward magnificence.

3 Money is on the screen, not just in terms of production design but also as subject matter. The almost mute Alex is an orphan of the streets, who can meet Michèle only because heartbreak and medical problems have led her away from a life of suburban comfort. Brought together through homelessness, the lovers cement their relationship by stealing from businessmen at sidewalk cafés and blowing the money on a good time. Their relationship later comes apart when Michèle recalls – and Alex realizes – that her poverty is voluntary.

4 The classes meet in a moment of carnivalesque misrule. To complete the atmosphere of intoxication, theft, fireworks, and water-skiing, *Les Amants du Pont-Neuf* makes Alex a street performer, who specializes in acrobatics and fire-eating. As in a festival or World's Fair, these popular amusements mingle with edifying presentations: of great paintings (glimpsed by Michèle during a nocturnal visit to the Louvre) and uplifting music (a cello sonata by Kodaly, which Michèle hears unexpectedly in the subway).

5 Everything is flammable – from the air in front of Alex's mouth to the image of Michèle's face, pasted up in the subway on missing-person

posters. Follies are known to dramatize their instability through violent outbursts of a varied nature: explosion, dismemberment, flood, avalanche, insurrection. But only fire transforms what it destroys, brightening as it consumes. Fire plays throughout *Les Amants du Pont-Neuf*, as the ruling element of folly.

6 As it goes up in flames, the picture seems to resolve into a portrait of the artist. Dedicated filmgoers knew that Carax had twice before cast Denis Lavant as a lovestruck unfortunate named Alex, who could be seen as a surrogate for the director. Many people also knew that Carax and Juliette Binoche had been lovers whose affair ended during the shooting of *Les Amants du Pont-Neuf*.

How was one to interpret this information, especially in relation to the film's great expense? *Les Amants du Pont-Neuf* cost a reported 160 million francs, or about $28 million, a figure that gradually took on a note of scandal. Yet two contemporaneous French productions, Maurice Pialat's *Van Gogh* (1991) and Claude Berri's *Germinal* (1993), cost about as much; they just didn't play out as hallucinatory versions of the filmmaker's own story. To harsher critics, *Les Amants* seemed the self-indulgence of a money-burning narcissist. To the more sympathetic, the film was an act of generosity, in which Carax, dimly visible behind the screen, poured largesse upon his characters, as if trying through sympathetic magic to enrich all the world's homeless.

In production for three years beginning in 1989, with filming interrupted twice for periods of several months, *Les Amants du Pont-Neuf* opened in France in the fall of 1991. The response from auteurist critics ran from warmly favorable (in *Positif*) to rapturous (in *Cahiers du Cinéma*). But the French public, which usually prefers its super-productions to be American, did not rush to see the glorification of a couple of bums; and even if they had, Carax had spent a handsome initial budget three times over.

His film could scarcely hope to earn back its investment through the domestic box office alone. Revenues from broadcast and videocassette sales were limited, since the picture can come alive only on a big screen. The last, best hope was for overseas revenue; and then the American market disappeared when Vincent Canby of *The New York Times* reviewed *Les Amants du Pont-Neuf* on the occasion of its showing in the 1992 New York Film Festival. He delivered a sound, Apollonian judgment; but nothing short of Dionysian frenzy would have emboldened a distributor's heart.

Indwelling spirit of the folly

'I discovered through the New Wave that there could be a very strong relation between director and actress through the camera, and that's when I bought myself a camera and started,' Carax once told an interviewer. 'I thought I could meet people by making films. Meet *actresses*.' Here (somewhat aggravated by the sexual urgency of youth) is the inner life of the folly. I believe it is a spirit revealed in its highest form in Jacques Tati's *Playtime*: a film in which nothing happens for two and a half hours, except that people find ways to get together despite a setting designed to keep them apart.

'It's probably the smallest script ever to be made in 70 mm,' Tati told Penelope Gilliatt in the late 1970s, a decade after the debacle of the film's release. *Playtime* may also be the smallest script for which the filmmaker constructed his own city.

Reproducing the modern architecture he intended to mock, Tati went in 1965 to Vincennes, outside Paris, and built a set that came to be known as Tativille. A group of International Style skyscrapers sprang up, at least to the height of a few stories, each installed with working elevators and escalators and automatic glass doors. To facilitate filming, production designer Eugène Roman had the buildings fitted with movable walls, which could be swung away to accommodate various camera setups. Some buildings were also mounted on rails, so they could be moved into different configurations on Tativille's streets, where real automobiles ran and real traffic lights blinked and real water pipes and electrical cables ran beneath the pavement.

Two power stations served the little town; a central heating system made each building comfortable for the cast and crew. A hundred construction workers labored for five months to build the set, using 11,700 square feet of glass, 38,700 square feet of plastic, 31,500 square feet of timber, and 486,000 square feet of concrete. To pay for this modernist everywhere-and-nowhere, La Défense built slightly before its time, Tati took out bank loans of about 4 million francs (or $800,000), putting up as collateral his home in St. Germain-en-Laye and his production company, Specta Films. All this, so he could bring together dozens of the most varied people, few of them professional actors, for the best time imaginable.

Within the opening few minutes of *Playtime*, a gleaming, soulless, echoing set of corridors slowly fills with human life: two nuns, a middle-aged couple fretting over nothing of consequence, a nurse with a baby, a cleaning man with a dustpan and broom but nothing to sweep up, men in military uniforms, brisk young airline stewardesses, a photographer, a scattering of businessmen, a very important person in a very large hat, and (all at once) two dozen excited women who prove to be American tourists.

They were genuine Americans: wives of U.S. officers posted to France, whom Tati had recruited *en masse*. The costumes were genuine, too; Tati asked the women to wear their own clothes. They were sure to feel more comfortable that way; besides, no one could have improved on this riot of checks and prints and flowered hats, which clashed so happily against the architecture. The only inauthentic element in the American group was its pretty laggard, Barbara (Barbara Dennek), who in real life was not an officer's wife. She was the *au pair* for a family who lived near Tati.

Out of Orly Airport the tourists spill (the all-purpose building having been that, rather than a hospital or an office tower), to ride into a Paris that looks identical to Orly Airport, or a hospital, or an office tower. Delighted anyway, the group happily snaps photos of a Paris that is indistinguishable from New York.

Meanwhile, a Parisian wanders lost amid the skyscrapers, trying unsuccessfully to meet someone on business. This Parisian is Tati's popular alter ego, M. Hulot. But even though Hulot is the person the audience would pay to see, even though he represents the author and real-estate developer of *Playtime*, he sticks out only slightly among the multitude of other characters. Hulot is not the star, as Tati told Gilliatt; there is no star. 'The film is about everybody.' And so, in a sequence typical of the long shots that fill Tati's wide-screen format with bustling detail, Hulot is lost among a swirl of businessmen, who carry him into an elevator, to be disgorged into a crowd of visitors to an international trade show, where he bumbles about, bemused by the gadgets that delight the two dozen Americans.

By this point *Playtime* already has offered a gathering of nations and a babble of tongues. Its architecture has developed strange powers of eclecticism (the Eiffel Tower suddenly floats into view, impossibly reflected in a skyscraper's glass door); its many characters have sampled a fair's commercial wares. All that is missing is a fair's revelry. Tati supplies this element at the high point of *Playtime*, an hour-long sequence set in a shiny new restaurant and nightclub called the Royal Garden.

Neither royal nor a garden, the place is all glass walls and sharp-edged, polished surfaces, like a paradise of Cartesian geometry too pure to admit any souls. A few workmen are still touching up the paint and laying a carpet; the *maître d'* fusses, trying to get the debris out of sight; waiters smoke and smooth their hair. When the first customers arrive – they are a middle-aged English couple in formal dress – the room somehow feels even emptier than before.

But, as at the beginning, the space fills anyway, and keeps filling, and fills to overflowing, until it turns into Tatisian paradise: a simmer of conviviality that bubbles through every part of the 70 mm frame. So many people invade the room that the bouncer can no longer keep out Hulot (who is not in evening clothes) or impecunious youths (who wander in from curiosity) or a cheerful drunk (whom friendly hands soon plant at the bar). The band segues from hard bop to African drumming; the American tourists get up and dance along with everybody else, including Barbara, including Hulot. It's as if three hundred vaudeville acts were being performed simultaneously. No wonder that the front door eventually breaks, the air conditioning breaks, a chair breaks, the seams break on all the waiters' uniforms, and a section of the ceiling breaks, dropping a jumble of multicolored lumber into one corner of the room, which immediately turns into a Russian Constructivist paradise. When the band quits, having decided this party is too wild, the revelry doesn't end; it escalates. The world's most lovably raucous American comes forward – a man who wants to buy everything in sight, just so he can give it away – and recruits Barbara to play the piano, and a redheaded French contralto steps in to croon, and here and there people begin to sing, happy in the corporate architecture they've shredded into streamers and confetti.

Tati spent seven weeks filming this sequence – as long as most directors take to shoot an average film. On *Playtime* as a whole, he worked for three years and spent a total of about 15 million francs, or $3 million, all out of his own pocket. He wanted people to get the full effect, so he at first insisted on showing *Playtime* only in 70 mm, which few theaters in France were equipped to do. He did eventually release a 35 mm print – just in time for the events of May 1968 to overtake those on the screen. The movie houses temporarily lost their customers; Tati lost his house and the rights to his films. It took him nine years to pay off the banks.

In the year he won back his films, 1977, Penelope Gilliatt found him in good spirits, despite his reverses. The worst he would say was that 'I had a bad year or two after *Playtime* . . . but at least I had never killed anybody.' In fact, he had given life. I imagine him about to begin a take in the Royal Garden, as he looked out over the heads of his cast – they were all so much shorter than he was – toward the cameras and the banks of lights and the grips waiting to move things around. At the moment before 'Action,' he was a god. And at the moment after, he was just another reveler in the crowd he'd called up, dancing in one small corner of the building he'd constructed. Apollo and Dionysus in one, ruiner of his own temple of false reason, he danced in pure innocence and paid his debts in full and died full of honor in 1982. 'I would like to make people smile and to give them a choice,' was how he explained himself to Gilliatt. Such was his folly.

We then walked to the Pantheon. The first view of it did not strike us so much as Ranelagh, of which he said, the '*coup d'oeil* was the finest thing he had ever seen' ... Sir Adam expressed some apprehension that the Pantheon would encourage luxury. 'Sir, (said Johnson,) I am a great friend to publick amusements; for they keep people from vice.'

JAMES BOSWELL,
THE LIFE OF SAMUEL JOHNSON

Acknowledgments

Thanks first of all to those who got me to write this book. Mary Lea Bandy and Laurence Kardish of The Museum of Modern Art got me thinking about follies by asking me to suggest a subject for an exhibition. My list of films for MoMA later turned into a nucleus of prose when a fellow reviewer, Elizabeth Pincus, introduced me to Jane Greenwood of Cassell, who then startled me by asking for the whole book. My warmest thanks to all of them; to Janet Joyce, Marion Blake, Charlotte Ridings, and Roz Hopkins, who guided the book through publication; and to those who offered material support. I have benefited from the spontaneous generosity of the Grand Street Foundation and the unending indulgence of my employer, Luisa Kreisberg, who would rather be a patron of the arts than a boss.

Thanks to all those who contributed their knowledge and understanding. These pages might have been blank without the help of Charles Silver and Ron Magliozzi of The Museum of Modern Art, and the staff of the New York Public Library for the Performing Arts. Melissa Riley offered her expertise as a researcher, tracking down a key detail about the elusive Walter L. Hall. Gillian Anderson took time to speak with me about D.W. Griffith's use of music. Tom Luddy very kindly allowed me to interview him about Coppola, Herzog, and *I Am Cuba*. Kent Jones gave me valuable information on Leos Carax and contemporary French cinema. Special thanks go to David Ansen, Phillip Lopate, Jonathan Rosenbaum, and David Sterritt for their comradeship, insights, and encouragement, and to Elliott Stein, Russell Merritt, Richard Koszarski, and Dennis Doros for uncomplainingly letting me pick their brains.

A number of people went out of their way to help secure the illustrations. My thanks to Nicholas Olsberg, Suzelle Baudouin, and Pierre Richard Bernier of the Centre Canadien d'Architecture/Canadian Center for Architecture in Montreal; Patricia Akre of the San Francisco History Center, San Francisco Public Library; Mary Corliss and Terry Geesken of The Museum of Modern Art Film Stills Archive; Catherine Verret; Rosine Handelman; and the staff of Photofest.

I owe a vast debt to all the editors who have made *The Nation* a home. Thanks, in chronological order, to Betsy Pochoda, Maria Margaronis, Julie Abraham, Elsa Dixler, Art Winslow, John and Sue Leonard, Molly Rauch, and Margaret Lee. Thanks as well to Victor Navasky, Katrina vanden Heuvel, and the *Radio Nation* team: Max Bloch, Marc Cooper, and Peter Rothberg. To Ben Sonnenberg, editor *hors de concours*, I owe the opening citation from Erasmus and a habit of looking over my shoulder. He hovers by the left one, gazing down on my prose in sorrow and pity.

For four years, The Film Society of Lincoln Center and the New York Film Festival gave me the best seat in the world for looking at movies. Thanks to Richard Peña (who convinced me that *Kolberg* had a place in the book), Joanne Koch, Wendy Keys, Joanna Ney, and all the friends on the fourth floor.

Gratitude beyond calculation goes to the friends and family members who for a year kept me properly watered and on occasion pushed me into the light. I won't set down a list; too many did too much, and a thank-you is too little reward. But I will name Bali Miller, who is a wonderful teacher of madness. Dear Bali: *Je t'aime à la folie.*

Bibliography

Abel, Richard, *French Cinema: The First Wave, 1915–1929*. Princeton: Princeton University Press, 1984.

Anderson, Gillian B., '"No Music until Cue": The Reconstruction of D.W. Griffith's *Intolerance*.' *Griffithiana* no. 38/39, October 1990.

Anderson, Susan Heller, '"Apocalypse Now" Film Stuns Cannes.' *The New York Times*, May 21, 1979.

Annenkov, Georges, *Max Ophuls*. Paris: La Terrain Vague, 1962.

Bach, Stephen, *Final Cut: Dreams and Disaster in the Making of 'Heaven's Gate'*. London: Faber & Faber, 1986.

Bahr, Fax and George Hickenlooper, *Hearts of Darkness: A Film Maker's Apocalypse* (film). 1991.

Barry, John D., *The City of Domes: A Walk with an Architect about the Courts and Palaces of the Panama-Pacific International Exposition*. San Francisco: John J. Newbegin, 1915.

Barsacq, Léon, *Caligari's Cabinet and Other Grand Designs: A History of Film Design*, revised and edited by Elliott Stein. New York: New York Graphic Society, 1976.

Bazin, André, *What Is Cinema?*, vol. 1, selected and translated by Hugh Gray. Berkeley: University of California Press, 1971.

Behlmer, Rudy (ed.), *Memo from David O. Selznick*. New York: Viking Press, 1972.

Bernstein, Matthew, *Walter Wanger: Hollywood Independent*. Berkeley: University of California Press, 1994.

Beylie, Claude, *Max Ophuls*. Paris: Editions Pierre Lherminier, 1963, revised 1984.

Blank, Les and Maureen Gosling, *Burden of Dreams* (film). 1982.

Bourguinon, Thomas, 'L'amour en Seine: "Les Amants du Pont-Neuf"'. *Positif*, November 1991.

Bowser, Eileen, *The Transformation of Cinema, 1907–1915*. New York: Scribner's, 1990.

Braithwaite, David, *Fairground Architecture*. London: Hugh Evelyn, 1968.

Braudel, Fernand, *The Wheels of Commerce: Civilization and Capitalism 15th–18th Century*, vol. 2, translated by Siân Reynolds. New York: Harper & Row, 1982.

Breskin, David, *Inner Views: Filmmakers in Conversation*. Boston: Faber & Faber, 1992.

Brodsky, Jack and Nathan Weiss, *The Cleopatra Papers: A Private Correspondence*. New York: Simon & Schuster, 1963.

Brown, Karl, *Adventures with D.W. Griffith*. New York: Farrar, Straus & Giroux, 1973.

Burch, Noël, *Marcel L'Herbier*. Paris: Editions Seghers, 1973.

Cagin, Seth, 'The Wrath of the Aguaruna.' *Soho Weekly News*, February 20, 1980.

Cohen, Jean-Louis, *Scenes of the World to Come: European Architecture and the American Challenge 1893–1960*. Paris: Flammarion; Montreal: Canadian Centre for Architecture, 1995.

Corrigan, Timothy (ed.), *The Films of Werner Herzog: Between Mirage and History*. New York: Methuen, 1986.

Cowie, Peter, *Coppola*. London: André Deutsch, 1989.

Cozarinsky, Edgardo, 'Foreign Filmmakers in France,' in *Rediscovering French Film*, edited by Mary Lea Bandy. New York: The Museum of Modern Art, 1983.

Douglas, Ann, *Terrible Honesty: Mongrel Manhattan in the 1920s*. New York: Farrar, Straus and Giroux, 1995.

Dumenil, Lynn, *The Modern Temper: American Culture and Society in the 1920s*. New York: Hill & Wang, 1995.

Ebert, Roger, 'Herzog's dreams a challenge, not a burden.' *Chicago Sun-Times*, January 16, 1983.

Eder, Richard, 'A New Visionary in German Film.' *The New York Times*, July 10, 1977.

Elsaesser, Thomas, *New German Cinema: A History*. New Brunswick: Rutgers University Press, 1989.

Erasmus of Rotterdam, *Praise of Folly*, translated by Betty Radice. London: Penguin Books, 1971.

Fischer, Klaus P., *Nazi Germany: A New History*. New York: Continuum, 1997.

Freund, Andreas, 'Jacques Tati and His Movies Return after Enforced Vacation.' *The New York Times*, February 19, 1977.

Gabler, Neal, *An Empire of Their Own: How the Jews Invented Hollywood*. New York: Crown, 1988.

Geduld, Harry M. (ed.), *Focus on D.W. Griffith*. Englewood Cliffs: Prentice-Hall, 1971.

Geist, Kenneth, *Pictures Will Talk: The Life and Films of Joseph L. Mankiewicz*. New York: Scribner's, 1978.

de Giannoli, Paul, Interview with Marcel L'Herbier. *France-Soir*, May 8, 1978.

Gilbert, Douglas, *American Vaudeville: Its Life and Times*. New York: Dover, 1963, reprint of 1940 edition.

Gilliatt, Penelope, 'Playing' (profile of Jacques Tati). *The New Yorker*, January 27, 1973.

Gitlin, Todd, Review of *Fitzcarraldo*. *Film Quarterly*, winter 1983–84.

Goldman, Albert and Evert Sprinchorn (eds), *Wagner on Music and Drama*, translated by H. Ashton Ellis. New York: Dutton, 1964.

Goodwin, Michael and Naomi Wise, *On the Edge: The Life and Times of Francis Coppola*. New York: Morrow, 1989.

Groth, Catherine D., 'Madame Maeterlinck at Home.' *Harper's Bazaar*, November 1911.

Grout, Donald Jay with Hermine Weigel Williams, *A Short History of Opera*, 3rd edition. New York: Columbia University Press, 1988.

Guérin, William Karl, *Max Ophuls*. Paris: Cahiers du Cinéma, 1988.

Hanson, Bernard, 'D.W. Griffith: Some Sources.' *The Art Bulletin*, December 1972.

Harding, James, *Jacques Tati: Frame by Frame*. London: Secker & Warburg, 1984.

Harlan, Veit, *Im Schatten meiner Filme*. Gütersloh: Siegbert Mohn Verlag, 1966.

Harris, Neil, 'Expository Expositions: Preparing for the Theme Parks,' in *Designing Disney's Theme Parks: The Architecture of Reassurance*, edited by Karal Ann Marling. Montreal: Canadian Centre for Architecture; New York: Flammarion, 1997.

Haskell, Molly, *From Reverence to Rape: The Treatment of Women in the Movies*, 2nd edition. Chicago: University of Chicago Press, 1987.

Hobsbawm, Eric, *The Age of Capital, 1848–1875*. London: Weidenfeld & Nicolson, 1975.

Hoffmann, E.T.A., *Tales of E.T.A. Hoffmann*, edited and translated by Leonard J. Kent and Elizabeth C. Knight. Chicago: University of Chicago Press, 1969.

Horak, Jan-Christopher, 'W.H. or the mysteries of walking in ice,' in Timothy Corrigan, *The Films of Werner Herzog*.

Horowitz, Joseph, *Wagner Nights: An American History*. Berkeley: University of California Press, 1994.

Hull, David Stewart, *Film in the Third Reich: A Study of the German Cinema 1933–1945*. Berkeley: University of California Press, 1969.

Jones, Barbara, *Follies and Grottoes*. London: Constable, 1953 (rev. 1974).

Kaes, Anton, with Martin Jay and Edward Dimendberg (eds.), *The Weimar Republic Sourcebook*. Berkeley: University of California Press, 1994.

Kehr, Dave, 'Movie minus One' (review of *Playtime*). *Chicago Reader*, July 22, 1983.

Koning, Hans, Review of *Fitzcarraldo*. *Cineaste*, vol. xii, no. v.

Koszarski, Richard, *An Evening's Entertainment: The Age of the Silent Feature Picture, 1915–1928*. New York: Scribner's, 1990.

——, *The Man You Loved to Hate: Erich von Stroheim and Hollywood*. New York: Oxford University Press, 1983.

Kracauer, Siegfried, *From Caligari to Hitler: A Psychological History of the German Film*. Princeton: Princeton University Press, 1947.

Kreimeier, Klaus, *The Ufa Story: A History of Germany's Greatest Film Company 1918–1945*, translated by Robert and Rita Kimber. New York: Hill & Wang, 1996.

Langlois, Gilles-Antoine, *Folies, Tivolis et attractions: les premiers parcs de loisirs parisiens*. Paris: Délégation à l'action artistique de la Ville de Paris, 1991.

Lawson, Carol, 'Herzog Jungle Film Halts as Ill Robards Leaves'. *The New York Times*, March 23, 1981.

Leblanc, Georgette, *Souvenirs: My Life with Maeterlinck*, translated by Janet Flanner. New York: Dutton, 1932.

Leiser, Erwin, *Nazi Cinema*, translated by Gertrud Mander and David Wilson. London: Secker & Warburg, 1974.

Lewis, Jon, *Whom God Wishes to Destroy . . . : Francis Coppola and the New Hollywood*. Durham, NC: Duke University Press, 1995.

Lista, Giovanni, 'La componente futurista ne "L'Inhumaine"', in *Marcel L'Herbier*, edited by Michele Canosa. Parma: Pratiche Editrice, 1985.

Lungstrom, Janet, '*Metropolis* and the Technosexual Woman of German Modernity,' in *Women in the Metropolis: Gender and Modernity in Weimar Culture*, edited by Katharina von Ankum. Berkeley: University of California Press, 1997.

McGilligan, Patrick, *Fritz Lang: The Nature of the Beast*. New York: St. Martin's Press, 1997.

McMillan, James F., *Housewife or Harlot: The Place of Women in French Society 1870–1940*. New York: St. Martin's Press, 1981.

Maland, Charles J., *Chaplin and American Culture*. Princeton: Princeton University Press, 1989.

Martin, Floyd W., 'D.W. Griffith's "Intolerance": A Note on Additional Visual Sources.' *Art Journal*, fall 1983.

Merritt, Russell, 'D.W. Griffith's *Intolerance*: Reconstructing an Unattainable Text,' in *Film History*, vol. 4, no. 4 (1990).

Moses, Montrose J., 'The Wife of Maurice Maeterlinck.' *Metropolitan*, March 1912.

Neumann, Dietrich (ed.), *Film Architecture: Set Design from Metropolis to Blade Runner*. New York: Prestel, 1996.

Noble, Peter, *Hollywood Scapegoat: The Biography of Erich von Stroheim*. London: Fortune Press, 1950 (reprinted by Arno and The New York Times, 1972).

O'Brien, Geoffrey, 'Werner Herzog in Conversation with Geoffrey O'Brien.' *Parnassus: Poetry in Review*, vol. 22, nos. 1 & 2.

Penman, Ian, 'Boy Shoots Girl' (profile of Leos Carax). *The Face*, September 1987.

Ramsaye, Terry, *A Million and One Nights: A History of the Motion Picture through 1925*. New York: Simon & Schuster, 1926.

Rentschler, Eric, *The Ministry of Illusion: Nazi Cinema and Its Afterlife*. Cambridge, MA: Harvard University Press, 1996.

Rosen, Charles, *The Classical Style: Haydn, Mozart, Beethoven*. New York: Norton, 1970.

Rosenbaum, Jonathan, *Greed*. London: British Film Institute, 1993.

Sandford, John, *The New German Cinema*. New York: Da Capo, 1982.

Sanzio, Alain and Paul-Louis Thirard, *Luchino Visconti Cinéaste*. Paris: Editions Persona, 1984.

Schatz, Thomas, *The Genius of the System: Hollywood Filmmaking in the Studio Era*. New York: Pantheon, 1988.

Schickel, Richard, *D.W. Griffith: An American Life*. New York: Simon & Schuster, 1984.

Schulte-Sasse, Linda, *Entertaining the Third Reich: Illusions of Wholeness in Nazi Cinema*. Durham, NC: Duke University Press, 1996.

Servadio, Gaia, *Luchino Visconti: A Biography*. New York: Franklin Watts, 1983.

Speer, Albert, *Inside the Third Reich*, translated by Richard and Clara Winston. New York: Macmillan, 1970.

Spotts, Frederic, *Bayreuth: A History of the Wagner Festival*. New Haven: Yale University Press, 1994.

Stirling, Monica, *A Screen of Time: A Study of Luchino Visconti*. New York: Harcourt Brace Jovanovich, 1979.

Taylor, Ronald, *Richard Wagner: His Life, Art and Thought*. London: Panther Books, 1979.

Thomas, Bob, *Selznick*. Garden City: Doubleday, 1970.

——, *Thalberg: Life and Legend*. New York: Doubleday, 1969.

Thomson, David, *Showman: The Life of David O. Selznick*. New York: Knopf, 1992.

Truffaut, François, 'Abel Gance, désordre et génie.' *Cahiers du Cinéma*, 1955.

Vidor, King, *A Tree Is a Tree*. Hollywood: Samuel French, 1981.

Villiers de l'Isle-Adam, *Tomorrow's Eve*, translated and with an introduction by Robert Martin Adams. Urbana: University of Illinois Press, 1982.

Welch, David, *Propaganda and the German Cinema 1933–1945*. Oxford: Clarendon Press, 1983.

Werner, Gösta, 'Fritz Lang and Goebbels: Myth and Facts,' in *Film Quarterly*, spring 1990.

White, Susan M., *The Cinema of Max Ophuls: Magisterial Vision and the Figure of Woman*. New York: Columbia University Press, 1995.

Williams, Alan, *Max Ophuls and the Cinema of Desire: Style and Spectacle in Four Films*. New York: Arno Press, 1976.

——, *Republic of Images: A History of French Filmmaking*. Cambridge, MA: Harvard University Press, 1992.

Index

Index

Index